Hoosier Hysteria!

Author Bob Williams (standing left) with three old Indianapolis Star cronies in the 1940s—Bob Collins, Jack Overmyer and Corky Lamm. (Photo by Maurice G Burnett, Indianapolis Star.)

Hoosier Hysteria!

ndiana High School Basketball

Bob Williams

Icarus Press
South Bend, Indiana
1982

HOOSIER HYSTERIA!
Copyright© 1982 by Bob Williams

The author and publisher wish to acknowledge Craig McKee and Mark Schneider of *The Indianapolis Star* for their work on the Larry Bird, Howard Sharpe, and Carmel chapters.

In addition, thanks go to the following people and organizations for all their assistance in acquiring photographs and research materials for the book: *The Indianapolis Star, The Indianapolis News,* The Indiana High School Athletic Association, the Indiana Basketball Hall of Fame (especially Herbert F. Schwomeyer, historian for the Hall of Fame, who authored the forerunner of this book, entitled *Hoosier Hysteria: A History of Indiana High School Basketball*), Anderson Newspapers, *Kokomo Tribune, Michigan City News-Dispatch, Plymouth Pilot-News* (Jan Garrison, photographer), *DuBois County Herald, Muncie Star, Rochester Sentinel,* Purdue University, and Indiana State University.

3   4   5   6   7   87   86   85   84   83   82

Icarus Press, Inc.
Post Office Box 1225
South Bend, Indiana 46624

Library of Congress Cataloging in Publication Data

Williams, Bob, 1923–
   Hoosier hysteria!

   Includes index.
   1. Basketball—Indiana—History. 2. School sports—
Indiana—History.   I. Title.
GV885.72.I6W54   1982   796.32'362'09772   8-15463
ISBN 9-89651-300-9
ISBN 0-89651-301-7 (pbk.)

*This book is dedicated with love
to a supporting cast second to none—
Florence, Beth, and Bobby Williams.*

Contents

Foreword

Many fine sportswriters covered high school athletic events in Indiana during my tenure as commissioner from the years 1962 to 1976. Most, however, covered a local area for their circulation. I know of no one who covered the entire state better than Bob Williams.

You have to love athletics, have complete knowledge of the games and their rules and be able to be impartial in judgments. These are characteristics of Bob.

It was a pleasure to travel Indiana from Gary to Jeffersonville, Angola to Evansville and to many points in between to basketball, football and other athletic events. I visited every high school in the state while I was commissioner. It seemed every place I went that Bob had been there or was there. This was true of not only the largest schools but also those with the smallest enrollments.

If any school had a good athlete or team, you could be sure that Bob would be on the scene. His comments about athletes and coaches are always fair and constructive.

Bob was not always right in picking a state champion but his batting average is above that of many other writers. At least he has more knowledge of the abilities of the teams than anyone I know.

Much criticism of officiating in sports writeups has always concerned me. I appreciate the fact that Bob has been very fair in this matter. I never heard that he blamed the outcome to a sports event on the officials. He is more interested in the ability of a player or team.

The fact that Bob is one of very few sportswriters who has been installed in the Indiana Football Hall of Fame and served as a director in the Basketball Hall of Fame since it was opened is proof of the high regard that coaches and directors of these organizations hold for Bob.

It was a pleasure always to have him telephone me because most of the time he had found a well-coached team or special player he thought I should go see.

Bob is welcomed in every school because school administrators and coaches recognize his excellent coverage and the publicity afforded their schools. Oftentimes this leads college scouts and others to take notice of an outstanding athlete. Many of these college scouts consult Bob concerning the attitude and ability of particular athletes.

As they say about the mailmen, snow, rain, flood, etc., does not keep Bob from his duties. Not all events are covered from a comfortable press box. I recall being holed up in Michigan City after my wife and I had attended a basketball game one night and found Bob and his wife Florence waiting out the snow storm in the same motel.

The Indianapolis Star has many subscriptions because Bob's column "Shootin' the Stars" is so widely read. Seldom a week goes by during the seasons that he does not have a story concerning some outstanding athlete. I'm sure these are proud moments for the athlete, his coach, school and community.

I appreciate his fairness, his honesty, his ability and personal friendship.

Phil N. Eskew
Commissioner Emeritus
Indiana High School Athletic Assn.

Introduction

Greensburg is known for two things—a tree growing out of the courthouse steeple and Bob Williams. The tree was there first, but just barely.

Williams and the tree run even in two areas—they have watched the same number of Greensburg state high school basketball championships and neither can go too long without water. After that, though, it's advantage Williams.

We all knew that, sooner or later, somebody would write a comprehensive book about Indiana high school basketball. And it certainly follows the form chart that the author would be Bob Williams. No man is more qualified.

Bob has watched basketball since the days when he used to climb a ladder an take the ball out of peach baskets in the Greensburg gym. His love of the game has taken him almost everywhere in Indiana where there are 10 kids and two hoops—come to think of it, though, that *is* everywhere. To paraphrase Will Rogers, he never saw a basketball game he didn't like.

Read his columns in *The Indianapolis Star* and you know this is a man who loves his work. And for nearly 40 years he has shared his enthusiasm with his readers.

Heywood Broun called sports, "the world of wonderful nonsense." But it always has made sense to Bob. And with his clear writing style he has helped us understand the complexities, chuckle over the transgressions, shout with the winners and cry with the losers.

And he always has kept it in perspective; it's a game. Cities may declare war, families may split, coaches may have their bags packed for a trip to Stroke City, but Bob always is there, calmly walking through the minefield. When our emotions finally return to room temperature, he again quietly reminds us that it's just a game.

A newspaperman stands or falls on his reputation. And Bob

Williams' veracity is unquestioned. It's simply accepted that if Williams writes something it's true.

Over the years Bob has been more than an observer; he has been a chronicler of events. He has made high school sports his life as much as his career. He worked 10 years, in print and behind the scenes, for a high school football playoff. It led to his Football Hall of Fame induction in 1974. He has served as a director of the Indiana Basketball Hall of Fame since it was founded in 1962.

Now he has labored for three years and given birth to a book on the great Hoosier preoccupation. This could lead to a book for the medical libraries, explaining why he didn't gain a pound during the gestation period.

From time to time, Bob has tantalyzed me with some sparkling chapters from his book. I'm anxious to read it all between covers.

I know I'm going to enjoy the game. I'm, sure you will, too.

Bob Collins
Indianapolis Star

HOOSIER HYSTERIA!

1908-1909

Barr Kann Barnhart-Captain Foglesong Agster Brackett Shafer Reagan-Coach

Rochester's Guy Barr (left, with haughty demean) scored a state record 97 points on December 11, 1908, in a 139–9 romp over hapless Bremen. Second place in individual-game scoring goes to Snowden Hert of Newberry and Tim Saylor of White's Institute, both of whom scored 90. Barr was a member of the first Rochester team in 1906–7 and later played on an unbeaten team at Purdue in 1911–12. Hugh Barnhart, a teammate and close friend of Barr's also scored more than 40 in the same Bremen "contest" played in the old second floor Armory Hall gym at Rochester. Barnhart (who celebrated his 90th birthday in July 1982) recalls that the playing floor was enclosed by a wire fence. Rezin Reagan (far right) was both principal and coach. And Rochester took its nickname of Zebras from the kind of uniforms worn in this picture.

1

Birthplace of Champs
Wears a Muncie Trademark

From Charley Secrist and Jack Mann in the early years to Jack Moore and Ray McCallum, the familiar purple-and-white legions of Muncie Central have come storming out of the North Central Conference to put their trademark on the Hoosier state's high school basketball showcase.

Sixteen times the tradition-rich Bearcats have gone to the Final Four in Indiana's $2 million state tournament, 12 times they have appeared in the month-long classic's championship game, and seven times Muncie walked off with the huge IHSAA trophy. Five different coaches have had a big hand in this incredible, record-setting, sweep—no other school has been blessed with more than four state titles.

Pete Jolly coached Muncie's first two state titlists in 1928 and 1931. Secrist sank the memorable game-winning shot from behind the midcourt line as the Bearcats edged Martinsville's defending champs in the 13–12 state title bout in 1928. Jolly, who coached the Bearcats for 13 seasons with an outstanding 263–101 record, came back three years later with another state titlist. Jack Mann (6–7) was one of the state's first big men, and Mickey Davison was singled out by Coach Jolly as the finest player he ever had. Muncie capped a 25–6 season with a 31–23 win over Greencastle for the title.

Art Beckner was the coach in 1951 when Muncie posted a 26–4, record and turned back Evansville Reitz in the 60–58 state tourney final. Jay McCreary took over the next year and the 25–5 Bearcat crew downed Indianapolis Tech with Mr. Basketball Joe Sexson in the 68–49 title tilt. McCreary compiled an excellent 131–34 record in his six seasons at Central.

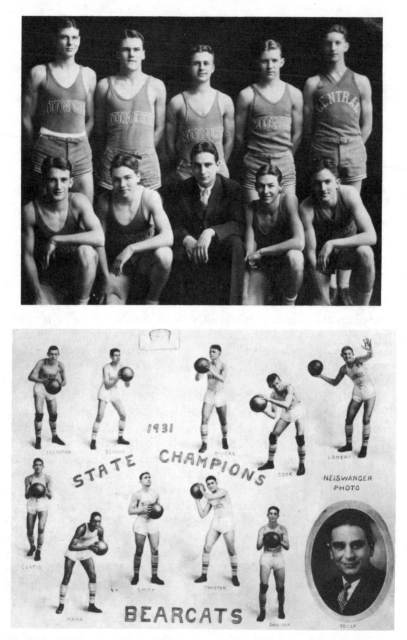

Top: The 1928 Muncie Central champs. Front row: Glenn Wolfe, Francis Reed, Coach Jolly, Ralph Satterlee, Carleton Walsh; back row: Charles Secrist, Hays Young, Eugene Eber, Robert Parr, Robert Yohler. Bottom: the 1931 championship team.

Another McCreary-coached Muncie outfit was upset by Milan's giant killers in the historic 1954 state tourney final, 32–30.

When McCreary went on to become head coach at Louisiana State University, he was succeeded by John Longfellow, who took an unbeaten Bearcat team to the State Finals in 1960. Muncie was the favorite but East Chicago Washington, coached by John Baratto, ended a 28–game Bearcat winning streak in the state championship struggle, 75–59.

Dwight (Ike) Tallman put together Muncie's fifth state champ in 1963 after Longfellow was forced out by illness. Mr. Basketball Rick Jones, Mike Rolf, and Glinder Torain led the Bearcats to a 65–61 win over South Bend Central for the crown. Muncie's only loss in a 28–1 record had been to the same South Bend team during the regular season.

Bill Harrell won back-to-back state championships at Muncie in 1978–79 following a successful career as a Kentucky state championship coach and in the college ranks with Morehead State in the Ohio Valley Conference. Coming to Muncie from Nebraska, where he had been a basketball assistant for four years, he returned Muncie's famed Bearcats to the state title trail with his disciplined four-corner offense and the help of two gifted backcourt magicians—Jack Moore and Ray McCallum.

Jack Moore, a 5-foot 9-inch bundle of skill and daring, became the first Muncie Central player ever to earn the prestigious Trester Award when he led the 27-3 Bearcats to a record sixth state title April 15, 1978. Moore exploded for 34 points in the afternoon when Muncie cut down Elkhart Central in an 89–85 slugfest, then came back with 27 at night to orchestrate a spine-tingling overtime win over Terre Haute South, 65–64.

Terre Haute South and Merrillville also battled one extra period before South's Braves could escape with a 54–53 nod in the other matinee encounter. Cam Cameron's jumper for South with only 34 seconds of regulation time remaining sent it into the overtime at 49–49.

Bill Harrell, the transplanted Kentuckian who won the bluegrass state title in 1966, celebrated the first of his two straight Indiana championships. Two desperation shots from midcourt by Rich Wilson of Terre Haute sent the final game into overtime in a 62–62 deadlock and reduced Muncie's lead in the extra period to 65–64 with one second on the board. Moore's 27-point performance including 13–of–16 at the charity line was backed by standout forward Jerry Shoecraft with 15 and 6–5 center Jon Carmichael with 11. Kevin Thompson, Tony Watson, and Will Uzzell all had 14 for South's runnerup ball club.

Moore, who went on to become an all-Big Eight player at Nebraska, was called "the best guard I ever coached" by Harrell. "In fact, he's the best I've ever seen and, baby, I've seen a lot of great ones." Jack handled Coach Harrell's 4-corner offense in a masterful way, and he went on to set the same tempo when the Indiana All-Stars scored their two-game sweep over Kentucky in the Blind Fund series which followed in June.

Asked if he felt responsible for taking charge of the Muncie team, Moore said, "Well, I'm a senior and

Jack Moore (11) lays one up for Indiana in the Indiana-Kentucky game.

the younger guys just sorta look to the seniors. I guess that's the reason they look to me or to Jerry Shoecraft. And what can you say about Jerry? He's played just great every game."

"Billy Keller, retired manufacturer of basketball excitement, accepted the prestigious Joe Boland Award for his important contribution to youth, . . . And a youngster named Jack Moore spent Saturday at Market Square Arena perpetuating the legend of Billy Keller and other diminutive basketball stars so dear to the hearts and memories of Indiana fans," the *Indianapolis Star* marveled.

"Moore bears a slight physical resemblance to Charley Hodson, who with Jerry Lounsbury formed an excellent half-pint backcourt combination in the early '50s when Jay McCreary's fast-breaking Muncie horde was devastating the North Central Conference.

"Moore doesn't end the contest wearing as much floor as Keller used to, but he has many of the old Westsider's competitive instincts. He has a good feel for the ball and a talent for finding the open man. He knows when to shoot it, when to let it go, and when to peel it and eat it.

"Conditioning and hard work are important. But they only help you hone the skills you already have. Nonetheless, I have never seen a great one who didn't have pure instinct. They know—and sometimes they don't even know why—when the ball is coming out of the crowd. Show me the greatest coach you ever watched [or any combination] and he can't teach that.

"Moore dribbles in a crouch, which brings him down to about 5–5, and pounds the floor like a machine gunner. Like Keller, he will pass off the dribble and fire the thing through some scary openings in the defense.

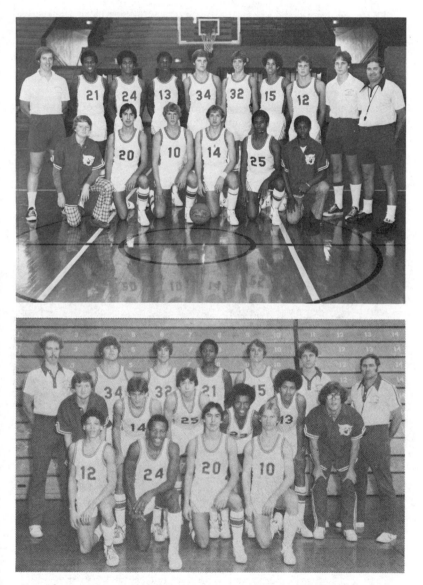

Top: The 1978 Muncie Central champs. Front row: team manager Gary Kern, Steve Avila, Robert Hoogenboom, Jack Moore, Bernard White, team manager; back row: Assistant Coach Rick Peckinpaugh, Troy Bridges, Darnell Ledsinger, Jerry Shoecraft, Wally Sparks, Jon Carmichael, Jim Armstrong, Brent Booher, Assistant Coach Brian Smith, Coach Bill Harrell. Bottom: Muncie's 1979 team. Front row: Ray McCallum, Fred Long, Steve Avila, Greg Mohler; second row: manager Gary Kern, Vance Sherrer, Rick Rowray, Freeman Galloway, Rick Leavell, manager Jeff Boyle, Coach Bill Harrell; third row: Assistant Coach Rick Peckinpaugh, Wally Sparks, Jon Carmichael, Troy Bridges, Mark Abrell, Assistant Coach Brian Smith.

"After watching the afternoon prelims, I wouldn't have wagered a devalued penny on Terre Haute South's chances against Muncie Central. But the Braves, who had to go extra innings to get past muscular Merrillville, threw up a zone defense that I can only call gorgeous," the writer continued. "They destroyed Muncie's rhythm and actually controlled the tempo of the game most of the way.

"The Terre Haute defense kept Moore from being spectacular. So he merely was efficient—efficient enough to penetrate the zone when Muncie was desperate, score 27 points, hit Muncie's last two points in regulation time and add the free throws that gave the Bearcats a 65–64 overtime victory."

One year later Harrell set out proving that his speech about Jack Moore being the best guard he ever saw might have been a bit premature because Ray McCallum and the 1979 Bearcats, with a 24–5 record, staged one of the finest encores anyone could ever hope to witness.

Mrs. Bill (Pam) Harrell, wife of the Muncie Central coach and a chemistry teacher at the school, pours a winning mixture with Troy Bridges, Jon Carmichael and Ray McCallum from the 1979 state championship team.

"Muncie Central mixed great team play with superlative individual accomplishment and superb coaching to win its second straight Indiana basketball championship," Bob Barnet wrote in the *Muncie Star.*

"The Bearcats turned back Anderson in a nerve-tearing final game, 64–60, for the seventh state crown for a school that long ago established the record. It was the second straight for Bill Harrell, who lost four of five starters and seven of 12 team members from the team of 1978 but came back loaded for Redskins."

Once again Muncie had to go overtime to move past Terre Haute South in the afternoon rematch of 1978's state championship rivals, 60–55. Anderson ended tiny Argos' string of 28 straight victories in the other semifinal clash, 74–64. Central's Bearcats shot .558 from the field and .941 at the foul line, hitting 16 of 17 free throws with four starters in double figures. Anderson held a slim 32–28 lead at halftime and it was 45–42 in favor of Muncie at the end of three quarters.

The Bearcats got an amazing performance from McCallum, although an ankle injury took him out of the lineup briefly with 3:33 to go in the third quarter. Central held a 41–38 lead at the time.

Muncie Central's Troy Bridges (21) and Jack Moore (14) scramble with Terre Haute's Richard Wilson for a loose ball during the 1978 state championship game, won by Muncie.

"Patient and smart and always under the firm control of a master coach, the Bearcats met every challenge offered by an Anderson team that was ready to bid strongly for a championship that has escaped the school since 1946. Anderson also won the state title in 1935 and 1937," Barnet explained.

"The Bearcats scored only two field goals in the final quarter, one by Jon Carmichael and one by Ray McCallum, who re-entered the game at the start of the period, but fought off the Indians with cold precision as they nursed their slim leads and made them grow with amazing shooting from the foul line.

"Steve Avila made six fouls in a row in the final quarter and

Bridges four in a row. The purpleclads had made 10 straight before McCallum finally missed the second of two shots.

"Anderson outscored the Bearcats from the field in the last quarter, nine baskets to two, and in the entire game, 29–24, but could not win because the Bearcats refused to miss from the line. The Bearcats committed only six personals against 17 for the Indians and Anderson was allowed to shoot only two foul shots, making both."

McCallum, who won the hearts of the Market Square Arena crowd just as Jack Moore had done the preceding year, made seven of nine from the field and 4-of-5 free throws for his team high 18 points. Troy Bridges scored 14 points, Carmichael 12, and Avila 10.

Henry Johnson kept Anderson in a threatening position with his 22 points on 11 of 16 shooting from the floor.

McCallum also popped 26 points on 10 of 11 from the field in the overtime win over Terre Haute in the afternoon. Carmichael added 17 points and Bridges 11 as the Bearcats took narrow leads of 29–27 at the half and 45–43 at three quarters.

Jim Bogle scored 22 and Kevin Thompson 15 for South's Braves but they couldn't match Muncie's .511 accuracy from the field.

Muncie became the first team in history to win back-to-back state titles twice. The school won it in 1951 and again in 1952 as it added to its amazing string of state championships. Frankfort is closest to Muncie's seven state titles—the Hot Dogs have four.

Coach Harrell told the huge gang of writers and sportscasters that he thought the 1979 championship effort had been more demanding than 1978. "It was because I wanted this team to win so badly," he confessed. "All year long, they've compared us to last year's team. They just worked too hard to come off second best in a comparison. Last Oct. 15, I told them I thought they had the potential to be the best team I'd ever coached, but I told them they could get there only if they were willing to work."

Harrell felt for a short time that they weren't listening but he changed his mind. "We just weren't patient enough on offense," he said. "We'd throw one up in the last few minutes in a lot of games instead of working for the shot. Then, along about the middle of February, we got more patient—I decided they'd been listening after all."

When his team was down by eight points, Harrell told reporters, he made a defensive change that turned things around. "We went from a matchup zone to a man-to-man. That caused Anderson not to get the shots they had been getting. We got their offense spread out a little more, and it gave us some opportunities we hadn't had before."

Terre Haute's Cam Cameron was named Trester Award winner,

and Harrell coached the Indiana All-Stars in the series with Kentucky; McCallum went on to have a brilliant college career with Ball State in his Muncie hometown.

Muncie Central state championship coaches Jay McCreary and Pete Jolly were inducted into the Indiana Hall of Fame in 1970. Front row: A. L. (Pete) Phillips, John Ward and Frank Barnes; back row: McCreary, Hall of Fame historian Herb Schwomeyer, and Jolly. Barnes coached Shelbyville's state champs in 1947.

Charley Secrist fired the most famous shot in the history of the Indiana basketball tournament in the opinion of most Muncie fanatics. He threw a field goal from the center of the floor in the final game of the 1928 tourney and Muncie Central beat Martinsville with its Johnny Wooden, 13–12, to win the school's first championship.

Those who study Hoosier Hysteria still mention that Muncie-Martinsville classic and Secrist's electrifying bomb from the center circle as the game neared its end. Of course, about 2,000 good folks from Milan would argue the point about the most famous shot because it was Milan's Bobby Plump who cast the game clincher against another mighty Muncie ball club in the 32–30 windup of the 1954 tourney.

Secrist was the Muncie center for that 1928 epic, Glen Wolfe and Bob Yohler were the forwards, and the guards were Gene Eber and Hays Young. Sixth man who saw a lot of action was Bobby Parr.

At 6–5, Secrist was one of the first big men who have become IHSAA legends down through the years. Jack Mann of Muncie's 1931 state champs was another. Big men weren't so plentiful in those days, and Secrist was an outstanding player as well as a tall one. He was picked at center on everybody's all-state team.

In those years they played three games in a single day in the 16-team finals, and the Bearcats got ready for their final battle against Martinsville by beating a great Anderson team in the morning, 38–37. Then the Bearcats crushed a good Bedford crew, 40–20. The final game brought together the two teams that had battled for the state championship the previous year, with Martinsville, coached by Hall of Famer Glenn Curtis, pulling out a tight 26–23 decision at the Indianapolis Exposition Building.

Curtis kept Wooden and three others from the 1927 state title winner, and he faced a young man destined to become one of Hoosierland's most successful coaches, Pete Jolly, for the 1928 state title. Only Secrist and Eber returned from the 1927 Muncie state finalist.

As the game neared its end Martinsville held the lead at 12–11 and Secrist turned an ankle. Walter Fisher, a young Bearcat football, track and wrestling coach only one year out of Indiana University, was helping the basketball squad by serving as trainer. He came out to tape Charley's ankle and the Bearcats clustered around Coach Jolly. Hays Young recalled it this way: "Martinsville had Tackett, the back guard, jumping center that night, and during the time out Sec [Secrist] said: 'I've noticed that every time we jump, Tackett turns his back and starts toward the back-guard position. I think I can get the jump and I'll tip the ball to myself. I'll watch for Glen [Wolfe] and Bob [Yohler] to get open and I'll get a pass to the open man. You guys be ready, because I can get the ball.' But something else happened before Secrist had a chance to run his play. We took too much time taping his ankle, and when we asked Curtis for a courtesy timeout because of the injury he refused·to give it to us. That meant that Martinsville got a technical foul shot—but Wooden missed it.

"The ball went up at center then, and sure enough, Secrist got the tip, grabbed the ball himself [this was permitted then under the rules] and looked around for Glen and Bob. Both were completely covered, so Secrist just threw the ball toward the basket from the center circle. He told me later that he wanted to get it up on the board so he could run under and try a follow shot. There weren't many seconds left and he figured he had to get the ball close to the goal somehow. Everybody was surprised, especially Secrist, when the ball went through the basket. We were ahead, 13–12, but it wasn't over.

"The ball went back to the center circle and this time Martinsville got the tip. They got it to Eubanks, who was only six or seven feet from the basket. He got his shot away, but it hit high on the backboard, and Bob Yohler fought his way under to grab the rebound. The game ended then, and we had the ball and the state championship."

Top: Muncie's 1951 champs. Front row: James Mace, Charlie Mock, Tom Harrold, Bruce Benbow; back row: Charlie Hodson, Jerry Lounsbury, Jerry Doublas, Carlos Miller, James Burt, Jim Sullivan, Danny Thornburg, Tom Raisor. Bottom photo: the 1952 version. Front row: Marvin Dick, Jerry Lounsbury, Charlie Hodson, Calvin Grim; second row: Jack Hawley, Danny Thornburg, Tom Raisor, Carl Miller; back row: Coach McCreary, Gerald Wright, jesse Rhodes, James Burt, Jim Sullivan.

Sports Editor Barnet turned back the pages on the closing seconds of still another memorable game, in which the Bearcats won their third state title, in 1951. Art Beckner, who starred on Muncie's state runnerup in 1923, was the Muncie coach and his Bearcats downed Evansville Reitz in a 60–58 barn burner.

"The score was tied at 58–58 and five seconds showed on the time board when Charley Mock leaped high and cut loose a one-hander from behind the foul circle.

"The ball banked cleanly through the strings and Muncie Central was the Indiana prep basketball champion for the third time."

Barnet mentioned that there were striking similarities between Beckner's team and the skilled mechanics of Bill Harrell's ball club in 1978. Both were often forced to give away height to their opponents.

"The 1951 team was smart and well-coached and every game plan was based on ball control," Barnet added. The same description applied to the 1978 team. The 1951 crew was calm and poised and blessed with reserves so good that the Bearcats, this time under Jay McCreary, survived heavy graduation losses and came back to win the championship again in 1952.

"The 1951 team was not the favorite in the state finals despite a good record that included 16 victories in 20 games. Actually, neither Central nor Reitz was supposed to be in the final game. Indianapolis Crispus Attucks, led by giant Willie Gardner, and Lafayette Jeff were supposed to fight that battle, but Reitz took out Attucks, 66–59, and the Bearcats clawed Jeff, 51–41.

"Reitz, a big team built around center Jerry Whitsell and forward Merle Reed, leaped out to a 17–11 lead over the Bearcats at the end of the first quarter but the calm, unhurried purpleclads had the lead at 31–30 at the half and 44–40 after three periods. Charley Hodson, another of those '51 supersubs who was to become a regular the following year and later co-captain the Indiana University team under Branch McCracken, hit a field goal with 2:43 to go to make it 56–51 and it appeared the ball-control specialists from Muncie were home free. Reed and Whitsell hit for the Panthers and with 2:04 remaining the Bearcat lead was one point, 56–55. With 1:34 to play Don Henry scored for Reitz and now Reitz was ahead, 57–56. Beckner sent Charley Mock back into the game bearing a burden of four fouls."

Tom Harrold's archer returned Muncie to a 58–57 lead, but the Bearcat joy subsided when Jim Sullivan fouled Phil Byers and the latter sank the tying free toss for 58–58. The lead had changed hands 15 times, and the score was tied seven times.

Muncie got the break it needed with 17 seconds to play when Jerry Marvel was called for traveling. Mock threw the ball in for the Bearcats, and then it was one pass after another until Mock broke loose

Muncie's 1963 champs. Front row: manager Mike Neese, Curt Hofheinz, Rick Jones, Mike Rolf, Andy Higgins, Glinder Torain, Billy Ray, manager Larry Icerman; back row: Principal John Huffman, athletic director Fred McKinley, Dick Hochstetler, Ollie Hill, Dave Baker, Marty Echelbarger, Dave Green, Larry Whittington, Coach Dwight (Ike) Tallman, Assistant Coach Ralph Zurbrogg.

just outside the key. Harrold hit him with a rifle pass, Mock faked once and then leaped high in the air for his state title winning jumper. It put Muncie ahead 60–58, and Bearcat rooters went wild.

Tom Harrold led all state tourney scoring through the last four games with 69 points, one more than Whitsell for Reitz, and Harrold was rewarded later when the state's writers and broadcasters named him Mr. Basketball for the All-Star team. Danny Thornburg was an All-Star the next year, Jerry Lounsbury and Charlie Hodson in 1953.

It should also be remembered that the 1951 team suffered a severe jolt when regular center Charley Ross became ineligible because of age during the week of the Kokomo Semistate. Jim Burt moved up to fill that gap and alternated the rest of the way with Jim Sullivan, whose contribution was especially important in the tournament—he shot 25 times and hit the mark on 14 baskets.

One of the most powerful Muncie Central ball clubs, if not the most powerful, mowed down all comers in 1960, then suffered a startling 75–59 loss at the hands of East Chicago Washington in the state championship game. Mr. Basketball Ron Bonham, John Dampier, and Jim Davis formed the Big Three for the Bearcats, who crushed Bloomington by a 102–66 score in the afternoon. East Chicago barely slipped past Fort Wayne Central, 62–61. Nobody gave East Chicago's Senators even an outside chance that night, but it was a much different story. East Chicago led 38–37 at the halfway mark and the lead changed hands 14 times in the second period. Muncie held its last lead at 41–38 early in the third quarter, and the Senators were in complete command the rest of the way.

Bonham, who scored a tourney record 40 against Bloomington in the afternoon, got 21 of his 29 points in the first half of the East Chicago tilt. He fouled out for the first time in 85 varsity games with 3:07 to go and East Chicago hanging onto a 61–55 advantage.

Coach John Longfellow huddles with John Dampier (50) and Ron Bonham during 1960 State Finals. Bonham was Muncie's all-time scoring leader.

Bonham's 69-point total for two State Finals games and his 40-point single game still are tournament records, Carmel's Dave Shepherd scored 40 in the 1970 state championship tilt to tie Bonham's single-game high, Pete Trgovich of Washington had 40 the next year, and Scott Skiles of Plymouth equalled his two-game total of 69 in the 1982 State Finals. The 6–5 Blond Bomber, who had a successful college career at Cincinnati and played pro ball with the Boston Celts, set another tourney record with 53 in the regional round. His 106-point tourney output for four games ranks among the top 10. He is Muncie's all-time scoring leader with 2,023 in three seasons for a 24-plus average.

In his senior year Bonham scored 803 points, averaging 28–plus, and he played an average of 24 minutes as the Bearcats destroyed one opponent after another with an average victory margin of 30. He was a 47 percent shooter from the field and grabbed 369 rebounds. Davis played with three teams in the NBA, and Dampier for the Washington Generals.

Muncie's loss to East Chicago Washington, one of the state tourney's all-time great upsets, was a bitter disappointment for Coach Longfellow, who put together a superb 53–2 record in the 1959–60 seasons. State title-bound Crispus Attucks had taken out Muncie in the 1959 Semistate in a 64–61 cliff-hanger.

Phil Dawkins who scored 21 points, Trester Award winner Bob Cantrell, and big Jim Bakos were the East Chicago big guns. Bakos scored just four points in the afternoon, but against Muncie he was a 17-point, 15-rebound giant on the boards. Hall of Fame coach John Baratto summed up East Chicago's position best: "We had everything to gain [in this game against favored Muncie]. If we were going to lose, we would lose to the best."

It was Muncie's fifth defeat in a state championship game—setting still another record for Hoosier Hysteria.

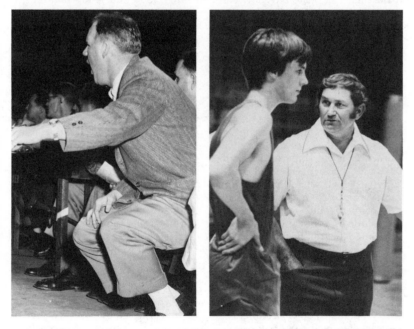

Two Muncie Coaches in action: Jay McCreary (left) and Bill Harrell. With Harrell is Batesville's Curt Clawson, whom Harrell coached as an all-star.

Muncie, Indiana, Star
December 28, 1981

Once again the bell has tolled, and Pete Jolly is gone.

His sudden passing on Christmas Day took another of those teacher-coaches whose strength and determination helped Hoosiers fight on during the grim years of the Great Depression and in World War II.

Through the late 1920's, the decade

of the Thirties and the first few years of the 1940's they taught young men—and their families—that life is often hard but victory over adversity can be achieved if hearts are stout and men and women possess the will to try again.

On basketball court and football field and in the arenas of other sports they taught by word and example that victory is better than defeat as long as it is fairly and honorably won and that defeat comes to all humans and must be accepted with grace and dignity.

By helping make it possible for Indiana high schools to offer low-cost entertainment of exceptional quality and strong appeal, they helped lift the spirits of families pounded by a terrible depression. Often it was the only entertainment available.

When the great war came many of these coaches and their athletes went away to fight their nation's battles. Their performances in this most demanding of all competitions proved that they, as athletes, had learned lessons vital to their survival and that of their homeland.

Indiana high school basketball in those years was in the hands of a race of giants and Raymond (Pete) Jolly stood as tall as any man. Nearly all of them, and surely Jolly, came from working families of the type hit hardest by depression. They knew what it meant to do without things and knew that athletes who sometimes tired in practice were weary because they were hungry.

Nearly all these coaches were college graduates and teachers because they had earned a measure of assistance as athletes. They were grateful for what athletics had done for them.

Jolly had served in the U.S. Navy during World War I, then returned to New Castle High School because Frank E. Allen, the New Castle principal and later superintendent of

Muncie schools, convinced him that a man needed to complete high school and go to college. At Purdue the young Jolly had played varsity football and basketball. Allen died recently at the age of 90 and Jolly said of his older leader: "Everything I have, everything I am, I owe to him."

_____

VALUED CONTRIBUTIONS

One needs only to walk along the rows of portraits at the Indiana Basketball Hall of Fame to become aware of the impact those coaches of the 1930's and 1940's had on Indiana high school basketball.

They were great men, determined men, and knew the hopes and dreams and heartbreak of the Depression Kids who made up their teams.

Everett Case of Frankfort and Anderson, John Adams of Vincennes, Cliff Wells of Logansport, Howard Sharpe of Terre Haute, Glenn Curtis of Martinsville, Tim Campbell of Indianapolis Tech, Burl Friddle of Washington and Fort Wayne South, Orville Hooker of New Castle, Archie Chadd of Anderson, Marion Crawley of Washington and Lafayette Jeff, Chester Hill of Kokomo, Murray Mendenhall of Fort Wayne, Woody Weir of Marion—there were so many, and so many are gone now. They taught their classes and coached their teams and wherever they worked they were respected community leaders. As coaches, they were among the all-time greatest.

Muncie Central High School had sent out great basketball teams before Pete Jolly came. Maurice B. Murray's fine teams had reached the championship games of 1923 and 1927. Raymond Myrick and others had turned out fine football teams before young Walter Fisher came from Indiana University in the autumn of 1927-28, the year Jolly arrived. The two of them and other dedicated coaches made Muncie Central respected in every sport, in every season.

Jolly's magnificent record as a basketball coach is among Indiana's great sports achievements. He won the 1928 state championship with the first team he ever coached and in the first four years of his tenure as Bearcat coach his teams played the championship game three times, with the 1931 squad winning the school's second state crown.

It is noteworthy that only three members of his 1928 championship team still live. They are Gene Eber, Francis Reed and Ralph Satterlee.

In 13 seasons as Muncie Central basketball coach, Jolly sent out teams that won 263 games while losing only 101, a remarkable record. His entire coaching career was spent at this school. His final year of coaching was 1939-40.

The man whose teams twice won the Hoosier basketball championship was confident some of his others would win. His 1930 team, built around Mickey Davison and Jack Mann, was beaten in the championship game by Washington, 32-21. The title-bound Bearcats took Washington out of the tourney in the quarterfinals the following year.

Jolly's 1932 team and Orville Hooker's New Castle team were ranked at the top in Hoosier prep basketball. Billy Thoman hit a long shot in the afternoon game of the Muncie Regional as the gun cracked and New Castle went on to win its only state championship.

In 1933 a team led by all-stater Fred Kleinfelder made it to the 16-team state finals and beat Franklin, then was beaten by Fort Wayne North, 28-24.

His 1937-38 team, a quick crew

that included Sonny Brown, Henry Young, Billy Campbell, Lee Monroe, Jim Carnes, Jack Comer, and Billy Myers, was one of Jolly's favorites because of its speed and precision. He thought this one was going all the way but Fort Wayne South, bound for the championship, took out the Bearcats in the final game of the Muncie Semi-State, 37-33. Muncie Central had won 26 while losing only four.

It is noteworthy that these four teams that did not win the Hoosier championship won a total of 89 games while losing 30. In 13 years, Pete Jolly never had a losing season.

THE CHESS MASTERS

Basketball was a careful game, a game of tactics, a chess game when Pete Jolly coached. The run-and-shoot game was practiced by only a few like Murray Mendenhall of Fort Wayne Central. Other coaches ran only when they had players with great speed and the ball-handling skill to match.

These coaches of the 1930's and early Forties planned carefully for every game but always "the tournament" was the goal.

Pete coached through the era of the stall game and in the stands nerves were drawn tight because a single shot, a single basket, meant so much in this type of play.

To those who followed the Bearcats—and that included all Muncie residents except those who cheered for Burris, only other school in town—one of the greatest thrills in sport came when Pete Jolly rose from the bench, took a step toward the sideline, and sent his purpleclads storming downcourt with a single wave of his right hand.

Spectators came up screaming. The coach was tired of watching that other team hold the ball. The Bearcats were going after them!

Pete Jolly was a great coach. More important, he was an honest, honorable man, a good teacher, a friend who always had time to help a high-schooler look for a summer job in those depression years.

He and his lovely Doris were among Muncie's best-liked, most-respected citizens in the years they lived among us.

— Bob Barnet

Muncie Central

Season Record (28–2)
1927–28

Muncie Central	29	Huntington	19
Muncie Central	35	Anderson	28
Muncie Central	33	Indianapolis Tech	18
Muncie Central	35	New Castle	34
Muncie Central	45	Martinsville	40
Muncie Central	26	Bedford	21
Muncie Central	33	Frankfort	24
Muncie Central	47	Shortridge (Indianapolis)	25
Muncie Central	56	Richmond	28
Muncie Central	32	Vincennes	38
Muncie Central	30	Logansport	32
Muncie Central	37	Lafayette	17
Muncie Central	44	Kokomo	24
Muncie Central	28	Gary Emerson	26
Muncie Central	32	Lebanon	23
Muncie Central	52	Marion	16
Muncie Central	49	Rochester	31
Muncie Central	35	New Castle	20
Muncie Central	41	Brazil	33
Muncie Central	29	Marion	14

Sectional (Muncie)

Muncie Central	69	Cowan	16
Muncie Central	51	Yorktown	19
Muncie Central	33	Royerton	11
Muncie Central	35	Eaton	14

Regional (Muncie)

Muncie Central	23	New Castle	17
Muncie Central	33	Mt. Comfort	28

State Finals (Indianapolis, Butler Fieldhouse)

Muncie Central	18	Evansville Central	10
Muncie Central	38	Anderson	37
Muncie Central	40	Bedford	21
Muncie Central	13	Martinsville	12

Season Record (24–5)
1930–31

Muncie Central	33	Hartford City	25
Muncie Central	22	Frankfort	27
Muncie Central	24	Huntington	27
Muncie Central	32	Anderson	17
Muncie Central	30	Indianapolis Tech	17
Muncie Central	16	New Castle	20
Muncie Central	29	Martinsville	14
Muncie Central	26	Anderson	25
Muncie Central	35	Bedford	27
Muncie Central	30	Frankfort	28
Muncie Central	22	Richmond	14
Muncie Central	33	Vincennes	26
Muncie Central	21	Logansport	23
Muncie Central	21	Kokomo	19
Muncie Central	29	Lebanon	12
Muncie Central	24	Marion	26
Muncie Central	43	Rochester	12
Muncie Central	28	New Castle	14
Muncie Central	26	Marion	23
Muncie Central	38	Fort Wayne South	35

Sectional (Muncie)

Muncie Central	33	Harrison Township	18
Muncie Central	43	Gaston	14
Muncie Central	43	Eaton	16

Regional (Muncie)

Muncie Central	23	New Castle	21
Muncie Central	31	Union City	24

State Finals (Indianapolis, Butler Fieldhouse)

Muncie Central	37	Kendallville	16
Muncie Central	21	Washington	19
Muncie Central	23	Logansport	17
Muncie Central	31	Greencastle	23

Season Record (26–4)
1950–51

Muncie Central	47	Winchester	27
Muncie Central	52	Shelbyville	37
Muncie Central	42	Richmond	27
Muncie Central	60	Logansport	50
Muncie Central	51	LaPorte	44
Muncie Central	69	Hammond	49
Muncie Central	61	Anderson	48
Muncie Central	41	Marion	48

Muncie Central	59	Lafayette Jeff (Overtime)	58
Muncie Central	67	South Bend Central	61
Muncie Central	60	Anderson	62
Muncie Central	60	Bedford	61
Muncie Central	69	Indianapolis Tech	42
Muncie Central	36	New Castle	44
Muncie Central	60	Dayton (Ohio) Stivers	46
Muncie Central	64	Kokomo	45
Muncie Central	55	Vincennes	53
Muncie Central	56	Frankfort	52
Muncie Central	35	Fort Wayne South	33
Muncie Central	51	Marion	49

Sectional (Muncie)

Muncie Central	44	Selma	21
Muncie Central	67	Gaston	34
Muncie Central	55	Burris (Muncie)	38
Muncie Central	77	Eaton	42

Regional (Muncie)

Muncie Central	70	Cambridge City	26
Muncie Central	57	Middletown	44

Semifinal (Kokomo)

Muncie Central	60	Kokomo	44
Muncie Central	53	Auburn	39

State Finals (Indianapolis, Butler Fieldhouse)

Muncie Central	51	Lafayette Jeff	41
Muncie Central	60	Evansville Reitz	58

Season Record (25–5)
1951–52

Muncie Central	68	Shelbyville	49
Muncie Central	52	Winchester	41
Muncie Central	56	Logansport	53
Muncie Central	51	LaPorte	33
Muncie Central	41	Richmond	43
Muncie Central	53	Hammond	34
Muncie Central	70	Terre Haute Gerstmeyer	39
Muncie Central	49	Anderson	42
Muncie Central	63	Lafayette Jeff	45
Muncie Central	62	South Bend Central	64
Muncie Central	50	Anderson	46
Muncie Central	64	Bedford	47
Muncie Central	69	Indianapolis Tech	46
Muncie Central	59	Vincennes	70
Muncie Central	57	New Castle	49
Muncie Central	48	Kokomo	57
Muncie Central	36	Frankfort	43
Muncie Central	60	Marion	51
Muncie Central	59	Richmond	41
Muncie Central	44	Marion	40

Sectional (Muncie)

Muncie Central	83	Harrison	31
Muncie Central	61	Royerton	36
Muncie Central	49	Center	24
Muncie Central	71	Muncie Burris	56

Regional (Muncie)

Muncie Central	72	New Castle	49
Muncie Central	50	Richmond	39

Semifinal (Muncie)

Muncie Central	64	Auburn	39
Muncie Central	62	Kokomo	60

State Finals (Indianapolis, Butler Fieldhouse)

Muncie Central	68	New Albany	67
Muncie Central	68	Indianapolis Tech	49

Season Record (28–1)
1962–63

Muncie Central	82	Hartford City	53
Muncie Central	84	Fort Wayne North	77
Muncie Central	66	Logansport	45
Muncie Central	78	Richmond	55
Muncie Central	90	Hammond	65
Muncie Central	73	Shortridge (Indianapolis)	46
Muncie Central	93	Elkhart	51
Muncie Central	72	New Castle	51
Muncie Central	90	Richmond	70
Muncie Central	61	Lafayette Jeff	53
Muncie Central	74	Anderson	63
Muncie Central	66	South Bend Central	71
Muncie Central	76	Muncie Southside	63
Muncie Central	76	North Central	50
Muncie Central	58	New Castle	53
Muncie Central	71	East Chicago Washington	56
Muncie Central	77	Kokomo	66
Muncie Central	75	Frankfort	63
Muncie Central	75	Marion	72

Sectional (Muncie)

Muncie Central	73	Yorktown	46

Season Record (27–3)
1977–78

Muncie Central	103	Monroe Central	48
Muncie Central	85	Delta	50

Muncie Central	79	Logansport	60
Muncie Central	62	Richmond	50
Muncie Central	62	Fort Wayne Wayne	61
Muncie Central	73	Muncie North	59
Muncie Central	70	Blackford	59
Muncie Central	72	Kokomo	45
Muncie Central	74	Marion	78
Muncie Central	65	Lafayette	54
Muncie Central	58	Indianapolis Washington	60
Muncie Central	47	Anderson (4 overtimes)	49
Muncie Central	67	Muncie South	44
Muncie Central	79	New Castle	67
Muncie Central	77	Kokomo	60
Muncie Central	51	Highland	42
Muncie Central	30	Madison Heights	28
Muncie Central	79	Marion	71
Muncie Central	62	Indianapolis Tech	59

Sectional (Muncie)

Muncie Central	49	Yorktown (3 overtimes)	41
Muncie Central	50	Muncie North	47
Muncie Central	75	Muncie Burris	32

Post-Sectional
(Approved by I.H.S.A.A. because of weather delay)

Muncie Central	84	Winchester	68
Muncie Central	69	Indianapolis Wood	61

Regional (New Castle)

Muncie Central	57	Jay County	41
Muncie Central	53	Richmond (2 overtimes)	52

Semistate (Indianapolis Hinkle Fieldhouse)

Muncie Central	84	Connersville	64
Muncie Central	70	Indianapolis Tech	66

State Finals (Indianapolis Market Square Arena)

Muncie Central	89	Elkhart Central	85
Muncie Central	65	Terre Haute South (overtime)	64

Season Record (24–5)
1978–79

Muncie Central	105	Delta	57
Muncie Central	79	Jay County	57
Muncie Central	69	Logansport	45
Muncie Central	47	Richmond	48
Muncie Central	53	Fort Wayne Wayne	48
Muncie Central		Muncie North (Forfeit)	
Muncie Central	98	Blackford	60
Muncie Central	92	Lebanon	62
Muncie Central	48	Bloomington South	46
Muncie Central	60	Lafayette Jeff	51
Muncie Central	96	Indianapolis Broad Ripple	74
Muncie Central	86	Anderson	77
Muncie Central	57	Muncie South	63

Muncie Central	48	New Castle	57
Muncie Central	64	Kokomo	59
Muncie Central	71	Anderson Highland	64
Muncie Central	75	Madison Heights	66
Muncie Central	55	Marion	66
Muncie Central	69	Indianapolis Tech	65
Muncie Central	64	Kokomo Haworth	45

Sectional (Muncie)

Muncie Central	87	Cowan	34
Muncie Central	63	Muncie South	38
Muncie Central	61	Muncie North	48

Regional (New Castle)

Muncie Central	56	Richmond	54
Muncie Central	93	Jay County	70

Semistate (Indianapolis Hinkle Fieldhouse)

Muncie Central	70	Rushville	59
Muncie Central	47	North Central	46

State Finals (Indianapolis Market Square Arena)

Muncie Central	60	Terre Haute South (overtime)	55
Muncie Central	64	Anderson	60

2

Anderson's Attendance Tops in Good Times and Bad

Anderson crowned the last of its three state high school basketball champs in 1946—Charlie Cummings was coach and Jumpin' Johnny Wilson was Indiana's Mr. Basketball.

Archie Chadd was the coach years ago when Anderson's Indians won their first two championships in 1935 and 1937.

Anderson's 1935 state champs. Front: Richard Baker, Clemens Ruh, Robert Clutch, Robert Morgan, William Jackson; back row: Keith Lambert, Bill Goss, Milton P'Simer, Charles Hartley, William Southworth.

The 1937 state champs from Anderson. Front: Managers Gibson and Stanley;
second row: Frank Clemons, Bill Goss, Russell Higginbotham, James Hughes,
Charles Richardson, Walter Davis; back row: Manager Coffin, Frank Caldwell,
Richard Hull, Coach Archie Chadd, Ora Davis, Morris Wood, Assistant Coach
Carl Bonge.

Norm Held and Ray Estes put together one state title contender
after another for the last 20 years. Held's Anderson ball club was a
64–60 loser to Muncie Central in the 1979 state championship game,
and two years later Vincennes Lincoln nipped the Indians, 54–52, in
the final game. An Estes-coached Anderson outfit dropped a 99–95
recordbreaker to South Bend Adams in the 1973 State Finals, after
which New Albany walked off with the championship trophy in an
84–79 title match with Adams.

Anderson's supremacy has been challenged in modern times by
two very talented neighbors. Madison Heights and Highland have
been ranked high in the polls consistently and now the three Anderson
schools combine each year to stage one of the most competitive sectional tournaments in the entire state.

Madison Heights was ranked No. 1 in 1981 but never got out of the
Anderson Sectional. Highland was No. 1 the preceding year when
head coach Bob Fuller suffered a fatal heart attack at mid-season and
Jerry Bomholt took over.

Phil Buck took Madison Heights all the way to the 1972 State
Finals losing to Gary West in the afternoon, 75–67.

Highland, coached by Butch Stafford, and Madison Heights
brought the Madison County seat still more recognition by winning

back-to-back Hall of Fame Classic tournaments in 1980 and 1981. Highland met Anderson in the 1981 Hall of Fame final before a record turnout in Anderson's Wigwam.

Highland was a 65–60 winner in the Hall of Fame windup, and George Allen of the Scots set a tourney record with 39 points in the 76–75 afternoon win over South Bend LaSalle.

Once again it was an underdog Madison Heights club that came out of the Anderson Sectional. Madison Heights nipped Highland 67–66 on two foul shots by All-Indiana All-Star Stew Robinson after time had elapsed. Robinson was fouled shooting from long range as the game ended, and it turned what appeared to be a certain Highland victory into defeat.

This is the brand of exciting Anderson basketball that has packed the Wigwam time after time for the big city rivalries as well as sectional and regional play.

Anderson leads all Hoosier Hysteria in attendance figures every year in good times and bad times, selling almost 6,000 season tickets for home games. The Wigwam seats 8,988 (second only to New Castle's 9,325) and the SRO signs are up frequently for the crucial North Central Conference head-knockers against old rivals like Muncie Central, Marion, Lafayette, and Richmond.

Of course, Anderson's backyard battles with Madison Heights and Highland are a sports promoter's dream. You couldn't find a ticket for one of those classics at any price.

Orville Hooker (who coached New Castle's only state titlist in 1932) put Anderson in the 16-team state tournament six times in his 10-year coaching career with the Indians, but it wasn't until Archie Chadd came to town that Anderson climbed to the top.

Chadd played three years for Tony Hinkle at Butler University and

Anderson's 1946 champions. Front: Paul Bevelhimer, Vaughn Voss, John Cochran, Isaac Weatherly, James Vanderbur, Bob Ritter, Stage; back row: Hamilton, Stodttlemeyer, Clyde Green, Robert Spearman, John Wilson, Richard Roberts, Donald Armstrong, Harry Farmer.

Charles Cummings (left) coached Anderson's 1946 state champs. On the right is Coach Norm Held from a more modern era.

captained the Bulldogs his senior year in 1928. He began his coaching career at Canton, Illinois, where he had a state runnerup in the Illinois tournament in 1933.

Archie moved to Anderson in 1934 and in just his second year took the Indians to their first state championship in 1935. He put together a 22-9 record and defeated unbeaten tourney favorite Jeffersonville in the 23-17 state championship game. Jeffersonville had won 31 straight led by the formidable 1-2 punch of Ernie Andres and Bill Johnson—the two Hall of Famers.

Anderson had some close calls along the way to the state windup, and the closest came against Shelbyville in the semifinal clash at Butler Fieldhouse. Shelbyville led Anderson by five points with only 90 seconds to go.

A tremendous rally by Anderson caught the Golden Bears and sent the game into overtime. Dick Baker was the Anderson hero, hitting the game-tying bucket for a 28-28 deadlock to send it into the extra period and then also scoring the clincher just before time ran out in overtime. Anderson won, 30-28.

Anderson seized an early 8-point lead on Jeffersonville in the final game and was never headed. Bob Clutch and William Jackson were the leading scorers for the Indians with eight points each.

The 1935 tourney was the last of the famed 16-team State Finals, and it also was the year that Camden defeated Delphi, 22-19, in seven overtimes in the Delphi Sectional. It is not the state record—Swayzee defeated Liberty Center, 65-61, in the 1964 Marion Regional in a game that required nine overtimes.

Anderson lost to Frankfort in the State Finals the next year, but the

Winston Morgan, Stew Robinson and Brad Duncan led Madison Heights to a No. 1 ranking in 1981. Robinson set Anderson schools' 1,656 career scoring record.

Indians came back in 1937 to wear the crown for the second time in three seasons. Anderson was 33–23 winner over the Happy Hunters from Huntingburg in the final game.

Walter Davis had a team high 11 points for Anderson in the final and Russ Higginbotham scored 11 in the afternoon when the Indians advanced with a 28–16 victory over Rochester.

Anderson carved out another outstanding 26–7 record on the way to its second state title. "Our 1937 team was much taller than the 1935 ball club and we didn't go into the tournament as the favorite either time," says Chadd, who coached Anderson for nine years and then served as School Superintendent through 1953.

Archie won eight sectionals, six regionals, and three Semistate tourneys in his nine years with the Indians. His overall coaching record at Anderson was 165 wins and only 67 losses.

Nicknamed Little Napoleon, Chadd played man-to-man defense all the way and used a set offense patterned mostly from what he learned under Hinkle at Butler. "You found some teams who tried to run with the ball at times but usually everybody stuck with some kind of a pattern—they made too many errors trying to run.

"Our crowds in those days were pretty big too, and after we won in 1935, we almost always played before a full house of 5,000 in the old Anderson gym. Our games with conference teams like Muncie, Indianapolis Tech and Logansport almost always drew huge crowds.

"I still watch the high school game whenever I can. State tourney tickets are hard to get so most years I see the state tourney on television. I went over to Anderson for this year's Hall of Fame Classic [1982], and it was a fine tournament. I was impressed with the record crowd and by the excellent play of all four teams.

David Moore, Kendrick Lewis and Andre Morgan made up the nucleus of Anderson's team that was ranked No. 1 during the early going in 1982. Morgan has been tabbed by many as one of Anderson's all-time best.

"You still have to get excited about basketball's popularity in the state of Indiana. When I played at Bainbridge [Chadd's hometown and his retirement home], we had many crowds of maybe 2,000 people in a town of 500. You could say the same thing about many small towns all over the state. This is the reason Indiana high school basketball gained so much respect all over the country. Others find our dedication to basketball a bit hard to understand."

Charlie Cummings came to Anderson (from Crawfordsville) because he felt that it was the best coaching job in Indiana. "It was a pressure job, but the best job always is," said Cummings, who now lives in Arkansas. "The fans were intensely interested, and as a result they were critical."

As Chadd had stated previously, "I was fortunate. I had 65,000 people to help me coach. But they were wonderful and the players were marvelous."

Cummings coached Anderson for just four years (1942–46) and wound up with a state championship in 1946 and an overall tab of 78–26. Anderson's third state title winner had a 22–7 record and was an impressive 67–53 winner over Fort Wayne Central in the final game.

George Allen, Kyle Paschal and Danny Zachary formed Highland's Big 3 in 1982.
The Scots knocked off No. 1 and 2 teams in the Hall of Fame classic in December
1981, and Allen set a one-season record for Madison County with 730 points.

Johnny Wilson, a 6-1 leaper, was the first to score 30 in a state
championship game. Anderson was probably the first fast-break ball
club to nail down a state championship and start a new basketball
trend.

Fort Wayne also favored the running game led by Bobby Milton,
who scored 30 in the afternoon when Central downed little Flora,
61-50. Wilson was Indiana's Mr. Basketball, and Anderson's Bob Ritter also was named to the All-Star team. So was Milton.

Wilson tallied 17 in the tourney opener and Anderson slipped past
a strong Evansville Central crew, 39-36.

"There was then and still is much tradition with the addition of
two more schools in Anderson," says Cummings who started out as a
coach in Cartersville and Webb City (Missouri) before moving to the
Hoosier state where he was coach and athletic director at Crawfordsville from 1937 to 1941.

"Opponents feel that tradition from the big crowds and even the
pictures that line the walls in the Anderson Wigwam. When Bob
Freeman [Anderson track and swim coach for several years] came to
us, he told me how Indianapolis Tech teams would come up here and
see all those pictures on the walls and it almost made them shiver.
Freeman was an outstanding athlete at Tech."

Madison Heights and Highland have built their own traditions
rapidly under successful coaches like Phil Buck and the late Bob Fuller,
succeeded at Highland by Butch Stafford. Highland already has had
two unbeaten regular seasons to go with its 1982 Hall of Fame Classic
tourney winner.

"On some nights, we can have 15,000 people watching basketball

—in the same town at three schools. Where else can you find this kind of enthusiasm?" Held asks.

Estes agrees. "There is no doubt that the city of Anderson has shown the greatest talent of any community per capita in the last 20 years. We've had a number of outstanding individuals. The kids are raised in that tradition."

Ray Tolbert of Madison Heights was Mr. Basketball in 1977 and Anderson's Roy Taylor was co-Mr. Basketball with Steve Collier of Southwestern Hanover in 1974. All three Anderson schools put blue chip players on the Indiana All-Star team in 1982—namely Andre Morgan of Anderson, Stew Robinson of Madison Heights, and Danny Zachary of Highland.

Buck won five of his first six Anderson sectionals after he arrived on the Madison Heights job in 1967, and Fuller coached Highland to 113 victories in six years after taking over the Scots in 1973. Stafford became the new kid on the block after Fuller's death, and he promptly carved out a 39–8 record in his first two years.

Anderson's Sectional is recognized as one of the strongest almost every year and four times from 1974 to 1982 the sectional featured teams that were either No. 1 in the state wire service polls or unbeaten. Madison Heights was No. 1 with a 21–1 record in the 1981 sectional. Highland ended the regular season with a 20–0 perfect slate in 1980, Highland was 20–0 going into the 1976 sectional and Anderson was rated No. 1 with 20–0 at sectional time in 1974.

"You know," comments Alexandria principal Shorty Burdsall, who in 1963 coached Alex to the last Anderson sectional title won by a

The left photo shows Roy Taylor (right) of Anderson, Indiana's Mr. Basketball in 1974, which he shared with Southwestern's Steve Collier. On the right is Madison Heights' Ray Tolbert, Mr. Basketball in 1977, who later starred on an NCAA title winner at Indiana University. He is shown here with Marion's three-time state-title-winning coach Bill Green.

county school, "you won't find any other place like this. You try to tell people about this place, and they just don't believe it until they see for themselves. Nine thousand people for a sectional final involving only two schools. You wonder where all of those people come from."

"If you're going to coach high school basketball, this has got to be the place," says Anderson Coach Held. "I always wanted to coach where basketball is more than just another extracurricular activity. Here basketball is a community affair."

It is said that there are a dozen or so people who have held season tickets to Anderson games for 50 years or more. They say that Lawrence Eckhardt has been a season ticketholder for 65 years, Albert George 63 years, Paul Whelchel and Boyd Howenstine for 60 years each.

Many Anderson people and others in Central Indiana remember the first Wigwam that stood to the West of the present high school from 1924 until a fire swept the building in 1958. The gym seated 6,078 and was looked on as one of the state's finest basketball arenas in the early years.

Madison Heights volunteered the use of its gym after fire gutted the historic Anderson basketball hall, and Coach Ick Osborne took the Indians crosstown for three years to practice and play all home games in the Heights gym.

One year after the fire Anderson began construction on the present $2.1 millon Wigwam, which contained over 133,000 square feet of space to accommodate several phys-ed classes at once, with balconies for additional physical ed work, a cafeteria and Olympic-size swimming pool. The regular seating capacity is 8,116, and additional bleachers up that figure to 8,998 for sectional and regional tourneys.

Anderson defeated Madison Heights in a scorching 67–66 comeback on dedication night in the 1961–62 season. Estes, Woody Neal and Held have been the only Anderson coaches in the first 20 years for one of Hoosierland's most popular basketball palaces. Held has compiled an outstanding 132–47 record in his seven seasons with the Indians.

"Anderson is a big town, but the people are very close and they are very loyal to their schools, churches and families—like a small town," Madison Heights coach Buck points out. "It's an excellent place to coach, and I don't know why the interest in Anderson is so great. Unless it's because all the fans are so well-informed on the game of basketball. They keep in touch through their service clubs and exchange clubs where all of the coaches go to speak the year around.

"Our kids live extremely close together; they go to church together and attend the same dances. They live across the street from each other in some cases and yet they go to different high schools. This is the reason you have so much tension when tourney time comes.

The Wigwam—seating capacity: 8,998. (Photo courtesy of Anderson Newspapers, Inc.)

"I don't have to tell you that it gets awful competitive and everybody gets pretty worked up over their basketball. But to my knowledge we've never had a crowd control problem or any trouble whatever with the players on the floor. It's a very unusual thing."

Buck said, "When I first came to Madison Heights the school played a much weaker schedule, but the school board told me they wanted to build up the schedule. I coached Frankfort for five years and was very close to the North Central Conference which in my opinion is tops. Now, we play all but one of those NCC ball clubs, and our schedule is one of the toughest you'll find.

"Of course, I was also informed in a nice way not to expect to win this sectional. Anderson never lost its own sectional, and playing the Indians on their own floor still isn't something that you look forward to with much joy.

"But they changed the boundaries right after I took the Madison Heights job, we began to get some of the very talented black athletes, and a short time later Highland came into the city school system. Highland also started to climb rapidly, and the city's growth is in that direction.

"So, I don't think you'll ever see the time again where any one Anderson school dominates the sectional. We've won it seven times in 16 years, and it's a real dogfight every year no matter what's happened during the regular season.

"When you win the Anderson sectional, you've really done something and quite often it's the strongest sectional in the whole state. There's a lot of pressure, but it's just a great place to be in athletics.

"Our press coverage in Anderson ranks right up there with the best and this also helps to make it pleasant for all of us coaches. We're very lucky that way, and in other towns it's something you have to worry about."

Buck's overall record reads 405–57 in 28 years of coaching—one year at Flora, six at Rossville, five with Frankfort and 16 at Madison Heights. His Madison Heights record is 251–135.

A survey of season ticketholders was taken in recent years and six players were listed as all-time greats in Anderson. They were Johnny Wilson, Steve Clevenger, Louis Graves, Roy Taylor, Rod Freeman, and Henry Johnson. Since that time the names of Andre Morgan (Anderson), Bobby Wilkerson, Stew Robinson and Ray Tolbert (Madison Heights), and George Allen, Danny Zachary, and Jeff Gary (Highland) have turned out one big headline performance after another. Wilkerson starred on Indiana University's unbeaten NCAA champs in 1976 and Tolbert for the 1981 NCAA champs.

Some have said that Morgan might be the greatest Anderson talent of all time. Indiana University's Bobby Knight reportedly called Robinson the state's best high school backcourt player in his 10 years at I.U. Allen set a one season scoring record for all Madison County cagers.

Anderson hasn't had a state title winner since 1946, and perhaps this is the most unbelievable twist of all, because the talent and the interest continues to rank second to none. It's like a time bomb just waiting to explode, and it's going to take more than an economic crisis to keep Anderson fans away from the Wigwam.

Madison County's Career
Scoring Leaders

Mark Barnhizer, Lapel	1,829	1974
Stew Robinson, Madison Heights	1,656	1982
Bruce Yeagy, Summitville	1,409	1959
Don Wagner, St. Mary's	1,375	1964
Roy Taylor, Anderson	1,374	1974
Dave Benson, Alexandria	1,362	1972
Steve Clevenger, Anderson	1,298	1963
Rod Hicks, Elwood	1,275	1961
Jack Rector, Madison Heights	1,267	1968
Darrell McQuitty, Elwood	1,262	1959
Ray Tolbert, Madison Heights	1,259	1977
Rod Freeman, Anderson	1,258	1969
Phil Leisure, Elwood	1,250	1975
Kevin Wright, Frankton	1,250	1982
Rick Lantz, Highland	1,248	1977
Chris Falker, Madison Heights	1,244	1976
Tony Marshall, Anderson	1,207	1974
Ron Schoeff, Markleville and Pendleton	1,195	1969

Andre Morgan, Anderson	1,158	1982
Mike Waller, Summitville and Madison-Grant	1,153	1970
Winston Morgan, Madison Heights	1,135	1981
John Mengelt, Elwood	1,130	1967
Bob Heady, Frankton	1,107	1961
Jeff Gary, Highland	1,106	1981

One-Season Totals

George Allen, Highland	730	1982
Mark Barnhizer, Lapel	686	1974
Mark Barnhizer, Lapel	658	1973
Stew Robinson, Madison Heights	638	1982
Todd Jones, Pendleton	620	1967
Jeff Gary, Highland	618	1981
Bruce Yeagy, Summitville	617	1959
John Mengelt, Elwood	611	1967
Dave Benson, Alexandria	607	1972

Anderson

Season Record (22–9)
1934–35

Anderson	14	Frankfort	12
Anderson	17	Kokomo (Double Overtime)	19
Anderson	31	Lebanon	33
Anderson	30	Marion	33
Anderson	15	Logansport	21
Anderson	40	Richmond	26
Anderson	25	Marion	23
Anderson	22	Logansport	15
Anderson	15	New Castle	25
Anderson	26	Indianapolis Technical	25
Anderson	16	Muncie Central	21
Anderson	25	New Castle	17
Anderson	23	Frankfort	21
Anderson	19	Kokomo	11
Anderson	27	Franklin	19
Anderson	21	New Castle	31
Anderson	30	Jeffersonville	32
Anderson	25	Lafayette Jeff	28
Anderson	34	Muncie Central	18
Anderson	36	Franklin	16
Anderson	32	Bedford	19
Anderson	36	Connersville	12

Sectional (Anderson)

Anderson	32	Alexandria	10
Anderson	41	Lapel	17
Anderson	43	Markleville	22

Regional (Indianapolis Tech)

| Anderson | 28 | Fortville | 15 |
| Anderson | 39 | Ben Davis | 21 |

State Finals (Indianapolis, Butler Fieldhouse)

Anderson	31	Brazil	22
Anderson	33	Nappanee	23
Anderson	30	Shelbyville (Overtime)	28
Anderson	23	Jeffersonville	17

Season Record (26–7)
1936–37

Anderson	28	Plainfield	22
Anderson	20	Frankfort	24
Anderson	26	Marion	17
Anderson	35	Lebanon	27
Anderson	23	New Castle	29
Anderson	27	Fort Wayne Central	39
Anderson	24	Lafayette Jeff	22
Anderson	25	Marion	20
Anderson	36	Shelbyville	24
Anderson	24	Muncie Central	19
Anderson	21	New Castle	31
Anderson	25	Logansport	30
Anderson	38	Richmond	31
Anderson	41	Crawfordsville	26
Anderson	24	Muncie Central	17
Anderson	26	Greencastle	28
Anderson	20	Frankfort	22
Anderson	27	Kokomo	20
Anderson	21	New Castle	14
Anderson	32	Muncie Central	19
Anderson	40	Indianapolis Tech	16
Anderson	21	Shortridge (Indianapolis)	6

Sectional (Anderson)

Anderson	55	Frankton	15
Anderson	14	Elwood	6
Anderson	21	Alexandria	16

Regional (Anderson)

| Anderson | 25 | Fortville | 10 |
| Anderson | 29 | Plainfield | 21 |

Semifinal (Indianapolis Technical)

| Anderson | 23 | Crawfordsville | 21 |
| Anderson | 26 | North Vernon | 15 |

State Finals (Indianapolis, Butler Fieldhouse)

| Anderson | 28 | Rochester | 16 |
| Anderson | 33 | Huntingburg | 23 |

Season Record (22–7)
1945–46

Anderson	39	Greenfield	24
Anderson	34	Lapel (Overtime)	36
Anderson	37	Marion	28
Anderson	42	Lafayette Jeff	30
Anderson	30	Muncie Central	29
Anderson	51	Marion	36
Anderson	32	Muncie Burris	10
Anderson	32	New Castle (Overtime)	34
Anderson	32	New Castle	29
Anderson	38	Kokomo	36
Anderson	41	Logansport	32
Anderson	22	Fort Wayne Central	49
Anderson	27	Richmond	30
Anderson	35	Indianapolis Tech	27
Anderson	45	Indianapolis Shortridge	20
Anderson	31	Muncie Central	21
Anderson	31	Shelbyville	36
Anderson	32	Frankfort	31
Anderson	29	Kokomo	31
Anderson	21	New Castle	35

Sectional (Anderson)

Anderson	40	Elwood	21
Anderson	57	St. Marys (Anderson)	38
Anderson	50	Lapel	33

Anderson

Anderson	51	Eden	33
Anderson	45	Tech (Indianapolis)	39

Semifinals (Indianapolis, Butler Fieldhouse)

Anderson	43	Lawrenceburg	32
Anderson	67	Crawfordsville	39

State Finals (Indianapolis, Butler Fieldhouse)

Anderson	39	Evansville Central	36
Anderson	67	Fort Wayne Central	53

3

Oscar Robertson, Ray Crowe, and the Crispus Attucks Era

Ray Crowe has been introduced frequently and installed in Indiana's Basketball Hall of Fame in 1968 as one of Hoosier Hysteria's all-time greats even though his varsity coaching career at Indianapolis Crispus Attucks High School was a brief one.

Crowe produced the first Indianapolis state champ in 1955, as well as the Hoosier state's first unbeaten state titlist in 1956, and he just missed a third straight championship the next year, losing to unbeaten South Bend Central in the Hinkle Fieldhouse windup.

Ray's phenomenal overall record in seven short seasons with Crispus Attucks from 1951 to 1957 was 179 wins and only 20 losses (89 percent). He started out with a loss to Evansville Reitz in the 1951 State Finals, reached the Sweet Sixteen six times out of seven, and lost in the Indianapolis Sectional only once.

One gets the impression that the Crispus Attucks coach had pretty good talent ticking off such superstars as Oscar Robertson (the inimitable Big O), Hallie Bryant, Willie Gardner, Willie Merriweather, Albert Maxey, Ed Searcy, Bill Brown, and Bailey Robertson (Oscar's older brother).

And when Ray gave up coaching in 1957 he didn't leave a bare cupboard. Two years later Bill Garrett (who starred for Shelbyville's state champs in 1947) took Crispus Attucks to its third state title in 1959, becoming only the third man to win a state championship ring as both a player and a coach. Burl Friddle was first, playing on the old Franklin Wonder Five and then coaching both Washington's Hatchets to a state championship in 1930 and Fort Wayne South in 1938. Jay McCreary was second as a member of Frankfort's 1936 state champs and coach of Muncie Central's 1952 state titlists.

Crispus Attucks didn't build a suitable gymnasium until 1966, so it should be remembered that Crowe had to whip some mammoth adversities on the way to the mountain top. Ray's Crispus Attucks teams never played a game on the home floor. Later on that was to work in their favor because many games were played in spacious 14,900-seat Butler Fieldhouse before huge crowds. It socked big dollars into the school's athletic and general funds. Not to be forgotten either was the fact that Attucks played all of its tournament games there in what amounted to home-floor surroundings. Opposing coaches didn't relish the thought of facing Crispus Attucks on the Butler floor at tournament time.

For the first few years Coach Crowe had some very serious problems putting together a desirable schedule. Not many of the established hardwood powers in the state would schedule the all-black Indianapolis school until Attucks' tournament success made it extremely profitable for everybody.

Old Hall of Famer Howard Sharpe was one of the first to put Crispus Attucks on his Terre Haute Gerstmeyer schedule—it paved the way and others followed his example. A game with Crispus Attucks meant instant cash, and it usually meant a defeat for your team.

Sharpe's gesture was appreciated by Coach Crowe and his players so much that Oscar Robertson remembered to thank the old Terre Haute master at the time of Robertson's 1982 Hall of Fame induction. "This will come as a surprise to Coach Sharpe, but he was the first to put us on his schedule, and it's something that we have not forgotten," Oscar explained.

Two Indy Mr. Basketballs. On the left is George McGinnis of Indianapolis Washington (1969); on the right is Crispus Attucks' 1953 Mr. Basketball Hallie Bryant.

Oscar Robertson (second from left) was just a sophomore when Ray Crowe took Crispus Attucks to the Semistate in 1954. Crowe's long-time assistant Al Spurlock is on the right.

Howard was in the audience, having recovered fully from open heart surgery the previous summer, and he was pleased.

Oscar Robertson's credentials as Indiana high school basketball's greatest player have gone almost unchallenged. The 6–5 Oscar led Attucks to two straight state championships and a 45-game winning streak which still stands, averaging 28 points per game in 1955–56 and 24 for his three-year high school career with a single-game high of 62. His 39-point performance in the 79–57 state championship game win over Lafayette Jeff in 1956 was a state tourney record at the time, and he also set Indiana All-Star records of 41 points for one game and 75 for two games in the Blind Fund sweep against Kentucky.

Many of his records have since been rewritten, but Oscar's position in Hoosier Hysteria's highest echelon remains unthreatened. He was inducted in the Naismith Hall of Fame at Springfield, Massachusetts, and the Indiana Hall of Fame in the same year.

Robertson was a College All-American for three years at the University of Cincinnati, becoming the holder of 16 conference records, 15 school records, and 14 NCAA scoring records. He was the nation's leading scorer three straight years and the all-time major college scoring leader with 2,973 points.

Oscar averaged 33.8 at Cincinnati and was voted MVP in the College All-Star game three times. He was voted outstanding player in the 1959 East-West game, starred on the Pan-American team the same year, and was co-captain of the gold-medal-winning U.S. Olympic team in 1960.

Cincinnati compiled a standout 79–9 record in Oscar's three years on the team. He shot .535 from the field and also totaled 1,338 rebounds in the 88 games.

Moving on to the National Basketball Association, Robertson led Cincinnati and Milwaukee to the playoffs nine times and the Bucks to one NBA championship. He was named all-NBA 11 times in his 14 years of pro ball, was Rookie of the Year in 1961, All-Star Game MVP three times (in 1961, 1964, and 1969) and the league's MVP in 1964. He scored 26,710 points for a 25.7 average in 1,035 NBA games with a record of 9,887 assists and 7,694 free throws. You can also add to that amazing record 246 points scored in 12 All-Star appearances.

Coach Crowe skips over most of those brilliant stats and recalls Oscar's other more intangible talents. "Oscar had tremendous leadership qualities, and that's something you can't teach as a coach," Crowe recalls. "He was always the last one to leave the practice gym, and he would get very upset with others when they didn't work just as hard on their game. He could be equally effective inside or outside, depending on the situation.

Coach Crowe with 1955 state championship lineup—Oscar Robertson, Sheddrick Mitchell, Willie Merriweather, William Hampton and Bill Scott.

"Oscar also had a very good attitude and never lost his composure in tight situations even though he was always under much pressure as our most dangerous offensive threat. He almost never got into foul trouble [he only fouled out once in his entire high school career], and yet he was a good defensive player. More than once we had to put Oscar on the other team's toughest player in the second half, and we usually got the desired results."

Oscar's only disqualification with five fouls came in the 1956 State Finals against Terre Haute Gerstmeyer—Terre Haute fans had their hopes lifted when the Big O fouled out in the third quarter. But it turned out to be of no importance with the Tigers holding on for a 68–59 victory.

Asked to list his best Crispus Attucks players from more than two decades ago, Coach Crowe singled out Oscar Robertson, Merriweather, Bryant, Maxey, Gardner, Searcy, Brown, Bailey Robertson, and 1951 Trester Award winner Bob Jewell. No surprises, really.

Bryant, Gardner, Jewell, and Bailey Robertson were standout members of that 1951 State Finals ball club which lost a 66–57 heartbreaker to Reitz in the afternoon. "We were not ready, and that was my fault," conceded Crowe. "I made up my mind right then that we would be back, and the next time we would be ready."

Oscar Robertson, Merriweather, and Brown all excelled on the

Full house at Indianapolis' Butler Fieldhouse for the Indiana State Finals basketball show.

Action photos from Crispus Attucks-Gary Roosevelt state championship game in 1955 showing Bill Brown (#23) and Bill Scott (#14).

1955 state championship crew which bombed Gary Roosevelt with its high-scoring Wilson Eison in the 97–74 final game. Eison outscored Oscar 31–30 in that memorable shootout at Butler Fieldhouse.

Oscar was joined on the unbeaten state championship team one year later by Brown, Maxey, Searcy, and Stan Patton—another Indiana All-Star pick. The Tigers wound up with a spotless 31–0 record, and the two-year record of 62–1 had just the one blemish coming in a 58–57 barn burner on the road at Connersville.

Bryant was Indiana's Mr. Basketball in 1953, captained the Indiana University team as a senior, and then started a successful career as both player and field representative with the Harlem Globetrotters. Hallie and Bailey Robertson were his best outside shooters, better than Oscar, according to Crowe. Gardner was a 6–9 frontliner with unlimited potential who scored 22 points in that 1951 State Finals game against Reitz as a sophomore, but his high school eligibility was limited to just 37 games in two years (he was acting student manager as a senior), and after he signed a pro contract out of high school fate dealt the big guy another cruel blow. He developed a heart problem that ended his playing career.

Crowe estimates that Gardner's potential as an intimidating inside player might have been the closest thing to Oscar, if he could have played three years in high school. Willie averaged 19 points and scored 21 field goals in one game his sophomore year.

Coach Crowe receives the key to the city from Indianapolis Mayor Alex Clark. Star forward Willie Merriweather (wearing cap) is shown at left.

Oscar and Merriweather, who averaged 19.7, presented a formidable 1–2 punch for Attucks on the 1955 state title winner. Merriweather went on to become an excellent college player at Purdue University.

Maxey who took over most of the scoring responsibilities on the 1957 state runnerup outfit went on to gain college stardom at Nebraska. Searcy played college ball at Illinois one year and then for Southern Illinois. Brown's career at Tennessee State was cut short when he contacted polio, and Bailey Robertson played for Angus Nicoson at Indiana Central, where he wiped out all the Greyhound scoring records.

Crowe put at least one player on the Indiana All-Star team in each of his seven seasons, and in 1956 when Attucks wiped out all 31 opponents he had both Oscar Robertson and Stanford Patton on the All-Star roster. Searcy, who started out under Crowe's wing, also made the All-Star honor roll in 1958.

Bobby Edmonds, Larry McIntyre, Jerry Hazelwood, and Claude Williams were the big guns on the 1959 state championship team coached by Garrett. Attucks compiled a 26–5 record and crushed Kokomo with Jimmy Rayl by a 92–54 margin in the title match. Edmonds led Attucks scoring with 19 in the final game and McIntyre was voted to the All-Star team.

Crispus Attucks' 1955 state champs. Front: John Brown, Stanford Patton, William Brown, Oscar Robertson, Sam Milton; back row: Coach Ray Crowe, Willie Burnley, William Hampton, Willie Merriweather, Manager Douglas, William Scott and Sheddrick Mitchell.

Stan Patton (#15), Al Maxey and Ed Searcy battle Terre Haute Gerstmeyer on the boards during the 1956 State Finals. On the right it's all smiles for Bill Brown and Oscar Robertson as they hold the 1956 championship trophy.

Crowe mentions three games as being the most important in his career at Crispus Attucks. Oddly enough, he didn't list either of the state championship games as being one of the three best in his memory.

There was the unforgettable 71–70 Semistate win over No. 1 ranked Muncie Central in 1955, the 81–80 regional win over Anderson in 1951 with Bailey Robertson hitting the game clincher in the last seven seconds, and the 60–58 double overtime win over Shortridge for the 1955 city tourney title. Oscar Robertson delivered the sudden death tie breaker in the latter.

Crowe has said that while everybody thinks of his two state championship teams in almost any discussion of past state tourney winners, his 1957 team which fell just one game short of making it three in a row ranks high in his own mind as something special.

"Winning the state championship was a bigger thrill, of course, but there was a different kind of satisfaction in working with a group of boys who weren't supposed to do much and seeing them fool everyone," the former Crispus Attucks coach says.

Crowe admits that many people feel that his best coaching job came with that 1957 team, and he agrees. "In many ways, it was my most satisfying year."

Attucks began with a state record 45-game winning streak and only one starter back from the 1956 unbeaten state champ. He was the 6–3 Albert Maxey, who was destined to become one of the most versatile players in a long parade of Attucks blue chippers.

"It didn't take long to forget the streak," Crowe said. "We lost our very first game to Terre Haute Gerstmeyer, and everyone figured we would be in for a long season. We were young, with Maxey as our only senior starter.

"We used Ed Searcy, a 6–5 junior at forward; 6–5 junior Odell Donel at center; 5–8 Laverne Benson at one guard and alternated Jerry Hazelwood and Larry McIntyre [two sophomores] at the other guard."

Attucks lost to Tech in the city tourney but improved gradually and entered the sectional with a respectable 16–5 record.

"I think it took a while for us to get used to not having Oscar on the floor. We surprised everyone by beating Tech in the sectional, and then we added a few more surprises.

"In the State Finals, we knocked off the same Gerstmeyer team that had broken our winning streak in the season opener, 85–71. But in the state championship game that night we ran into a great unbeaten team from South Bend Central with Herbie Lee and the Coalmon brothers, John and Sylvester. And we got whipped, 67–55.

Attucks' 1959 state champs. Front: James Gholston, Larry McIntyre, Jerry Hazelwood, Donald Swift; second row: Bill Jones, George Dixon, Bobby Edmonds, Larry Young; third row: Claude Williams, Walter Smith, Coach William Garrett, Detroit Spencer and Jerry Trice.

Bill Garrett, who led Shelbyville to the 1947 state title as a player, coached Crispus Attucks to its third championship in 1959. Next to Garrett on the bench is Don Thomas, who later coached both Attucks and Shortridge.

"I always felt this team was overlooked, but they had a tough act to follow."

Crowe gave up coaching a short time after that final game and became the school's athletic director. "By the next season I wished I was coaching again," he confesses now. "It was one of the biggest mistakes of my life to quit. I've often wondered why I got out when I did, because I loved coaching. And I talked to many of the athletic directors at other schools about returning, but nothing ever materialized. I just think they weren't ready yet to have a black coach at most schools."

Crowe stayed on as athletic director for 10 years and in that time helped lay the groundwork for a modern gymnasium before he entered private business. He was elected to the Indiana Assembly for five terms and served as director of the Indianapolis Park Department for several years.

Ray has been asked many times if his success in other fields ever gave him as much enjoyment as he got from coaching. "No way," is his quick reply. "I never got the same kick out of my business experiences or my work in politics that I enjoyed in coaching. I believe that our teams in those days would still do all right today, and I believe that our best players were just as good.

"Our philosophy was the running game and to get down the floor before the defense could set up. We stressed offense and putting the ball in the basket. A lot of teams tried to hold the ball on us, and you see teams doing the same thing in the game today; but we'd go out after 'em whenever that happened. Our game was the fast break.

"I really believe there's still a place in the game for the small guard,

Oscar Robertson (right), one of Hoosier Hysteria's all-time greats, at the Hall of Fame banquet where he was inducted in 1982 along with Congressman Lee Hamilton (left) of Evansville and IU's great coach, Bobby Knight.

especially in high school. There are a lot of good basketball players who are overlooked every year because of their small size, and I'm not sure some couldn't have done better than some of the 6–4 or 6–5 players who were recruited."

Crowe believes that Indianapolis basketball is just as strong most years as the basketball played anywhere in Indiana. He credits the grade school program started by Superintendent H. L. Shibler in the late 1940s and early 1950s as having improved the quality for all Indianapolis schools.

At the same time Ray expresses his concern over declining attendance, particularly for inner-city schools. "We worried about it and had many meetings while I still was athletic director. Everybody was hurting, and it's still a serious problem. I can't believe it when you see only 2,000 for some of those sectional sessions at Hinkle Fieldhouse these days, compared to the sellouts of 15,000 we had 20–25 years ago," he observed.

"A lot of factors are to blame for the small crowds, including the economy and television. There are so many distractions now, and young people have changed a lot since I left coaching. We didn't have a lot of rules on our teams at Crispus Attucks, but the ones we had the players were expected to keep. I was strict in that sense, and I don't think I could change if I was still in coaching.

"I probably wouldn't be as strict as [Indiana University's] Bobby Knight, but they would have to go along with what I believe. I believe that Knight is the best coach in the college game anywhere—he's a likeable guy, and he sure gets results," Crowe said.

Crispus Attucks' lone loss in two state championship years is

Ray Crowe and his wife Betty were the main attractions in a Crispus Attucks reunion. All-time greats Hallie Bryant, Oscar Robertson and Willie Gardner (left to right) were on hand to greet the Crowes.

another classic story in itself. Connersville's small gym couldn't begin to hold the huge overflow crowd so the school's auditorium was equipped with loud speakers, and the radio play-by-play was piped in for those fans. The weather was cold and the ground covered with snow. Inside, the gym was like a bake oven and at half-time, when the exits were opened briefly for many fans to get a breath of fresh air, the playing floor was like a sheet of ice from the condensation. Players and referees alike were slipping and sliding the whole second half—it was like a skating rink.

Connersville, coached by Kenny Gunning, was primed for the big upset and played a near perfect first half to take an unexpected 13-point lead. It became clear in the opening seconds of the second half that the Spartans aimed to put the ball in the deep freeze to hang onto that lead.

Crispus Attucks nevertheless made up most of that deficit, led by the amazing Big O. Connersville took only four shots in the fourth quarter and hit all four, playing its stall game to perfection; but Crispus Attucks was threatening. Oscar had been held to three points in the first half, but he would get 19 in the second.

Robertson hit one from the side with just five seconds on the clock to cut the Connersville lead to one point, but that was the end of the story. Attucks stood helpless for five seconds as Connersville held the ball safely out of bounds until the final gun sounded.

It was the only Crispus Attucks loss in 63 games on the way to two state championships.

Ray Crowe's Record
(Won 179, Lost 20)

1951—Won 26, Lost 2 (lost to Evansville Reitz in State Finals)
1952—Won 20, Lost 2 (lost to Tech in Indianapolis Sectional)
1953—Won 23, Lost 4 (lost to Shelbyville in Indianapolis Semistate)
1954—Won 24, Lost 5 (lost to Milan in Indianapolis Semistate)
*1955—Won 30, Lost 1 (State Champion)
*1956—Won 31, Lost 0 (State Champion)
1957—Won 25, Lost 6 (lost to South Bend Central in state championship
        game)

Crowe's 1955 and 1956 state championship teams won 45 games in a row including tourneys—the Hoosier state's longest winning streak. Argos owns the longest regular-season streak, with 76.

Indianapolis Crispus Attucks

Season Record (31–1)
1954–55

Crispus Attucks	75	Fort Wayne North	64
Crispus Attucks	80	Sheridan	36
Crispus Attucks	57	Terre Haute Gerstymeyer	44
Crispus Attucks	76	South Bend Riley	62
Crispus Attucks	57	Indianapolis Tech	47

City Tourney

Crispus Attucks	73	Howe (Indianapolis)	60
Crispus Attucks	85	Washington (Indianapolis)	53
Crispus Attucks	60	Shortridge (Indianapolis)	58
		(Double Overtime)	
Crispus Attucks	63	Sacred Heart (Indianapolis)	44
Crispus Attucks	70	Fort Wayne Central	60
Crispus Attucks	88	Michigan City	69
Crispus Attucks	93	Shortridge (Indianapolis)	62
Crispus Attucks	84	Mishawaka	59
Crispus Attucks	72	Hammond Noll	71
Crispus Attucks	75	Washington (Indianapolis)	45
Crispus Attucks	57	Connersville	58
Crispus Attucks	82	Cathedral (Indianapolis)	39
Crispus Attucks	53	Manual (Indianapolis)	33
Crispus Attucks	90	Howe (Indianapolis)	61
Crispus Attucks	80	Bloomington University	36

Sectional (Indianapolis, Butler Fieldhouse)

Crispus Attucks	79	Washington (Indianapolis)	51
Crispus Attucks	87	Manual (Indianapolis)	36
Crispus Attucks	33	Broad Ripple (Indianapolis)	19
Crispus Attucks	73	Shortridge (Indianapolis)	59

Regional (Indianapolis, Butler Fieldhouse)

Crispus Attucks	95	Wilkinson	42
Crispus Attucks	76	Anderson	51

Semifinal (Indianapolis, Butler Fieldhouse)

Crispus Attucks	80	Columbus	62
Crispus Attucks	71	Muncie Central	70

State Finals (Indianapolis, Butler Fieldhouse)

Crispus Attucks	79	New Albany	67
Crispus Attucks	97	Gary Roosevelt	74

Season Record (31–0)
1955–56

Crispus Attucks	81	Fort Wayne Central	41
Crispus Attucks	98	Terre Haute Gerstmeyer	52
Crispus Attucks	55	Sheridan	36
Crispus Attucks	90	South Bend Riley	35
Crispus Attucks	87	Ben Davis (Indianapolis)	44
Crispus Attucks	59	Broad Ripple (Indianapolis)	46
Crispus Attucks	44	Indianapolis Tech	37
Crispus Attucks	75	Indianapolis Washington	55
Crispus Attucks	52	Shortridge (Indianapolis)	45
Crispus Attucks	46	Indianapolis Tech	39
Crispus Attucks	88	South Bend Adams	51
Crispus Attucks	123	Michigan City	53
Crispus Attucks	66	Shortridge (Indianapolis)	56
Crispus Attucks	55	Indianapolis Howe	24
Crispus Attucks	86	Gary Wallace	32
Crispus Attucks	67	Indianapolis Washington	62
Crispus Attucks	75	Connersville	49
Crispus Attucks	65	Cathedral (Indianapolis)	44
Crispus Attucks	64	Manual (Indianapolis)	40
Crispus Attucks	76	Sacred Heart (Indianapolis)	47
Crispus Attucks	52	Frankfort	42

Sectional (Indianapolis, Butler Fieldhouse)

Crispus Attucks	91	Beech Grove	30
Crispus Attucks	72	Howe (Indianapolis)	58
Crispus Attucks	57	Cathedral (Indianapolis)	49
Crispus Attucks	53	Shortridge (Indianapolis)	48

Regional (Indianapolis, Butler Fieldhouse)

Crispus Attucks	61	Anderson	48
Crispus Attucks	99	Hancock Central	43

Semifinal (Indianapolis, Butler Fieldhouse)

Crispus Attucks	67	Connersville	49
Crispus Attucks	67	Scottsburg	42

State Finals (Indianapolis, Butler Fieldhouse)

Crispus Attucks	68	Terre Haute Gerstmeyer	59
Crispus Attucks	79	Lafayette Jeff	57

Season Record (26–5)
1958–59

Crispus Attucks	51	Sheridan	44
Crispus Attucks	67	Terre Haute Gerstmeyer	52
Crispus Attucks	57	South Bend Central	50
Crispus Attucks	38	Broad Ripple (Indianapolis)	39
Crispus Attucks	52	Indianapolis Tech	44
Crispus Attucks	59	Evansville	55
Crispus Attucks	65	Manual (Indianapolis)	61
Crispus Attucks	58	Shortridge (Indianapolis)	61
Crispus Attucks	52	Lafayette Jeff	47
Crispus Attucks	69	Gary Lew Wallace	35
Crispus Attucks	77	Howe (Indianapolis)	55
Crispus Attucks	62	Martinsville	59
Crispus Attucks	75	Indianapolis Washington	61
Crispus Attucks	63	Connersville	74
Crispus Attucks	78	Cathedral (Indianapolis)	47
Crispus Attucks	74	East Chicago Washington	75
Crispus Attucks	82	Wood (Indianapolis)	54
Crispus Attucks	75	Shelbyville	59

Sectional (Indianapolis, Butler Fieldhouse)

Crispus Attucks	79	Broad Ripple (Indianapolis)	65
Crispus Attucks	89	Lawrence Central	44
Crispus Attucks	63	Shortridge (Indianapolis)	62
Crispus Attucks	78	Indianapolis Tech	68

Regional (Indianapolis, Butler Fieldhouse)

Crispus Attucks	60	Alexandria	53
Crispus Attucks	75	Southport	47

Semistate (Indianpolis, Butler Fieldhouse)

Crispus Attucks	82	Madison (Overtime)	80
Crispus Attucks	64	Muncie Central	62

State Finals (Indianapolis, Butler Fieldhouse)

Crispus Attucks	76	Logansport	50
Crispus Attucks	92	Kokomo	54

4

5 Unbeaten Champs
Destroy a Myth

For many years there was a strong feeling, among even the most successful coaches in Indiana high school basketball, that an unbeaten team could not go on to win the state championship—the pressure was too much.

Jeffersonville with Ernie Andres and Bill Johnson came close in 1935 before losing to Archie Chadd's Anderson Indians in the 23-17 final game, and big Clyde Lovellette led Terre Haute Garfield on an unbeaten journey in 1947 before losing to Shelbyville with Bill Garrett and Emerson Johnson in the state championship showdown, 68-58.

It was a Hoosier Hysteria myth that wasn't really erased until Oscar Robertson and his Crispus Attucks running mates came along in the 1950s, and many of today's best coaches still believe that going into the month-long tournament grind without a loss puts a terrible burden on any ball club.

One of Muncie Central's most powerful teams brought a perfect record to the Final Four in 1960, and the Bearcats led by high-scoring Ron Bonham crushed Bloomington in the afternoon, 102-66. Bonham bombarded 29 points in the championship game that night, but Muncie still watched its unbeaten record go up in smoke against East Chicago Washington, 75-59.

Old-timers still recognize that Muncie ball club as perhaps the strongest team to ever lose a championship game. New Albany's 1973 state champs had a 28-game perfect record spoiled by Broad Ripple of Indianapolis, 73-66, in the 1980 state championship game.

Robertson and Willie Merriweather teamed up in 1955 to bring Indianapolis its first state championship with a staggering 97-74 win over Gary Roosevelt in the title bout, and the next year the Big O returned to lead Crispus Attucks on its history-making unbeaten state championship march. Attucks became the Hoosier state's first unbeaten champion with an impressive 79-57 victory over Lafayette Jeff.

During those two remarkable 31–1 and 31–0 seasons, Crispus Attucks put together a 45-game winning streak including tourneys which still stands. The only loss in two years came on the road at the hands of Connersville (58–57) near the end of the 1955 regular-season schedule.

Hall of Fame Coach Ray Crowe still refers to Crispus Attucks' electrifying 71–70 win over Muncie Central in the 1955 Semistate final as one of his three biggest victories in an outstanding seven-year career. Muncie had been rated No. 1 and Attucks No. 2 by the pollsters.

One year later South Bend Central duplicated that drive to an unbeaten (30–0) state championship with a 67–55 triumph over Crispus Attucks in the final game. Elmer McCall became a two-time winner repeating his state title shot with South Bend in 1953. John Coalmon tied Oscar Robertson's state tourney record with a 4-game total of 106 points and South Bend blocked Crispus Attucks' strong bid to equal Franklin's Wonder Five, who swept three straight championships in 1920–22.

Indianapolis Washington (31–0), East Chicago Roosevelt (28–0), and East Chicago Washington (29–0) bracketed three straight unbeaten state championship performances from 1969 to 1971. All three were blessed with intimidating inside strength and were favored by the pollsters from the beginning.

Bill Green was in his first year as head coach at Indianapolis

Crispus Attucks' 1956 champion had the distinction of being the first unbeaten team in Indiana history. Front: Henry Robertson, William Brown, Lavern Benson, Albert Maxey, Sam Milton; back row: Assistant Coach Al Spurlock, Edgar Searcy, Odell Donel, Oscar Robertson, Stanford Patton, James Enoch, and Coach Ray Crowe.

Washington in 1969, taking over for Jerry Oliver who had moved on to Indiana University. Bill was to win two more state titles a little later with Marion in the North Central Conference in 1975–76.

George McGinnis (6–7) and Steve Downing (6–9) were the two big guns for Washington which won its first state title in 1965 with Billy Keller as leading scorer and Oliver doing the coaching. McGinnis set a state tourney record with 148 points in four games and averaged 32.7 with 1,014 for the full distance.

South Bend Central followed up Attucks with an unbeaten year for itself in 1957. Front: Joe Winston, Mike Sacchini, Lee McKnight, Herb Lee, Denny Bishop, Mohler Hobbs; back row: Principal Rupert Ferrell, Coach Elmer McCall, Lamar Gemberling, Sylvester Coalmon, Bill Floring, John Coalmon, and Assistant Coach Jim Powers.

Marion, Vincennes, and Gary Tolleston completed 1969's Final Four and the tournament cast owned an unbelievable combined record of 110–1. Tolleston was tagged with the lone defeat and it had come at the hands of a Chicago team.

Washington had to come from behind in the afternoon to down Marion, 61–60, in the tournament's outstanding game. Tolleston was 77–66 winner over Vincennes, and then Washington held off Tolleston at night in the 79–76 state title shootout.

McGinnis bombed 35 points and Downing 20 in the final against Tolleston. Big George also had 27 rebounds for the Continentals.

Bill Holzbach's towering East Chicago Roosevelt ball club featuring 6–8 Jim Bradley thumped Muncie Central, 90–75, and an underdog Carmel ball club, 76–62, in the 1970 State Finals. Bradley had 27 in the afternoon and 24 in the championship game as the Rough Riders overpowered both opponents.

Four Hall of Fame coaches met in the 1957 State Finals: Elmer McCall of South Bend Central's state champs, Howard Sharpe of Terre Haute Gerstmeyer, Marion Crawley of Lafayette Jeff and Ray Crowe of Indianapolis Crispus Attucks.

Dave Shepherd of Carmel set a 40-point championship game record, breaking the old record of 39 by Oscar Robertson in 1956; but the huge inside strength of Bradley and John Davis was just too much for the smaller Greyhounds.

East Chicago Washington broke the 100-point barrier eight times the next year on the way to the Hoosier state's third unbeaten state championship effort in a row. John Molodet's Washington crew beat Floyd Central in the afternoon, 102–88, and Elkhart in the final, 70–60.

It was the second state championship for the East Chicago school and Molodet called his starting five the best ever in Washington's brilliant hardwood history. Pete Trgovich and Junior Bridgeman were the forwards, Tim Stoddard was the center and Darnell Adell and Ruben Bailey were the guards.

Trgovich was the team's leading scorer, and he bombed a record-tying 40 points in the afternoon game against Floyd Central. Pete came back with 28 in the windup with Elkhart.

Trgovich and Stoddard went on to play for NCAA champions in

Indianapolis Washington star
Steve Downing in action in 1969.

college—Trgovich for Johnny Wooden at UCLA and Stoddard for
Norm Sloan at North Carolina State. Bridgeman played on an NCAA
finalist at Louisville.

These excerpts from the *Indianapolis Star* recall those five
unbeaten champions and some memorable final games.

Crispus Attucks
first unbeaten
state champion

Crispus Attucks, the greatest team in the history of Indiana
high school basketball, walked where none could find a path in
the 46 years of the state tourney.

The magnificent men of Ray Crowe, with the incomparable
Oscar Robertson scoring 39 points and smashing every scoring
record he could reach, walloped Lafayette, 79–57 [March 12,
1956], to win their second straight state championship.

When that last tick went off the clock, Attucks stood alone as
the only team ever to go the distance unbeaten. The Tigers finished with 45 straight victories over a two-year period—31 this
season.

Attucks won this just as it captured most of those other 44,
grabbing an early lead and then, with Oscar as the lever, applying
relentless pressure until the weary opponent could go no more.

The Tigers never trailed in this, one of the finest games in their brilliant two-year run.

Oscar's 39 points ripped up a single-game record that had stood since 1949 when Dee Monroe hit 36 points for Madison in a losing title game effort against Jasper. The four-game mark Oscar probably figured was simply out on loan. Gary Roosevelt's Jake Eison set the mark of 97 points and nosed out Oscar by two points in 1955 when Attucks nailed the first title for an Indianapolis school with a 97–74 win over Roosevelt in the final.

This time Robertson, in a red-hot duel with Lafayette's Ron Fisher, cut loose with a 17-point fourth quarter to close with a state record 106 points.

Before Attucks, two unbeaten teams made it to the final game and lost. Jeffersonville bowed to Anderson in the 1935 state title tilt and Terre Haute Garfield was disappointed by Shelbyville with Bill Garrett in the 1947 windup.

Marion Crawley of Lafayette could soothe the bitter disappointment in missing this bid for a fourth state title in the knowledge that there was little he or his Broncs could do to stop this perfectly drilled and fiercely competitive band of Attucks Tigers.

Lafayette rifled 19 of its 46 shots for a solid .404 percentage and under great pressure committed just four errors.

It would have been good enough against almost anyone but the Indianapolis powerhouse. Attucks blistered Broncho opponents with incredible .492 shooting on 32 baskets in 65 attempts and was charged with one less error.

It was Oscar's night. But all of those Tigers were great. Their names will be remembered now as long as high school basketball is played in Indiana. There was Bill Brown, the fantastic jumper,

Unbeaten state champs for 1969, Indianapolis Washington. Front: Alan Glaze, George McGinnis, Wayne Pack, Steve Downing, Louis Day, James Riley; back row: Assistant Coach Basil Sfreddo, Steve Stanfield, Abner Nibbs, Kenneth Carter, James Arnold, Kenneth Parks, Harvey Galbreath, and Coach Bill Green.

East Chicago Roosevelt's unbeaten 1970 champions. Front: James Rossi, Holland Fluellen, Cavanaugh Gary, Leonard Marks; second row: Chris Kouros, Mike Artis, Frank Suchecki, Woodrow Rancifer; back row: Coach Bill Holzbach, Darryl Brandford, James Bradley, John Davis, Napoleon Brandford, Assistant Coach Henry Zawacki.

and quiet, underrated Stan Patton and Al Maxey and Ed Searcy—names for the Hoosier sports Hall of Fame.

Attucks hit eight of 13 shots as it rolled to a 20–11 first quarter lead. . . . Lafayette still was within reaching distance, 44–36, with four minutes left in the third quarter. . . . Brown, playing with four fouls, then helped Oscar and Patton roll the Tigers into the fourth quarter with a prohibitive 56–41 advantage.

South Bend Central
ends Attucks bid
for three straight

South Bend Central, the giant of the North, slammed the door on Crispus Attucks' bid for a third straight high school basketball championship [March 23, 1957] with a convincing 67–55 victory that certified in every way claims that nothing in Indiana this season could tame those Bears.

The victory, South Bend's 30th of the season, made the Bears the second team in two years to go the distance unbeaten. It also ended a fabulous Attucks state tourney winning streak at 29 games. South Bend's John Coalmon scored 24 points. That gave him 106 for the last four games and tied the all-time record set [in 1956] by Oscar Robertson of Attucks.

The game presented a situation unmatched for drama, emotion and tenseness. Here was South Bend Central, the unbeatable, waiting to jump that one last obstacle. And here was Attucks, the defending champion, forgotten in pre-tourney talk, but back in the finals—proud, hungry, and determined to keep the Bears from going through unbeaten.

But the desire that carried the Indianapolis team through the tourney wasn't enough to stop Elmer McCall's poised, confident outfit. There was too much South Bend speed, too much South Bend rebounding.

There was just too much of everything for any Hoosier high school team to match this season.

The game was torrid and tight throughout the first half. Al Maxey, Odell Donel, and Ed Searcy shot Attucks into a 6–2 lead in the opening minutes. And it was 10–9, Atucks, with 1:42 left in the first quarter.

Then the terrific Herbie Lee, playing with one good ankle [the left one was sprained in the Semistate] and without his glasses about half the time (the shaft kept breaking), scored to give the Bears a lead they never lost.

John and Sylvester Coalmon, rebounding like mad, took it from there and ran the South Bend lead to 21–14 through the second quarter. But with 2:07 left in the half, Maxey and scrappy little Laverne Benson had Attucks challenging at 23–20. Always on the attack, Central slugged back and ran its lead to 29–22 at the intermission.

Central took almost complete charge of the game as the second half opened. Operating with the precision of a drill team, the Bears opened up a 35–22 lead before the third quarter was two minutes old.

East Chicago Roosevelt's Jim Bradley in an ebullient mood in 1970.

East Chicago Washington, unbeaten in 1971. Front: Nick Elish, manager, Francisco Sanchez, Ruben Bailey, Darnell Adell, Albert Pollard, Mike Monagan, Mike Andric, manager; back row: Coach John Molodet, Robert Smith, Alex Kountoures, Ulysses Bridgeman, Tim Stoddard, James Williams, Pete Trgovich, Marcus Stallings, and Milan Grozdanich.

Attucks reached down into its shoes for one last counter attack. Benson, Maxey, and Donel led the charge. Attucks cut the gap to 55–47 with five minutes to go and 59–53 with 3:30 showing on the clock.

This was the time when the Bears had to offer quick and definite proof of their right to succeed Attucks on the throne. And they left no doubt. Sylvester Coalmon sank two free throws and the Bears went into a fast, beautifully executed stall game and held the ball until Attucks stole it with 1:24 left.

This was South Bend's second state championship. Coach McCall gave the Bears their first in 1953, his first year as coach.

Washington's second
title fifth for
Indianapolis schools

Washington became the third unbeaten team in 59 years to rule the Hoosier high school basketball world [March 22, 1969] with a stubborn 79–76 victory over stubborn Gary Tolleston.

Big George McGinnis, a 6-7 Washington superstar, set a 148-point state tourney record for four games with 35 in the title clash. Washington nailed down its second state championship in five years and it was the fifth for Indianapolis schools, three being reeled off by Crispus Attucks in the 1950s.

First-year coach Bill Green's towering Continentals charged into a 16-10 lead near the end of the first quarter with eight straight points. Washington led the rest of the way and was ahead

Tim Stoddard, now a pitcher
with the Baltimore Orioles, is
shown in 1971 starring capacity
for East Chicago Washington.

by as much as 18 points one time in the third quarter.

Tolleston bounced back on the 47-point sharpshooting of
backcourt aces Henry Goodes and Donell Baity in the closing
minutes to eat up most of that big Continental cushion. But the
Blue Raiders who would soon consolidate with Gary West got no
closer than three points.

Washington wound up with a 31–0 clean sweep equalling the
Crispus Attucks record in 1956. South Bend Central was the only
other unbeaten state champ, crowned in 1957 with a 30–0 mark.
Tolleston lost for only the second time in 30 games.

No. 1 ranked Washington reached the championship bout
with a tense 61–60 comeback win over unbeaten Marion in the
afternoon thanks to a shot by 6–9 center Steve Downing with only 24 seconds on the clock.

Marion led Washington 56–46 with six minutes to go and it
took a brilliant 11-point blitz by the Continentals to turn it
around at 3:35. Marion regained a 60–57 lead before a shot by Jim
Arnold cut it to just one point. That set the stage for Downing's
clincher in the closing seconds.

Tolleston downed unbeaten Vincennes in the other afternoon
tilt, 77–66.

McGinnis cracked 14 of his 36 shots in the championship game
and grabbed 27 rebounds. Big George, who closed a brilliant high
school career with 1,014 points and a 32.7 average, topped the
128-point tourney record which belonged to Evansville North's
Bob Ford. The latter scored 128 in the 1967 tourney.

McGinnis and Downing, who was limited to three buckets by

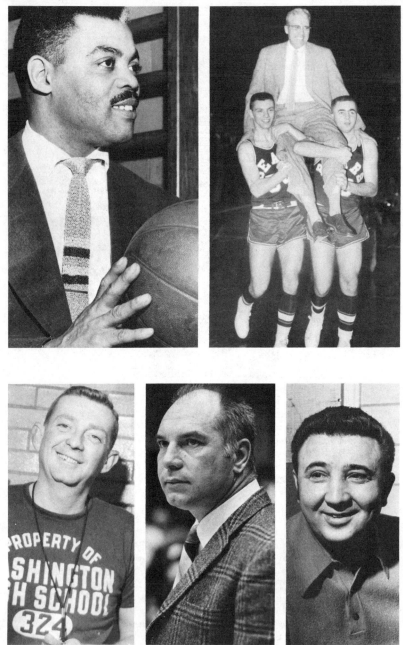

Coaches of the five unbeaten teams: top left is Ray Crowe of Indianapolis Crispus Attucks and top right shows an exuberant Elmer McCall of South Bend Central being carried off the floor by Bill Floring and Lamar Gemberling following Central's 67–55 victory of Crispus Attucks for the 1957 state championship. Above, left to right, are Bill Green of Indianapolis Washington, Bill Holzbach of East Chicago Roosevelt and John Molodet of East Chicago Washington.

Marion, teamed for 55 points and 45 rebounds—almost matching their average for the year. Downing added 20 points in the title tilt, lending strong support underneath for the Continentals.

One of the unsung heroes of this Washington state championship was peppery guard Wayne Pack who cracked three straight in the afternoon to help put the stopper on Marion and then came back with 13 points against Tolleston.

Most of the experts billed the Washington-Marion opener as the one for all the marbles, no matter what happened the rest of the way. There were two or three dangerous stretches in the second half where it looked like Washington believed the notices.

Tolleston threatened at 75–70 with 1:22 to go and 77–74 with less than one minute remaining.

East Chicago's
Rough Riders rustle
Shepherd's flock

Dave Shepherd's brilliant 40-point final game record couldn't keep heavily-favored East Chicago Roosevelt from becoming the fourth unbeaten champion in the 60-year state tourney history [March 21, 1970] with a 76–62 victory over outmanned Carmel.

Shepherd cracked 14 of his 39 shots from the floor and 12 out of 14 free throws to wipe out the great Oscar Robertson's 39-point mark for Crispus Attucks in 1956.

It was just a drop in the bucket against Roosevelt's towering Rough Riders led by 6-7 giants Jim Bradley and John Davis. Bradley with 24 points and Davis with 21 overwhelmed the Greyhounds on the boards even though underdog Carmel made it surprisingly close for better than three quarters.

Roosevelt led only 14–12 at the quarter, 32–29 at the half and 49–42 at three quarters. But that staggering 67–31 rebound advantage took its terrible toll on Carmel as the game wore on.

Shepherd, the gifted 5–10 son of Carmel Coach Bill Shepherd, went down smoking. He ripped in the last two in the last seconds to close out a sensational prep career with a single season record of 1,079 for Indiana preps.

He also had a 37.4 average going into the State Finals and became the Sweet Sixteen's third highest scorer with a four-game total of 125.

Roosevelt, ranked No. 1 by the pollsters all year, crushed fourth-ranking Muncie Central in the afternoon by a shocking 90–75 margin. Carmel advanced with a hard-fought 76–62 win over little Loogootee.

For a short time, it looked like Roosevelt might have suffered a slight letdown following the big bout with the North Central Conference champs. But the Rough Riders led all the way and maybe they just figured they could nail it down whenever the time was ripe.

Bill Holzbach's Roosevelt ball club joined Crispus Attucks [1956], South Bend Central [1957] and Indianapolis Washington [1969] as the four unbeaten state champs. This was Roosevelt's first trip to the Sweet 16 and the Rough Riders didn't blow it.

Bradley got his 24 points and a Sweet 16 total of 107 with 11 of 22 from the field and two of four free throws. Big Brad lived up to all his notices and those comparing him to the incredible McGinnis can't be too far wrong.

Bradley, Davis, and Napoleon Brandford collected 49 rebounds compared to Carmel's meager team total of 21.

They said in the program that Bradley is 6-7 and so is running mate John Davis. "Actually, John is about 6-9, I guess," Bradley confessed later in the locker room. "I'm 6-8½." And at 6-8½ he handled the ball so smoothly and so deftly that one wag called him "the best guard in the state."

Jim Bradley couldn't sleep Friday night [on the eve of the state championship], and now 200 college coaches won't sleep all week. In two ball games he scored 51 points and grabbed 42 rebounds.

East Chicago Senators
3d straight unbeaten
to climb Mount IHSAA

Mighty East Chicago Washington climbed Mount IHSAA [March 20, 1971] to take its place alongside four other unbeaten state basketball champions with a 70-60 victory over Elkhart.

Washington blazed to a 12-0 lead in the first three minutes and led all the way. Coach John Molodet's Senators became the third straight unbeaten state champ and the fifth since 1956.

Underdog Elkhart, on its first trip to the championship round, got away to a terrible start missing its first nine field attempts in each of the first two quarters. But the Blazers battled back in the second half to put some pressure on the state's No. 1 ranked team.

Elkhart, trailing 38-22 at half-time, trailed only 52-48 near the end of the third quarter and 56-54 with 4:36 to play in the fourth period. Washington then nailed down its 29th straight victory and first state championship since 1960 with a five-point flurry in the last 28 seconds.

Pistol Pete Trgovich, who resembles Pete Maravich, was the triggerman for the champs, drilling 28 points in the final game and a record-tying 40 against Floyd Central in the 102-88 afternoon clash.

Trgovich's 40 tied a tourney record set by Muncie Central's Ron Bonham in 1960 and tied by Carmel's Dave Shepherd in 1970.

Washington's 344 points in the last four games of the Sweet 16 set another tourney record, erasing the 330 by Gary Tolleston in 1969. The Senators tied still another tourney record with 102 against Floyd Central.

Trgovich, 6-7 Tim Stoddard and 6-5 Ulysses (Junior) Bridgeman made up the tall Washington front line which dominated the game completely in the first half. Elkhart appeared to be all but out of it (38-22) when the two ball clubs headed for the dressing room at the halfway mark.

Carl Macon, Elkhart's 6–5 rebounding workhorse, John Babcock and Joe LeFevre sparked Elkhart in the third quarter. Bill Davis also hit four straight buckets in the third quarter and Elkhart outscored the Senators, 26–16. Suddenly it was 54–48 in favor of the Senators.

"I thought we had a little letdown after getting out to that big lead in the first half," Coach Molodet confessed later. "I think the kids thought they could win it easily and relaxed just a little too much.

"We did make some late changes. We told the kids they were going to have to hit that defense and the boards. I knew we were tired but I told the kids—they are just as tired as we are."

Elkhart had every reason to be exhausted because the Blazers had to go three overtimes in the afternoon to get past New Castle, 65–60.

Indianapolis Crispus Attucks

Season Record (31–0)
1955–56

Crispus Attucks	81	Fort Wayne Central	41
Crispus Attucks	98	Terre Haute Gerstmeyer	52
Crispus Attucks	55	Sheridan	36
Crispus Attucks	90	South Bend Riley	35
Crispus Attucks	87	Ben Davis (Indianapolis)	44
Crispus Attucks	59	Broad Ripple (Indianapolis)	46
Crispus Attucks	44	Indianapolis Tech	37
Crispus Attucks	75	Indianapolis Washington	55
Crispus Attucks	52	Shortridge (Indianapolis)	45
Crispus Attucks	46	Indianapolis Tech	39
Crispus Attucks	88	South Bend Adams	51
Crispus Attucks	123	Michigan City	53
Crispus Attucks	66	Shortridge (Indianapolis)	56
Crispus Attucks	55	Indianapolis Howe	24
Crispus Attucks	86	Gary Wallace	32
Crispus Attucks	67	Indianapolis Washington	62
Crispus Attucks	75	Connersville	49
Crispus Attucks	65	Cathedral (Indianapolis)	44
Crispus Attucks	64	Manual (Indianapolis)	40
Crispus Attucks	76	Sacred Heart (Indianapolis)	47
Crispus Attucks	52	Frankfort	42

Sectional (Indianapolis, Butler Fieldhouse)

Crispus Attucks	91	Beech Grove	30
Crispus Attucks	72	Howe (Indianapolis)	58
Crispus Attucks	57	Cathedral (Indianapolis)	49
Crispus Attucks	53	Shortridge (Indianapolis)	48

Regional (Indianapolis, Butler Fieldhouse)

Crispus Attucks	61	Anderson	48
Crispus Attucks	99	Hancock Central	43

Semifinal (Indianapolis, Butler Fieldhouse)

Crispus Attucks	67	Connersville	49
Crispus Attucks	67	Scottsburg	42

State Finals (Indianapolis, Butler Fieldhouse)

Crispus Attucks	68	Terre Haute Gerstmeyer	59
Crispus Attucks	79	Lafayette	57

South Bend Central

Season Record (30–0)
1956–57

South Bend Central	81	Gary Roosevelt (Overtime)	72
South Bend Central	55	Hammond High	40
South Bend Central	78	Shelbyville	37
South Bend Central	55	Michigan City	48
South Bend Central	66	Goshen	40
South Bend Central	62	Lafayette Jeff	39
South Bend Central	86	East Chicago Washington	53
South Bend Central	79	Seymour	52
South Bend Central	57	Lafayette Jeff	45
South Bend Central	95	Warsaw	41
South Bend Central	84	LaPorte	49
South Bend Central	69	South Bend Adams	43
South Bend Central	72	Muncie Central	58
South Bend Central	83	Logansport	37
South Bend Central	96	South Bend Riley	49
South Bend Central	87	South Bend Washington	43
South Bend Central	78	Anderson	51
South Bend Central	81	Mishawaka	75
South Bend Central	112	Fort Wayne North	46
South Bend Central	53	Elkhart	37

Sectional (South Bend)

South Bend Central	52	South Bend Adams	32
South Bend Central	77	Mishawaka	72
South Bend Central	44	Walkerton	26
South Bend Central	56	Lakeville	48

Regional (Elkhart)

South Bend Central	66	Elkhart	55
South Bend Central	89	Pierceton	42

Semistate (Fort Wayne)

South Bend Central	74	Fort Wayne South	50
South Bend Central	75	Noblesville	62

State Finals (Indianapolis, Butler Fieldhouse)

South Bend Central	54	Lafayette Jeff	36
South Bend Central	67	Crispus Attucks (Indianapolis)	55

Indianapolis Washington

Season Record (31–0)
1968–69

Indianapolis Washington	102	Hammond High	57
Indianapolis Washington	82	Shortridge (Indianapolis)	77
Indianapolis Washington	91	Northwest (Indianapolis)	48
Indianapolis Washington	84	East Chicago Washington	71
Indianapolis Washington	101	Lawrence Central	52
Indianapolis Washington	90	Warren Central	45
Indianapolis Washington	109	Cathedral (Indianapolis)	65
Indianapolis Washington	87	Southport	74
Indianapolis Washington	93	Terre Haute Gerstmeyer	48
Indianapolis Washington	104	Indianapolis Manual	58
Indianapolis Washington	90	Speedway	57
Indianapolis Washington	102	Scecina (Indianapolis)	72
Indianapolis Washington	90	Indianapolis Tech	57
Indianapolis Washington	97	Cathedral (Indianapolis)	66
Indianapolis Washington	90	Shortridge (Indianapolis)	68
Indianapolis Washington	80	Columbus	66
Indianapolis Washington	86	Wood (Indianapolis)	38
Indianapolis Washington	96	Broad Ripple (Indianapolis)	42
Indianapolis Washington	97	Howe (Indianapolis)	41
Indianapolis Washington	106	Ben Davis	67
Indianapolis Washington	71	Indianapolis Tech	47
Indianapolis Washington	92	Arlington (Indianapolis)	53

Sectional (Indianapolis, Hinkle Fieldhouse)

Indianapolis Washington	73	Indianapolis Tech	42
Indianapolis Washington	105	Broad Ripple (Indianapolis)	57
Indianapolis Washington	90	Crispus Attucks (Indianapolis)	64

Regional (Indianapolis, Hinkle Fieldhouse)

Indianapolis Washington	46	Shortridge (Indianapolis)	38
Indianapolis Washington	87	Warren Central	41

Semistate (Indianapolis, Hinkle Fieldhouse)

Indianapolis Washington	85	Silver Creek	64
Indianapolis Washington	96	Jac-Cen-Del	65

State Finals (Indianapolis, Hinkle Fieldhouse)

Indianapolis Washington	61	Marion	60
Indianapolis Washington	79	Gary Tolleston	76

East Chicago Roosevelt

Season Record (28–0)
1969–70

East Chicago Roosevelt	78	Gary Lew Wallace	58
East Chicago Roosevelt	68	Mentone	48
East Chicago Roosevelt	73	Valparaiso	59
East Chicago Roosevelt	57	Crown Point	44
East Chicago Roosevelt	96	Chicago Hirsch	61
East Chicago Roosevelt	71	Gary Roosevelt	60
East Chicago Roosevelt	102	Highland	76
East Chicago Roosevelt	57	Huntington	55
East Chicago Roosevelt	87	Munster	56
East Chicago Roosevelt	73	Whiting	46
East Chicago Roosevelt	76	Portage	48
East Chicago Roosevelt	86	Hammond Morton	63
East Chicago Roosevelt	68	Hammond Noll	57
East Chicago Roosevelt	80	East Chicago Washington	57
East Chicago Roosevelt	75	Hammond Tech	63
East Chicago Roosevelt	85	Hammond Gavit	73
East Chicago Roosevelt	68	Hammond Clark	57
East Chicago Roosevelt	75	Hammond High	38
East Chicago Roosevelt	68	Warsaw	58
East Chicago Roosevelt	71	Gary Westside	67

Sectional (East Chicago)

East Chicago Roosevelt	68	Calumet	46
East Chicago Roosevelt	58	East Chicago Washington	55

Regional (Gary)

East Chicago Roosevelt	72	Gary Roosevelt	64
East Chicago Roosevelt	72	Hammond Clark	38

Semistate (Lafayette)

East Chicago Roosevelt	56	Lafayette Jeff	54
East Chicago Roosevelt	82	Michigan City	78

State Finals (Indianapolis, Hinkle Fieldhouse)

East Chicago Roosevelt	90	Muncie Central	75
East Chicago Roosevelt	76	Carmel	62

East Chicago Washington

Season Record (29–0)
1970–71

East Chicago Washington	92	Calumet	63
East Chicago Washington	109	Crown Point	67
East Chicago Washington	95	Hammond Gavit	43
East Chicago Washington	80	Terre Haute Gerstmeyer	60

East Chicago Washington	77	Gary Roosevelt	70
East Chicago Washington	100	Whiting	38
East Chicago Washington	73	Hammond Morton	50
East Chicago Washington	92	Hammond Clark	51
East Chicago Washington	98	Anderson	73
East Chicago Washington	90	Munster	39
East Chicago Washington	94	Warsaw	70
East Chicago Washington	91	LaPorte	59
East Chicago Washington	95	Valparaiso	77
East Chicago Washington	112	Kokomo	60
East Chicago Washington	105	Hammond High	55
East Chicago Washington	112	Hammond Tech	55
East Chicago Washington	89	East Chicago Roosevelt	59
East Chicago Washington	110	Michigan City	89
East Chicago Washington	106	Hammond Noll	73
East Chicago Washington	88	Gary West	85

Sectional (East Chicago)

East Chicago Washington	71	Gary Edison	39
East Chicago Washington	73	East Chicago Roosevelt	48
East Chicago Washington	87	Hobart	76

Regional (Gary)

East Chicago Washington	65	Hammond Clark	51
East Chicago Washington	94	Gary West	89

Semistate (Lafayette)

East Chicago Washington	93	Michigan City	79
East Chicago Washington	79	Rossville	67

State Finals (Indianapolis, Hinkle Fieldhouse)

East Chicago Washington	102	Floyd Central	88
East Chicago Washington	70	Elkhart	60

5

Stretch Murphy to Dave Colescott—Bill Green Puts New Life in Marion

Charles (Stretch) Murphy and Bob Chapman were the two great players mentioned most often in Marion hardwood history for a half century. They starred on the Marion basketball team that knocked off Johnny Wooden, Les Reynolds, and their Martinsville teammates, 30–23, for the 1926 state basketball championship. Murphy went on to become an All-American center at Purdue (on the same team with Wooden), and later both men were installed in the Indiana Hall of Fame—Murphy in 1963 and Chapman 13 years later.

Coached by Gene Thomas, Marion won 27 of its 29 games on the way to the school's first state title, losing only to Kokomo and Bloomington. Orville Hooker, Woody Weir, and Jack Colescott turned out numerous big winners in succeeding years at Marion. Weir won 163 games from 1947 to 1958 (he still leads all Marion coaches in total wins) and Colescott with his 122–34 overall record put the Giants in the State Finals two straight years in 1968–69.

Colescott's most talented ball club had a perfect 27–0 record spoiled by state title bound Indianapolis Washington with George McGinnis and Steve Downing in the 1969 State Finals. Downing's bucket in the closing seconds rescued Washington in a 61–60 nailbiter after Marion led by 56–46 coming down the stretch.

Ironically, Bill Green, who coached Washington's unbeaten champs in a magnificent 31–0 season, and Colescott's son David teamed up a short time later to bring Marion back-to-back state titlists in 1975–76. Marion cut down small-school power Loogootee, 58–46,

Marion's 1926 state champs. Front: Edward Heck, Hal Chasey, Glen Overman, Karl Kilgore, Zed Usher, Stephen Johnson; back row: Everett Chapman, Homer Davidson, Charles (Stretch) Murphy, Robert Chapman and Coach Gene Thomas.

for the 1975 state title and came back the next year to repeat with an 82–76 win over Rushville.

David Colescott, Marion's big gun on both teams (setting a school record with 1,529 career points), was voted Indiana's Mr. Basketball and Trester Award winner in 1976.

Green became just the fifth coach to put together three state title winners in Indiana. Only three have done better with four—Everett Case at Frankfort, 1925–39; Glenn Curtis with one at Lebanon in 1918 and three more at Martinsville from 1924–33; and Marion Crawley with two at Washington (1941–42) and two at Lafayette Jeff in 1948–64.

Griz Wagner coached the Franklin Wonder Five to three straight championships from 1920 to 1922. Bill Harrell also had three nailing down Muncie Central's sixth and seventh in 1978 and 1979, but Bill's other state title came in Kentucky with Shelby County in 1966.

Larry Liddle took over Marion with a phenomenal 113–22 record when Green left the coaching ranks for five years from 1977 to 1981, and Liddle's 1980 State Finalist team dropped a 71–69 heartstopper to state champ Indianapolis Broad Ripple on an incredible 57-foot shot by Stacey Toran as the final horn sounded.

Green left coaching following his second straight Marion state title in 1976 to pursue a job in the college ranks and look after his other business interests. He returned for the 1981–82 season when Liddle accepted Purdue-Calumet's attractive offer.

Led by Indiana All-Star Joseph Price and all-state junior James Blackmon, Marion ranked high in the polls all year with a classy 22–3 record and bowed out against Plymouth's state champs in the Fort Wayne Semistate. Marion lost in overtime, 56–55.

Price, a strong 6–5 forward recruited by Notre Dame, wound up his outstanding prep career with 1,492 points—second only to Colescott's 1,529. Blackmon seemed almost certain to become the most heavily recruited player in Marion cage history.

Marion's eight-year record from 1974 to 1982 was a phenomenal 186–31, including eight straight trips to the Semistate round. It was the longest unbroken string of Sweet 16 appearances for the Hoosier state.

Green increased his impressive coaching record in seven seasons with the Giants to 124–51. Only Weir had more victories with 163.

Green, a successful coach in the Indianapolis system at Park School, Sacred Heart, Cathedral, and Washington, was received by many Marion fans with mixed emotions when he took over the Giants in the early 1970s. A great many Marion diehards found it hard to forgive the man who kayoed an unbeaten Giant team for the 1969 state championship.

Oddly enough, Green and Jack Colescott (his predecessor on the Marion bench) had been old athletic products from Indiana Central College in the Capital City. Green was named Coach of the Year after his Washington state championship sweep in 1969 and headed for

A long time in coming, but 1975 was a sweet victory. The state champs are aligned as follows: front: Assistant Coach Dan Gunn and Coach Bill Green; second row: Manager Mark Prater, Dave Colescott, Doug Harris, kevin Pearson, Rob Acord, Bill Lester, Manager Mike Chin, Student Trainer Bill Mooney; back row: Dave Peak, Jess Alumbaugh, Ray Myers, Charles Jackson, Mike Flynn, Rob Oatess, Joe Neal, Cregg Baumbaugh, Trainer Dick Lootens.

The day following the 1975 victory.

Marion when Colescott became athletic director in 1970.

"It was a great challenge for me because I considered Marion one of the top coaching jobs in the state," Green said at the time. "My goal is to keep the program right where it's been under Colescott's guidance."

After Green coached Marion to two straight state championships in 1975-76, he pointed out that he was "particularly pleased for the Colescott family because Jack took a couple of outstanding teams to the State Finals [in 1968-69] and both times lost in the closing seconds."

Bill added that "Jack probably should have had a gold ring and now he has the satisfaction of watching his son [Dave] win a state championship ring."

By this time Coach Green had converted most of his critics in Marion where the pressures on both coaches and players rank second to none. When Dean Smith recruited Mr. Basketball Dave Colescott for North Carolina's NCAA powerhouse, he spoke of that pressure. "Dave Colescott won't play under as much pressure for us at North Carolina as he did in high school at Marion," Smith said.

Marion sells from 4,700 to 5,000 season tickets each year, and the entire community is devoted to the high school team and its players. Anderson would be the only school with more season ticket holders, and the coaching pressures in Anderson probably are slightly less than those in Marion.

Anderson's sectional is much tougher with the split to three strong basketball powers, and it's no longer a must-win proposition for coaches. Marion expects its teams to go to Fort Wayne for the Semistate every year, while a loss in the Anderson sectional becomes more and more predictable.

Marion teams won 20 or more for eight straight years, with 23–5 in the 1976 state championship year its poorest mark in that stretch.

Green recalls that Marion returned all five starters from a 14–10 team in 1975 with David Colescott being just a junior. It was a very intelligent ball club (all B-students or better) but not one with a lot of physical talent, according to the coach.

Coaches for the final four hold the championship trophy, later won by Marion: Bill Stearman (Columbus North), Jim Rosenstihl (Lebanon), Bill Green (Marion) and Jack Butcher (Loogootee).

Marion won the North Central Conference championship with a 7–0 record in league play, and the Giants got off to a sensational 16–0 start before suffering their only setback all year at the hands of Fort Wayne Snider, 73–66.

Marion had struggled to an 85–81 overtime win over visiting North Central of Indianapolis the preceding night and the Giants were a bit tired the next night on their trip to Fort Wayne. Marion hit only 6 of 28 shots in the first half and Snider seized a 31–24 lead at the intermission.

Several times during the second half Marion threatened to come from behind, and early in the fourth quarter the Giants trailed only 50–49. Snider exploded to a big 73–60 cushion at this point, and the loss prevented Marion from climbing to the No. 1 spot in the wire service polls.

Colescott, a tremendous team leader, averaged 18 points his junior year and 25 as a senior. Frontliner Kevin Pearson was the most under-

Top photo shows the 1976 champs. Front: Devol Tyson, Bob Wiesler, Rick Francis; second row: Dave Colescott, Jess Alumbaugh, Carlton Hayes, Jeff Bragg, Matt Dubuque, James Freshwater; top row: Coach Bill Green, Brad Haskell, Matt Pain, Mark Smith, Charles Jackson, Ray Myers, Jodan Price, Joe Neal and Assistant Coach Morris Smedley. Coach Green displays his two state championship rings for back-to-back victories in 1975 and 1976. He had won an earlier one in 1969 at Indianapolis Washington.

rated man on the 1975 state title winner and Marion's No. 2 offensive threat. Pearson was rewarded with a spot on the Indiana All-Star team for its series against Kentucky.

Marion ranked fifth in the state going into the sectionals where little Oak Hill greeted the Giants with perhaps their toughest battle in the entire month-long tournament. Colescott had the flu and played only sparingly in the first quarter. Rob Acord sank two free throws in the closing seconds for a narrow 48–46 decision.

Marion turned in one of its most convincing performances, wiping out a highly regarded Fort Wayne North outfit in the final game of the Fort Wayne Semistate, 82–61. The Giants led only 38–35 at the halfway mark, but a 28-point explosion in the third quarter buried the Redskins.

Green's famed matchup-zone defense and that third quarter blitz during which Marion drilled 11 straight shots put the Giants in the State Finals with 26 victories in 27 outings. Colescott hit five buckets without a miss in the quarter and the Giants reeled off 12 unanswered points in one flurry.

Marion led Lebanon with its famed Walker brothers almost all the way in the State Finals opener on the way to a 73–65 victory. Indiana All-Star Steve Walker, the Trester Award winner, displayed a deadly outside touch with 29 points for Coach Jim Rosenstihl's Lebanon crew, but Marion had superior balance.

Colescott led the team with 24 points followed by Acord with 16, Pearson with 14, and Doug Harris with 12. Marion boosted a small 31–29 lead at halftime to 47–40 at the end of three quarters. Lebanon couldn't come closer than 59–54 down the stretch.

Marion faced a much-different predicament in tiny Loogootee's patient ball control offense before a sellout 17,490 Market Square Arena crowd at night, but the Giants grabbed control in the second quarter and hung on for a brilliant 58–46 state title victory.

Nailing down its first state championship since 1926, Marion worked nervously through a low-scoring first quarter which found Jack Butcher's Loogootee outfit leading 7–6. Then Marion opened the second quarter with eight straight points and the smaller Lions had to play catchup the rest of the way.

This forced Loogootee, which finished with an outstanding 27–2 record, to change its game plan a bit. It was a game plan that Butcher had perfected for an unbelievable 50–27 rout of Columbus North on .604 shooting in the afternoon.

Once again Marion benefitted from brilliant offensive balance and its matchup zone defense that held opponents to a 57-point scoring average all year. Pearson scored 18 points and had 13 rebounds, Acord 12 points, Colescott and Harris 10 each.

Bill Lester contributed a game high 14 rebounds for the Giants, who ruled the boards by a wide 25–9 margin in the second half.

The Giants, who reached the championship game after four straight misses in 1947, 1950, 1968, and 1969, rolled to a 35–25 lead at

Trester Award winner Dave
Colescott is shown with his
parents after receiving his
plaque. His father Jack was
Marion's coach during an earlier
period. Colescott is seen in the
other photo dribbling downcourt
during the 1976 State Final.
Colescott was also named Mr.
Basketball in 1976.

the end of three quarters and lifted that to 46–32 early in the final session.

"We decided after the Snider game that we wouldn't lose any more," said Pearson, the Marion center who went on to play for Indiana Central and then began his own coaching career.

Jack Lake of the *Marion Chronicle-Tribune* wrote that "the Giants, in fact, played flawless basketball in their last 12 victories. . . . They had several close shaves but their strength was in teamwork and dedication.

"A variety of ingredients, of course, goes into the mix to produce such a spectacular campaign. For one, Bill and his athletes respected one another and developed the unique rapport so necessary for success. He always characterized his 1974–75 crew as intelligent, unselfish kids dedicated to winning. That may have been their major weapon."

Lake continued, "Even the most rabid Marion fans realistically hoped for a record in the neighborhood of 14-6, 15-5 or 16-4 on a regular schedule featured by tough duels against the North Central Conference's seven other members. But Bill Green, privately at least, had a dream."

" 'I told these kids when the season started that I was privileged to be one of maybe just 50 coaches in the state who could say we had a chance to take it all,' Green said. 'I felt we had a good chance all along and when we knocked off Anderson and Kokomo early in the year, it gave us a little momentum.' "

Green never varied his starting unit in Marion's 28-1 run to the IHSAA title—opening each game with the same five youngsters who also started at the end of the 1973–74 season. Rob Acord, Bill Lester, Kevin Pearson, Doug Harris, and Dave Collescott—every starter improved in his own way. Marion also developed a valuable bench headed by Mike Flynn, Tuffy Jackson, Cregg Baumbaugh, and Joe Neal.

Colescott was the only returning starter in 1976 and Green says now that it was probably his best job in 21 years of coaching. Green brought up four players from the reserves and the Giants were ignored by the pollsters at the start of the year.

Marion still carved out a 15-5 regular season led by Colescott with his 25-plus average and actually had a shot at the NCC trophy. A loss to Muncie Central in the season windup kept Marion from gaining at least a share of the conference crown.

Going to the state in 1975 helped a great deal in Coach Green's opinion, and it was a continuation of pride for the Giants. Five members of the 1976 team were on the state tournament squad the previous year, and they got their second ring.

And yet, apart from the extremely talented Colescott in the

backcourt, Marion didn't have state championship material. Green reminds that, besides Colescott, who went to North Carolina, Jeff Bragg was the only other player to sign with a major school. Bragg went on to Wright State—a Division II college.

Marion had a rough time slipping past Huntington North in the regional (74–70). One week later in the Fort Wayne Semistate the Giants nipped Anderson Highland in a 59–57 barn burner and then had to go overtime to down Fort Wayne North, 69–66.

Unranked Marion barely edged out highly regarded Jeffersonville in the State Finals at Market Square Arena, 49–47, on what was the fourth trip in five years to the Final Four for George Marshall's Jeff Red Devils.

Colescott rifled 25 points, Joe Neal 20, and Bragg 14 in the championship game as the fired-up Marion crew mowed down Rushville, 82–76. Rushville startled the big MSA crowd in the afternoon by upsetting tourney favorite East Chicago Washington 68–59 after the No. 1 ranked Senators led 33–12 early in the second quarter.

Colescott also was the big gun with 26 points in Marion's matinee win over Jeffersonville.

"Bill Green and his Marion Giants turned the 66th Indiana high school basketball tournament into a three-ring circus last night with a comeback 82–76 victory over first-time finalist Rushville in a see-saw windup," the *Indianapolis Star* reported in its March 28, 1976 editions.

"Marion became the first repeat winner since Crispus Attucks in 1955–56 before a sellout crowd of 17,490. It was the third gold ring for Coach Green and the third gold ring for Marion.

"Green's North Central Conference crew was forgotten by the pollsters and trailed Rushville by 25–13 near the end of the first quarter, but the Giants just wouldn't be counted out. They pulled ahead for the first time in the opening seconds of the last half at 48–46 and opened up a 73–67 lead midway in the fourth quarter.

"Heading the state championship march for the 23–5 Marion outfit was 6–1 backcourt ace David Colescott, only returning regular from last year's state title lineup, who netted 25 points. Colescott, a popular Trester Award winner in post-game ceremonies, also came through with nine assists and three steals.

"Rushville, fifth in the polls with a 26–1 record going into the hot-shooting final game, came about as close as you can get on a dandy game high 27–point blast by super guard Ricky Goins and 6–8 Brad Miley with 19.

"It was a disappointing finish for Coach Larry Angle's South Central Conference champs, but how can you find any fault with a team that shot 56 percent? Marion bounced back to trail only 46–44 at halftime despite Rushville's incredible 60 percent shooting in the first half. Four straight points by sub frontliner Carlton Hayes put the Giants ahead at the end of three quarters, 66–63.

"Rushville led just one more time in the first seconds of the fourth quarter on two straight buckets by Goins, 67–66. Five points by Colescott pumped the defending champs in front to stay, 73–67."

Colescott rifled nine of his 20 shots from the field and 7-for-9 at the foul line, but a deciding factor was the timely 17-for-26 gunning by the two unsung forwards, Neal and Bragg. They had combined for just 11 points in the afternoon in a 49–47 cliff-hanger against South Central Conference co-champ Jeffersonville.

Ricky Goins drilled 10 of his 17 and the hard rebounding Miley eight for 11 shots for the Lions. Miley wound up with 45 rebounds for the day, including what must have been a record 29 against East Chicago in the tourney opener.

Green and his assistant coach Moe Smedley credited the improvement of Bragg, Neal, James Freshwater, Ray Myers, Jess Alumbaugh, Matt Dubuque, and Tuffy Jackson for getting the Giants through the tourney. Except for Colescott, Marion had a lot of inexperience and had to work hard for victories.

By Hey, coach of Fort Wayne North, which lost an overtime to Marion the preceding week, said of Colescott: "I think he is a great penetrator, a great team asset and he knows how to get the ball down to the scoring person." He said Marion showed during the entire tournament "it had the poise in the closing period to hold onto victories."

Charles (Stretch) Murphy, who led Marion to its first state title in 1926, returned to MSA to see his first state tourney since he played fifty years earlier. He had predicted that Marion's experience from its 1975 state championship team would improve their chances, pointing to his own experience.

Murphy's state championship team in 1926 had learned some valuable lessons losing to Vincennes in the State Finals in 1925. "It helped us to have been through that final day of the tournament," Stretch agreed.

For Green, it was a wonderful turnaround with a team that had been riddled in the beginning by graduation and slowed often during the year by injuries and one suspension for a violation of team rules. Colescott was in traction with a painful back injury and before that had missed some playing time early with an ankle injury.

Assistant Commissioner Charles Maas of the Indiana High School Athletic Assocation described the Marion-Rushville final as "truly one of the great state championship games. Rushville played an excellent game and Marion is a fine champion."

A five-year layoff from coaching followed for Green, who was disappointed in his search for a place in the college game. But he authored a book explaining his now-famous matchup zone defense and was kept busy speaking at clinics and working with several college coaches who wanted to learn more about his defense.

Green spent much time with Digger Phelps and his Notre Dame team during the 1976–77 season. Digger beat UCLA's national champs that year and downed UCLA twice the next season. "He beat UCLA four of six times with the matchup," Green said.

"I sold the book to a lot of big time college coaches who would call me after they heard my presentation in different clinics. Don Casey of Temple asked me to come out for the same reason, and he uses it a lot."

Green still has a long-standing desire to be a Division I college coach someday because he is confident that his defense would be very effective. "Sixty percent of the success I've had in coaching comes from the matchup zone, but nobody uses it as a basic defense the way I do. I've always wanted to have that opportunity someday," he said.

For reasons that some find extremely hard to explain, the college coaching shot never came for the old redhead. Green searches for an answer. "It seems to me that coaching Indiana high school basketball for 20 years with some success would prepare a man for just about anything."

Bill handled the Indiana All-Stars in several games against Kentucky, Minnesota, and the touring Russians. Green returned to the high school ranks and the profession he loves most at Marion, and right away demonstrated that he hadn't lost his touch. Marion ranked in the state's top 10 all year long and went to the Semistate for the eighth straight time with an excellent 23-3 record, bowing out in overtime to Plymouth's state champs.

It was mostly a senior ball club, but the blue chip Blackmon returns and is recognized by some big time college scouts as the best point guard in the nation. Only time would tell how much longer Green would stay—his name has a way of popping up on every attractive job opening.

Marion

Season Record (27–2)
1925–26

Marion	61	Wabash	28
Marion	65	Warsaw	7
Marion	39	New Castle	11
Marion	29	Vincennes	26
Marion	40	Fairmount	27
Marion	26	Kokomo	37

Marion	56	Anderson	31
Marion	48	Peru	19
Marion	44	Kokomo	34
Marion	69	Akron, Ohio	26
Marion	60	Fairmount	29
Marion	52	Huntington	28
Marion	47	Martinsville	32
Marion	19	Bloomington	31
Marion	40	Muncie Central	39
Marion	40	Anderson	38
Marion	59	South Bend Central	27
Marion	45	Muncie Central	43
Marion	37	Wabash	27
Marion	59	Gary Froebel	37

Sectional (Marion)

Marion	61	Van Buren	12
Marion	37	Fairmount	32
Marion	65	Gas City	19

Regional (Kokomo)

Marion	47	Laketon	20
Marion	24	Kokomo	8

State Finals (Indianapolis, Exposition Building)

Marion	49	Nappanee	26
Marion	50	Fort Wayne Central	26
Marion	29	Evansville Central	22
Marion	30	Martinsville	23

Season Record (28–1)
1974–75

Marion	76	Wabash	36
Marion	68	Elkhart Central	50
Marion	73	Anderson	62
Marion	83	Tipton	56
Marion	65	Kokomo	49
Marion	61	Huntington	45
Marion	71	Blackford	65
Marion	87	Warsaw (Overtime)	80
Marion	83	Kokomo	71
Marion	72	Richmond	60
Marion	67	New Castle	57
Marion	79	Elwood	60
Marion	68	Lafayette Jeff	64
Marion	87	Madison Heights	56
Marion	64	Ft. Wayne Northrop	44
Marion	85	Indpls. North Central (Overtime)	81
Marion	66	Fort Wayne Snider	75
Marion	91	Logansport	71
Marion	76	Kokomo Haworth	50
Marion	78	Muncie Central	51

Sectional (Marion)

Marion	72	Mississinewa	50
Marion	48	Oak Hill	46
Marion	76	Elwood	57

Regional (Marion)

Marion	66	Norwell	44
Marion	73	Huntington	54

Semistate (Fort Wayne)

Marion	72	Columbia City	49
Marion	82	Ft. Wayne North	61

State Finals (Indianapolis Market Square Arena)

Marion	73	Lebanon	65
Marion	58	Loogootee	46

Season Record (23–5)
1975–76

Marion	73	Wabash	51
Marion	61	Elkhart Central	49
Marion	67	Anderson	68
Marion	96	Tipton	57
Marion	78	Kokomo	66
Marion	57	Huntington	56
Marion	66	Blackford	41
Marion	73	Muncie Central	48
Marion	74	Kokomo	63
Marion	61	Richmond	63
Marion	74	New Castle	62
Marion	60	Elwood	48
Marion	55	Lafayette Jeff	54
Marion	84	Madison Heights	89
Marion	61	Fort Wayne Northrop	62
Marion	87	North Central	74
Marion	72	Logansport	70
Marion	64	Kokomo Haworth (Overtime)	63
Marion	56	Muncie Central	62
Marion	70	Fort Wayne Snider	50

Sectional (Marion)

Marion	86	Oak Hill	51
Marion	77	Bennett	60

Regional (Marion)

Marion	74	Huntington	70
Marion	76	Logansport	59

Semistate (Fort Wayne)

| Marion | 59 | Anderson Highland | 57 |
| Marion | 69 | Fort Wayne North (Overtime) | 66 |

State Finals (Indianapolis Market Square Arena)

| Marion | 49 | Jeffersonville | 47 |
| Marion | 82 | Rushville | 76 |

6

Herman Keller—A New Beginning with Bosse

Herman Keller thought he was through with coaching varsity basketball when he moved from Boonville to Evansville Bosse in the early 1940s.

Harry King was Bosse's varsity coach at the time, Arad McCutchan was B-team coach, and Keller consented to take the freshman team. On that freshman club he had among others Julius (Bud) Ritter, Bryan (Broc) Jerrel, and Norris Caudell.

Fate took over a short time after Keller joined Bosse. King went to the army, the navy took McCutchan, and Herman suddenly moved up to the Bosse varsity job where he took over a team made up mostly of underclassmen.

You know the rest because an underdog Bosse ball club won the state championship in 1944, beating Kokomo 39–35 in the final game. Then virtually the same Bulldog crew came back the next year to repeat by knocking off South Bend Riley 46–36 for the title. Both state tournaments were played in Indianapolis' State Fairgrounds Coliseum.

Jerrel left for the army but Ward (Piggy) Lambert enrolled Ritter, Caudell, Jack Matthews, Norm McCool, and Gene Whitehead for Purdue. All but Ritter and Caudell left Purdue at the end of the first year. Caudell went on to captain the Boilermakers his senior year.

Bill Fox once wrote in his "Shootin 'Em and Stoppin 'Em" column for the *Indianapolis News* that Bosse used a precision passing game the likes of which had never been seen before in any state tournament.

Jerrel, a 5–8 backcourt wizard, was a passing master and Bosse's leading scorer in the 1944 season. All but Gene Schmidt returned the

Bosse's 1944 state champs on the steps of the school building. Seated: Bill Holman, Norris Caudell, Norman McCool, Irvin Schultz, Don Tilley; standing: Assistant Coach Arvel Kilpatrick, Gene Whitehead, Gene Schmidt, Jack Matthews, Julius (Bud) Ritter, Bryan (Broc) Jerrel and Coach Herman Keller.

next year and Ritter was the team's leading scorer. McCool was the replacement for the departed Schmidt.

Later on Keller served as Assistant Commissioner with the Indiana High School Athletic Association from 1961 to 1973, Ritter became one of Hoosier high school basketball's most successful coaches at Madison (where his teams won 61 straight regular season games in the early 1960s), and both were installed along with Jerrel in the Indiana Basketball Hall of Fame.

Ironically, Ritter's 1962 Madison ball club with Larry Humes as Indiana's Mr. Basketball went all the way to the Final Four and lost to another standout Bosse outfit which then won the school's third state championship against East Chicago Washington at night, 84–81.

Jim Myers (a Gimbel Award winner in 1939) coached Bosse's third state title winner, and the Bulldogs wound up with an excellent 26–2 record. Ritter's Madison team accounted for one of those two Bosse losses in a 59–51 contest near the end of the regular season. Bosse reversed that loss in the 79–75 first game of the State Finals.

Ritter's 1961 Madison team was unbeaten but lost to Bill Stearman and the Columbus Bulldogs in the Regional.

Now retired in Brown County, Keller recalls how Jeffersonville's Ed Lyskowinski sized up the young Bosse team as having state championship material when the two teams met at mid-season in 1944.

"Lyskowinski had a good team of his own at Jeffersonville, and we won by eight or nine points," Keller related. "After the game, Ed told me he thought our Bosse team had the talent to win a state title. I just laughed at him and really didn't think any more about it. Ed reminded me of his January prediction after we went on to win the championship in March.

"We were overlooked in the 1944 tournament by everybody because we lost seven games during the season. Sickness and injuries played a big part in many of those seven defeats. We didn't have our whole team together until late in the year."

Jerrel scored 17 points and Ritter 13 as Bosse came from 10 down in the second half to beat LaPorte, 41–38, in the second afternoon game of the State Finals. Kokomo was a 30–26 upset winner over tourney favorite Anderson in the opener. One of the most prominent members of that Anderson crew was a lad named Carl Erskine—you remember Carl as one of the National League's premier pitchers for the old Brooklyn Dodgers.

Jerrel and Caudell led the way for Bosse in the championship game combining for 21 points against Mr. Basketball Tom Schwartz and his Kokomo teammates. Jerrel led Final Four scoring with 28 in the two games.

Bosse fought Jasper for the No. 1 spot in the basketball polls almost all year long in 1945. Bosse beat Jasper 41–39 to take over No. 1 brief-

The 1945 state champs. Front: Bryan (Broc) Jerrel, Jack Matthews, Alfred Buck, Norman McCool, Don Tilley; back row: Coach Herman Keller, Gene Whitehead, Julius (Bud) Ritter, Bill Butterfield, Norris Caudell, Jim DeGroote, Assistant Coach Kilpatrick.

ly, but a 43–42 loss to Evansville Central (which Ritter missed due to illness) returned Jasper to the No. 1 position heading into the tournament.

Bosse survived a 38–37 scare against Evansville Memorial in the sectional that year and then didn't have another close call until a big Semistate rematch with Jasper in the old Indiana University Fieldhouse. There was a tremendous buildup for that Semistate showdown matching the state's No. 1 and No. 2 teams.

"It looked like the Game of the Year and was highly publicized because of our earlier game with Jasper and the season-long battle for top spot in the polls," Ritter explained. "But it didn't turn out to be the spectacular game that everyone expected. We led 15–0 at the end of the first quarter and the lop-sided final score was 55–32. Jasper played nothing but zone defense in those days, and our sharp passing game really helped us get good shots against the zone," Keller added. "It was

Bosse's Jack Matthews drives under for a lay-up in the 1945 State Finals game against Indianapolis Broad Ripple. Ralph Chapman (#12) of Broad Ripple and Bud Ritter (#11) of Bosse wait for the rebound. Bosse won 37–35 and then went on to beat South Bend Riley 46–36 in the evening for the championship.

Evansville's 1945 flood lent itself to this publicity photo of the state champs.

just one of those days when everything went right for us." It was a satisfying win for Bosse because the press had picked Jasper to win the tourney.

Bosse had perhaps its toughest test against Indianapolis' Broad Ripple in the opening game of the 1945 State Finals, with Ripple leading most of the first three quarters. Bosse caught up at 21–21 going into the final period and then scrambled out of it with a narrow 37–35 decision over the Rockets.

The Bulldogs took the lead at the start of the final period and stalled the last two minutes.

Caudell, a fluid 6–4 forward, was the big gun for Bosse in the Broad Ripple game with 15 points. Center Ralph Chapman scored 11 for Frank Baird's talented Broad Ripple losers, and little Max Allen of the Rockets was rewarded later with the Trester Award.

Bosse's 10-point win over South Riley Bend in the championship bout was almost anticlimactic. Ritter tallied 14 points and McCool 13 to lead the way for the Bulldogs against a stubborn Riley outfit which built its offense around Bob Whitmer.

Jerrel turned in another outstanding floor game for the Bulldogs and scored eight points.

Keller began his coaching career at Plainville in the same sectional with Washington's famous Hatchets. Little Plainville was a stubborn sectional loser to the Hatchets in 1930 when Jingles Englehart and Dave Dejernett started their march to the school's first state championship.

Bosse's 1945 champs amid adoring fans as they prepare to hop aboard the local fire truck en route to the celebration.

Herman coached at Boonville for 10 years and at Bosse for another 15, but he still can't remember his overall career record in numbers of victories. "I didn't care about the record and still don't. I coached for the fun of it and for the kids," he said.

Ritter, who became president and board chairman of the Indiana Basketball Hall of Fame in more recent years refers to his old high school coach as the Abe Lincoln of Indiana high school basketball. "He was an excellent coach but a very quiet man who kept us together. Herman Keller had a good system, and we were able to execute that system.

"Jerrel was a master ball handler and a tremendous set shot. For those times, we were a high-scoring ball club. We ran a lot of tip plays which Herman put in to make good use of our talents. Jerrel was a master at getting the ball to Caudell and me for an easy shot inside. We hit the 70s a few times and I averaged about 17 a game in my senior year—in those days that was pretty good.

"Broc Jerrel's dad [Rush Jerrel] had a lot to do with our success too because he coached all of us when we were just young kids. And when we were down to LaPorte in the 1944 state tourney game, he lectured us at half-time. He was a fine basketball player on his own at Sandborn."

Bosse's march to two straight state championships continued a wave of four state titles in five years for the South.

"In the last five years Indiana's southern goal shooters have been preeminent in the supreme court doings of Hoosierdom's favorite fling," Bill Fox penned. "Washington won in 1941 and retained its title

Bud Ritter, who starred on two Bosse state title winners, later became president of the Indiana Basketball Hall of Fame and chairman of the Hall of Fame Classic tourney. Here he is shown (second from left) with Hall of Fame officer Doxie Moore, Gary Emerson's Wallace Bryant, Coach Earl Smith and Frank Smith before the first Hall of Fame Classic in 1977. Emerson was tourney champ.

the next year, and now Bosse of Evansville, winner in 1944, has duplicated that feat.

"Five times in the 35-year history of our magnificent obsession of March, champions successfully have defended their crowns of the empire of IHSAA, and three of these are southerners—Franklin starting the southern supremacy with an incomparable string of three in 1920. Before that, Wingate and Lebanon performed this neat trick."

Of course, in later years Indianapolis Crispus Attucks, Marion, and Muncie all had repeat winners.

And Bosse almost put together a fourth state title winner being ranked No. 1 in the polls with an unbeaten 27–0 record going into the 1982 state tournament. Gary Roosevelt ended that drive in a one-point barn burner that was decided on a last-second shot.

Plymouth battled from behind to down Gary Roosevelt in two overtimes, 75–74, for the 1982 state championship.

When Bosse's Bulldogs put state titles back to back in 1944–45, big towns dominated the championship game for the second time. South Side of Fort Wayne defeated Hammond in 1938's title match. Three of 1945's Final Four represented cities having populations of more than 100,000.

"While Broad Ripple's Rockets did not reach the last game, it was agreed by most of the 11,555 persons who saw their matinee struggle against Bosse that Coach Baird's team was the second best team in the Coliseum," Fox observed.

"All year long this Bosse team was the target of every opponent. Never for a minute did it appear to lose faith in the teachings of its coach. Never for a minute did it appear to be a confused team. . . . If any team ever proved itself to be of championship caliber in the face of a stern test, Bosse did that against Broad Ripple's determined Rockets.

"The Broad Ripple boys built up leads of 8–6 at the quarter, 20–14 at the half—and the 13th and 14th Bosse points were in the air when the second quarter gun fired. This was a shot by Jerrel.

"Gradually, the Broad Ripple lead dwindled in the third quarter after Floyd Chafee had made it 22–14 with a pretty shot soon after the last half began.

Herman Keller coached Bosse's 1944 and 1945 state champs and Ray Eddy took Madison to its state title in 1950. Here they meet at the Kiwanis Roundup in Indianapolis in 1962. Bosse played Madison at Butler Fieldhouse the next day and went on to add a third state title. Eddy coached Purdue in the Big 10 for 13 years.

"Allen scored a field goal after Bosse had made a free throw, and then the Rockets fizzled a little. Bill Butterfield, tallest player on the Bosse team, started the rally by tipping in a rebound. Jack Matthews and Caudell then went under to score for Bosse. The score was tied by Caudell on an out-of-bounds play.

"Chafee scored and Jerrel tied it up at 27–27 as the third quarter ended. As the fourth quarter began, McCool scored on the third of three rebound attempts, and Bosse took the lead for the first time. A fast play with Matthews on the scoring end put Bosse four points ahead. Coach Baird sent Bob Gossman in to replace Allen. Then came the second of those two fatal out-of-bounds plays with Matthews throwing the ball in to Caudell. These two plays won the game.

"Broad Ripple did not have the height to combat the work of the slender but scrappy Caudell . . . Bosse, with Jerrel dribbling, started playing a possession game (with the score 36–31). The Indianapolis lads battled stubbornly to the wire but could come no closer than two the rest of the way," the sports editor of the *Indianapolis News* reported.

"When the Bulldogs carried off their second straight state title by beating Riley of South Bend, 46–36, it marked the final high school game for seven members of a great team—a machine many were comparing with the 1936 Frankfort squad, generally considered the best modern Indiana yardstick," Chris Hankemeier added in the *News*.

Baird, the Hall of Famer who coached Broad Ripple basketball for 17 years and baseball for 36 seasons, thought Bosse's experience was a big factor. "We were disappointed, but we lost to an outstanding team," the Broad Ripple coach admitted.

"I thought our defense on Bosse was excellent most of the way [Chapman held Ritter to just six points while scoring 11 himself], but Bosse was just too tough. Caudell's rebounding at both ends of the floor really hurt and once again Bosse's experience under pressure might have been the difference. They were well-coached and didn't seem to get rattled when we had the lead in the first half."

Considerably outweighed, Bosse resorted to its intricate set plays and fancy dribbling against Riley in the championship game. By halftime the Bulldogs were perched on a comfortable 26–15 lead, and it was 38–21 at the end of three quarters.

Bosse had simply too much speed and too much class for its South Bend opponent. Ritter, with seven field goals, and McCool with six were the two big guns in the championship clash. Governor Ralph Gates was on hand to congratulate the champs in traditional postgame ceremonies.

Broad Ripple led state tourney shooting with a .322 average for the Sweet 16, better even than Bosse's .304. Ripple's defense was one of the tourney highlights, checking Bosse with a sub-par 16–of–79 performance from the field (.203). It was almost good enough to pull off the upset.

All Evansville forgot a damaging weekend storm and receding floodwaters to take part in the welcome home party for Bosse the next day. Dozens of cars met Coach Keller and the champs at the outskirts of the city, escorted them to the school's athletic field and the same fire truck that was used in 1944 led the huge parade.

More than 100 automobiles made up the big parade to the high school, and a celebration followed for more than one hour. School was closed the following Monday in honor of the team, and the first of a series of parties was scheduled for later in the week.

Mayor Manson Reichert left his sick bed to take part in Sunday's homecoming for the champs.

Evansville Bosse

Season Record (19–7)
1943–44

Evansville Bosse	42	Mount Vernon	21
Evansville Bosse	46	Winslow	32
Evansville Bosse	35	Fort Branch	30
Evansville Bosse	38	Evansville Reitz	36
Evansville Bosse	25	Evansville Memorial	27
Evansville Bosse	36	Evansville Central (Overtime)	37
Evansville Bosse	35	Huntingburg	36
Evansville Bosse	48	Jeffersonville	39
Evansville Bosse	36	Sullivan	19
Evansville Bosse	29	New Albany	27
Evansville Bosse	37	Princeton	30
Evansville Bosse	32	Jasper	36
Evansville Bosse	46	Evansville Reitz	25
Evansville Bosse	32	Evansville Central	36
Evansville Bosse	27	Boonville	38
Evansville Bosse	28	Vincennes	30

Sectional (Evansville)

Evansville Bosse	62	Washington Township	20
Evansville Bosse	32	Evansville Reitz	25
Evansville Bosse	49	Lincoln (Evansville)	31
Evansville Bosse	46	Memorial (Evansville)	29

Regional (Evansville)

Evansville Bosse	38	Dale	22
Evansville Bosse	43	Boonville	35

Semifinal (Vincennes)

Evansville Bosse	46	Mooresville	33
Evansville Bosse	40	Washington	34

State Finals (Indianapolis, Coliseum)

Evansville Bosse	41	LaPorte	38
Evansville Bosse	39	Kokomo	35

Evansville Bosse

Season Record (25–2)
1944–45

Evansville Bosse	69	Mount Vernon	20
Evansville Bosse	37	Linton	36
Evansville Bosse	50	Fort Branch	24
Evansville Bosse	48	Evansville Reitz	17
Evansville Bosse	60	Princeton	28
Evansville Bosse	35	Evansville Memorial	31
Evansville Bosse	54	Evansville Central	28
Evansville Bosse	50	Huntingburg	21

Evansville Bosse	23	Jeffersonville	27
Evansville Bosse	53	Sullivan	28
Evansville Bosse	41	New Albany	29
Evansville Bosse	54	Lafayette Jeff	26
Evansville Bosse	41	Jasper	39
Evansville Bosse	35	Bedford	26
Evansville Bosse	47	Boonville	28
Evansville Bosse	38	Evansville Reitz	25
Evansville Bosse	42	Evansville Central	43
Evansville Bosse	41	Vincennes	16

Sectional (Evansville)

Evansville Bosse	44	Mount Vernon	20
Evansville Bosse	38	Evansville Memorial	37
Evansville Bosse	50	Evansville Central	35

Regional (Evansville)

| Evansville Bosse | 49 | Boonville | 37 |
| Evansville Bosse | 77 | Tell City | 44 |

Semifinal (Bloomington)

| Evansville Bosse | 44 | Bedford | 34 |
| Evansville Bosse | 55 | Jasper | 32 |

State Finals (Indianapolis, Coliseum)

| Evansville Bosse | 37 | Indianapolis Broad Ripple | 35 |
| Evansville Bosse | 46 | South Bend Riley | 36 |

7

Fort Wayne Up Front with 4 State Champs

Fort Wayne's sizeable contributions to the Indiana high school basketball history books rank right up front with Indianapolis, Gary, South Bend, Muncie, Anderson, Lafayette, Frankfort, and Evansville.

South Side's Archers, Northrop, and old Central High (which closed its doors in the early 1970s to make way for Northrop) have blessed the Summit City with four state titles. Three favorite sons have been named Indiana's Mr. Basketball for the traditional Blind Fund series with Kentucky and two others have been recipients of the state tournament's coveted Mental Attitude Award.

Hall of Famer Burl Friddle coached the first of South's two state championships in 1938—it was the first for Northern Indiana schools. Twenty years later Don Reichert came along with another Archer ball club still recognized as one of the Hoosier state's strongest champions.

Murray Mendenhall, another Hall of Famer, took his Fort Wayne Central crew all the way to the 1943 state championship. Murray Jr. was one of the individual standouts on that ball club providing Hoosier Hysteria with one of its best-known father-and-son combinations. Later on Murray Jr. would become a successful coach in his own right at South Side.

Bob Dille put the icing on his own brilliant career as both player and coach in 1974 when Northrop's Bruins marched to a state championship—in just the third year for the new school, located on Fort Wayne's north perimeter.

Fort Wayne's position as one of the hardwood sport's best known hubs has grown from five schools in the early years to 10 schools in modern times. A long parade of basketball greats learned their basics on the high school courts of Fort Wayne.

Mike McCoy of South Side's 1958 state champs, Willie Long who starred on South's 1967 State Finalist outfit, and Jim Master of Harding, who set a regular season record for Fort Wayne cagers in 1980, all wore the No. 1 uniform reserved for Mr. Basketball in the midsummer All-Star Classic.

Long established a career scoring record for Fort Wayne preps with 1,697 points. Central's Steve Sitko was named winner of the Gimbel Mental Prize for Mental Attitude in the 1935 state tourney, and Charles Nelson of South Side received the Trester Award (a successor for the Gimbel) in 1967.

Countless other individual greats have come out of Fort Wayne to reach both college and professional stardom. Johnny Bright, Bobby Milton, Paul (Curly) Armstrong, Herm Schaefer, Tom Bolyard, Johnny Kelso, Eugene Parker, Eddie Stanczak, Bob Cowan, Jim Glass, Dale Hamilton, Carl Stavreti, John Flowers (father and son), Tom Baack, and Walter Jordan are just a few that come to mind.

Fort Wayne hosts one of the state tournament's four Semistate shootouts each year at the Allen County Coliseum, and without exception it's a sellout. Five times in nine years from 1974 to 1982 the state title winner came out of the Fort Wayne Semistate.

Fort Wayne South's 1938 state champs. Front: Cook, John Chedester, Dale Hamilton, Robert Bolyard, Richard Frazell, Harold Kitzmiller; back row: Athletic Manager Davis, Hire, Donald Derry, James Glass, John Hines, Frank Belot, James Roth, Coach Burl Friddle.

Fort Wayne Central's 1943 champions. Front: Edwin Lindenberg, Robert Doty, Charles Stanski, Robert VanRyan, Murray Mendenhall, Jr., Robert Armstrong; back row: Manager Jeffrey, Max Ramsey, Assistant Coach Banet, Coach Murray Mendenhall, Principal Croninger, James Blanks, Raymond Chambers, Tom Shopoff and Manager Meyer.

1938—Fort Wayne South 34, Hammond 32

Burl Friddle's South Side Archers gave Northern Indiana its first state championship and ended a 27-year monopoly of the small towns with their hard-fought, 34–32 decision over Hammond in the 1938 final game.

The Northeastern Indiana Conference champions roared ahead in the second quarter after spotting Hammond's Wildcats a 7–0 lead at the outset. It was the second state title for Friddle who starred on Franklin's famed Wonder Five in 1920 and then coached Washington's Hatchets to a state championship 10 years later.

South Side's successful state title drive to a 29–3 overall record captured Hoosier Hysteria's first crown for a city with a population of more than 50,000.

Fort Wayne's only scare on the way to the State Finals came in a last-minute victory over tourney favorite Muncie in the semifinal round, with the Archers shaking off the mighty Bearcats for a narrow 37–33 victory.

South Side slipped past Columbus 40–34 in the state tournament's afternoon round, and then the greenclad Archers displayed the same amazing stamina against Hammond that had proved to be the deciding factor against Muncie one week earlier.

The Friddle-coached ball club seemed to grow stronger each

Fort Wayne South's 1958 state champions. Front: Tom Bolyard, Daniel Howe, Nicholas Demetre, Carl Stavreti, Richard Miller; back row: Coach Don Reichert, Mike McCoy, Bill Meyer, Larry Miller, Michael Simmons, James VaChon and Assistant Coach Scott.

quarter in the closest state championship contest since Muncie's one-point win over Martinsville in 1928.

Special credit went to hot-shooting Dale Hamilton with his six field goals and to 6-8½ center Jim Glass, who was singled out as the team's most-improved player by members of the working press. But they had plenty of support from a well-balanced offense against a strong Hammond crew which advanced in the afternoon with a 39–24 win over Bedford.

Glass lost 20 much-needed pounds with a siege of pneumonia and was not available as a regular until after the Christmas holidays. Used only sparingly until the start of tournament play four weeks earlier, the big center's accurate passing and ability to control rebounds turned out to be the steadying influence which enabled the champs to work so smoothly as a unit.

Gimble Prize winner Bobby Mygrants and George Sobek shot their Hammond team into that early 7-0 lead in the championship clash, and Fort Wayne didn't catch up until Bob Bolyard sank two free throws for a 17–15 lead just before the intermission. Johnny Hines and Hamilton combined to pace the Archers in the seesaw second half, with South Side taking a slim 27–24 lead into the fourth quarter. This pair hit two buckets just outside the foul circle to increase the Fort Wayne margin to five points early in the final period, 31–26.

Sobek wound up with a game high 13 points for Hammond and Mygrants had 12. Hamilton was Fort Wayne's leading scorer with 12 and Hines had nine. Glass was limited to just four free throws but his rebounding role was a determining force.

More important than South's scoring balance was the defense that forced 14 Hammond errors. Time after time the Archers picked off Wildcat passes while South Side was charged with only miscues in the title tilt.

1943—Fort Wayne Central 45, Lebanon 40

Coached by Hall of Famer Murray Mendenhall since 1924, Central's once-beaten Tigers brought Fort Wayne its second state championship in 1943 with a 45-40 victory over three-time state title winner Lebanon in the 1943 final game at the Indianapolis Coliseum.

Lebanon reigned as the Hoosier hardwood ruler in 1912, 1917, and 1918, but the Boone County squad was unable to match the scoring power displayed by Central under the direction of Mendenhall who starred at little West Newton in Indianapolis' Marion County 25 years earlier. Fort Wayne became the first city in the Hoosier state with two title-winning schools.

Fort Wayne Northrop got into the state champ picture in 1974. Front: Craig Klein, Neal Putt, Tony Casso, Tom Madden, Dennis Hetrick, Willie Spencer; back row: Assistant Coach Chris Stavreti, Mike Suttle, Mike Muff, Maurice Drinks, Walter Jordan, James Wimbley, Mark Fredrick, Assistant Coach Jim Klein, Coach Bob Dille.

Fort Wayne South's Mike McCoy, 1958's Mr. Basketball, is shown at left, and Mr. Basketball of 1967, Willie Long, is on the right.

Central avenged its only loss in a 27–1 season against neighboring Fort Wayne South before the end of the regular season and again in sectional play. South Side battled Central into overtime before the Tigers could gain a 25–24 nod in the sectional.

Robert VanRyan and Robert Armstrong led the way as Central downed Batesville in the afternoon, 33–24. Lebanon edged Bedford's Stonecutters in a 36–35 barn burner to qualify for a state title shot against Fort Wayne.

One of the standouts on that Lebanon ball club was Pete Mount, the father of Rick Mount who came along more than 20 years later to be recognized as one of the Hoosier state's all-time great scorers.

Ralph Houser and Pete Mount put Lebanon ahead in the opening minutes of the state championship clash but it was Fort Wayne, 15–11, near the end of the first quarter and Central's Tigers were hanging on-to a 26–21 cushion at the halfway mark.

Lebanon threatened at 28–26 during the third period before Fort Wayne surged into a more comfortable 38–29 lead at the end of three quarters. The game was close the rest of the way with Lebanon threatening at 40–38 but Fort Wayne's superior depth proved to be too much.

VanRyan scored 11 points and Murray Mendenhall Jr. had 10 to set the scoring pace for Fort Wayne. Houser tallied 14 and Mount 11 for runnerup Lebanon. Dave Laflin of Lebanon was rewarded with the state tournament's Gimbel Medal presented each year for mental attitude.

A driving attack by Coach Butch Neuman's Lebanon crew in the afternoon had offset the tournament's top individual effort by Center John Brennan who scored 21 points for the Stonecutters.

Bob Truitt's late bucket following a steal turned out to be the clincher. It gave Lebanon a 36–33 lead and then one last tip-in basket by Brennan for Bedford wound up scoring.

This was the first year for private, parochial and black schools in the IHSAA's state tournament. These schools were admitted for membership August 15, 1942 and eligible for participation for the first time in the 1943 tourney.

1958—Fort Wayne South 63, Crawfordsville 34

Fort Wayne South, with seven-foot center Mike McCoy and a team that raced over a basketball floor in seven-league boots, swamped Crawfordsville, 63–34, to capture the 48th State Tourney at Butler Fieldhouse.

McCoy, a young man with a reach of nearly 9½ feet and a basketball future that couldn't be brighter, dropped in 11 of his 22 shots and closed with 24 points. Danny Howe, 6–4, added 13 points to the South Side total and Tom Bolyard, 6–4, scored nine and contributed a tremendous rebounding job.

A heavy favorite all through the 1958 state tourney, South Side yanked off 40 rebounds to only 19 for outsized Crawfordsville. There were times when it appeared that the Archers were playing a game of keepaway at the backboards, tapping the ball back and forth over the baskets and over the heads of the Athenians.

The victory was South Side's 19th in a row and climaxed a stand-out 28–2 season record. It nailed down the Fort Wayne school's second state championship, and it came 20 years after the first state trophy dash in 1938.

Dick Haslam of Crawfordsville was named Trester Award winner, and the Athenians coached by Dick Baumgartner made the favored South Side giants hustle for three quarters. It was 12–12 at the end of the first period and South led only 28–22 at half-time. The Athenians cut that deficit to 32–27 midway in the third quarter before the roof collapsed.

Slick ball-handler Carl Stavreti began cutting and driving through the Crawfordsville defense. And McCoy continued to ram in those high percentage shots underneath, in an unspectacular but most effective way.

Crawfordsville could manage just one more basket in the third quarter, and it was pretty much academic after South Side entered the last period boasting a whopping 43–29 advantage over the outmanned enemy.

South Side cut loose with both barrels—fast breaks, driving lay-

The Big 3 of Northrop's 1974 state champs: Coach Bob Dille, Mike Muff and Walter Jordan. Both Muff and Jordan were named to the Indiana All-Stars and Dille coached the Stars. On the right is Jim Master of Fort Wayne Harding, 1980's Mr. Basketball.

ins, high hooks, and tips. By the 5:29 mark of the fourth quarter it was a 53–29 rout for Coach Don Reichert's South Side powerhouse.

Fort Wayne outclassed little Springs Valley (before Larry Bird) by a 55–42 score during the afternoon session, led by McCoy with 18 points, Stavreti with 15, and Bolyard's 14, Crawfordsville moved up with a 53–45 win over Muncie Central.

It had been written before the month-long state tourney grind began that South Side probably would go all the way if the Archers could wade safely through a rugged sectional tournament in their own backyard.

South had to work overtime to convince Central by a 60–56 score in the sectional, and it was the only really tough test the Archers encountered throughout the four week tournament schedule.

McCoy and Company drubbed Elkhart by a staggering 76–44 margin to reach the Final Four. McCoy was voted Mr. Basketball on the Indiana All-Star team, and Stavreti also was named for the series against Kentucky. Bolyard was No. 1 player in the Indiana-Ohio All-Star game hosted by Fort Wayne.

1974—Fort Wayne Northrop 59, Jeffersonville 56

Walter Jordan and his towering Fort Wayne Northrop teammates pulled out a tight 59–56 decision over Jeffersonville in the 1974 state championship classic played at Indiana University's Assembly Hall. It was the first trip to the Final Four for Northrop in just the third year for the Fort Wayne newcomer.

Bob Dille's Northrop ball club closed a sensational 28–1 season with a 26-game winning streak but the Bruins had to hold off a fierce zone press by the Red Devils at the wire. Jeff owned a 26–1 record going into the low-scoring defensive struggle and deadlocked Northrop for the last time at 53–53 with only 1:47 on the clock.

Wayne Walls, Jeffersonville's brilliant 6–6 forward, led game scoring with 25 points. It wasn't enough to overcome a well-balanced Northrop starting five that played the full 32 minutes without a substitution.

Jordan, Northrop's 6–6 answer to the Jeffersonville superstar, led Bruin scoring with 18 points—16 in the first three periods. Jordan had totaled 26 in the afternoon when Northrop downed Lafayette Jeff, 63–49.

Tom Madden came through with a strong 16-point backcourt effort for the champs, and 6–5 workhorse Mike Muff also hit double figures with 10. Both Jordan and Muff were named along with Walls to the Indiana All-Star team in June.

Jordan drilled nine of his 14 shots from the floor and Northrop wound up with 26 of 56 on target for .464, considerably better than Jeffersonville's 24 of 63 for a .381 average. Walls rifled nine of his 17 shots in another dandy 25-point effort for the Red Devils. Wayne also had a super 24-point game in the afternoon when Jeffersonville took out Franklin, 63–52.

Jordan fired in seven points in the 15–10 first period, and Muff added three buckets against Jeffersonville in the second quarter. Walls was the big gun as Jeff bounced back to tie at 22–22 with 2:37 to go in the first half and then deadlocked it twice more before the half-time buzzer sounded with the game knotted, 28–28.

Jeff grabbed its first lead at 33–30 in the first 90 seconds of the third quarter. Northrop bombed six of its first eight shots in the third period and the Bruins soon returned to a 40–37 lead. Northrop's tremendous rebounding strength began to assert itself, and it was 42–37 heading down the stretch.

Big Maurice Drinks popped Northrop's first fourth-quarter shot, and the Bruins had reeled off 10 straight points for a 44–37 edge. The Bruin defense also had limited Walls to just two baskets in the second half.

Jeff refused to go down without a stiff fight on its first final game appearance since 1935. Jordan collected his fourth foul, and the Red Devils trailed only 53–51. Mark Meyer's third basket in the fourth period tied the game for the last time at 53, but two Madden free throws regained a 55–53 lead for Northrop.

Northrop hung onto that slim lead in the closing seconds, although Jeff had the ball while trailing only 58–56 with less than 30 seconds to play. The Red Devils failed to capitalize on their final possession, and when Walls fouled out in the game's last two seconds, Madden tacked on a free toss for the 59–56 final margin.

A heavy snowstorm forced 350 Jeffersonville fans to spend the night in IU's Assembly Hall because most Southern Indiana roads were blocked. Eight busloads of Jeff rooters slept on the basketball court and in the wrestling room. Coach George Marshall and the Jeffersonville team already had departed before school officials decided to arrange for the fans to stay overnight.

Marshall's outstanding Jeffersonville teams appeared in the State Finals three times from 1972 to 1976, losing to the state champs each year. Connersville battled overtime to down the Red Devils in 1972, and Marion was a two-point winner over Jeff in 1976.

Fort Wayne South

Season Record (29–3)
1937–38

Fort Wayne Southside	42	LaPorte	39
Fort Wayne Southside	28	Rushville	24
Fort Wayne Southside	39	Kendallville	32
Fort Wayne Southside	30	Bluffton	20
Fort Wayne Southside	43	Fort Wayne Central Catholic	26
Fort Wayne Southside	29	Auburn	26
Fort Wayne Southside	27	Fort Wayne North	31
Fort Wayne Southside	25	Gary Froebel	23
Fort Wayne Southside	44	Hartford City	29
Fort Wayne Southside	41	Fort Wayne Central	36
Fort Wayne Southside	28	Connersville	24
Fort Wayne Southside	40	Elwood	24
Fort Wayne Southside	51	Huntington	34
Fort Wayne Southside	34	Goshen	31
Fort Wayne Southside	34	Fort Wayne North	15
Fort Wayne Southside	38	Decatur	20
Fort Wayne Southside	30	Fort Wayne Central	28
Fort Wayne Southside	25	Bedford	34
Fort Wayne Southside	33	Gary Horace Mann	31
Fort Wayne Southside	32	Brazil	28
Fort Wayne Southside	33	Gary Froebel	21
Fort Wayne Southside	24	LaPorte (Overtime)	25

Sectional (Fort Wayne)

Fort Wayne Southside	50	Huntertown	24
Fort Wayne Southside	68	Arcola	29
Fort Wayne Southside	62	Decatur	37
Fort Wayne Southside	23	Central (Fort Wayne)	15

Regional (Fort Wayne)

Fort Wayne South	38	Huntington	19
Fort Wayne South	54	Ridgeville	25

Semifinal (Muncie)

Fort Wayne South	39	Sheridan	13
Fort Wayne South	37	Muncie Central	33

State Finals (Indianapolis, Butler Fieldhouse)

Fort Wayne South	40	Columbus	34
Fort Wayne South	34	Hammond	32

Fort Wayne Central

Season Record (27–1)
1942–43

Fort Wayne Central	33	Muncie Central	27
Fort Wayne Central	54	New Castle	45
Fort Wayne Central	37	Hartford City	23
Fort Wayne Central	42	Central Catholic (Ft. Wayne)	21
Fort Wayne Central	36	Evansville Central	27
Fort Wayne Central	28	Fort Wayne North	25
Fort Wayne Central	61	Auburn	30
Fort Wayne Central	33	Hammond	31
Fort Wayne Central	53	Decatur	13
Fort Wayne Central	22	Fort Wayne South	26
Fort Wayne Central	45	Columbia City	27
Fort Wayne Central	60	Whiting	34
Fort Wayne Central	41	Fort Wayne North	30
Fort Wayne Central	46	Elkhart	34
Fort Wayne Central	58	Huntington	26
Fort Wayne Central	36	Fort Wayne South	30
Fort Wayne Central	66	Kendallville	35
Fort Wayne Central	35	Marion	25

Sectional (Fort Wayne)

Fort Wayne Central	58	Elmhurst	36
Fort Wayne Central	37	Fort Wayne North	34
Fort Wayne Central	25	Fort Wayne South (Overtime)	24
Fort Wayne Central	62	Huntertown	49

Semifinal (Muncie)

Fort Wayne Central	46	Monroe	24
Fort Wayne Central	44	Marion	23

State Finals (Indianapolis, Coliseum)

Fort Wayne Central	33	Batesville	24
Fort Wayne Central	45	Lebanon	40

Fort Wayne South

Season Record (28–2)
1957–58

Fort Wayne South	65	Bluffton	48
Fort Wayne South	65	Kendallville	32
Fort Wayne South	56	Concordia (Fort Wayne)	54
Fort Wayne South	67	New Haven	50
Fort Wayne South	81	Huntington	41
Fort Wayne South	62	Auburn	47
Fort Wayne South	74	Terre Haute Gerstmeyer	55
Fort Wayne South	58	Muncie Central	61
Fort Wayne South	78	Richmond	45
Fort Wayne South	53	Michigan City (Overtime)	56
Fort Wayne South	67	Elkhart	40
Fort Wayne South	63	Fort Wayne North	29
Fort Wayne South	54	Mishawaka	45
Fort Wayne South	72	Fort Wayne Central	64
Fort Wayne South	71	Muncie Burris	45
Fort Wayne South	70	Fort Wayne North	34
Fort Wayne South	70	Shortridge (Indianapolis)	63
Fort Wayne South	69	Gary Froebel	64
Fort Wayne South	77	Fort Wayne Central	67
Fort Wayne South	45	Fort Wayne Central Catholic	39

Sectional (Fort Wayne Coliseum)

Fort Wayne South	68	Leo	40
Fort Wayne South	67	New Haven	53
Fort Wayne South	60	Fort Wayne Central (Overtime)	56
Fort Wayne South	55	Concordia (Fort Wayne)	34

Regional (Fort Wayne Coliseum)

Fort Wayne South	61	Fremont	48
Fort Wayne South	68	Berne	51

Semistate (Fort Wayne Coliseum)

Fort Wayne South	71	Bluffton	49
Fort Wayne South	76	Elkhart	44

State Finals (Indianapolis, Butler Fieldhouse)

Fort Wayne South	55	Springs Valley	42
Fort Wayne South	63	Crawfordsville	34

Fort Wayne Northrop

Season Record (28–1)
1973–74

Fort Wayne Northrop	54	Fort Wayne North	52
Fort Wayne Northrop	69	DeKalb	48

Fort Wayne Northrop	56	South Bend Adams	59
Fort Wayne Northrop	70	Heritage	47
Fort Wayne Northrop	70	Warsaw	52
Fort Wayne Northrop	64	Fort Wayne Elmhurst	52
Fort Wayne Northrop	62	New Haven	37
Fort Wayne Northrop	55	Fort Wayne Wayne	42
Fort Wayne Northrop	52	Elkhart Central	32
Fort Wayne Northrop	63	Fort Wayne Wayne	51
Fort Wayne Northrop	61	Huntington	59
Fort Wayne Northrop	71	Fort Wayne Concordia	64
Fort Wayne Northrop	77	Fort Wayne Dwenger	55
Fort Wayne Northrop	75	Fort Wayne Luers	40
Fort Wayne Northrop	75	Fort Wayne Snider	47
Fort Wayne Northrop	92	Marion	64
Fort Wayne Northrop	67	Fort Wayne South	58
Fort Wayne Northrop	60	Penn	58
Fort Wayne Northrop	70	Garrett	48
Fort Wayne Northrop	47	Carroll	34

Sectional (Fort Wayne Coliseum)

Fort Wayne Northrop	70	Harding	44
Fort Wayne Northrop	75	Woodland	56
Fort Wayne Northrop	57	Carroll	47

Regional (Fort Wayne Coliseum)

Fort Wayne Northrop	67	Fort Wayne South	51
Fort Wayne Northrop	63	DeKalb	44

Semistate (Fort Wayne Coliseum)

Fort Wayne Northrop	55	Logansport	53
Fort Wayne Northrop	67	Anderson	52

State Finals (Indiana University)

Fort Wayne Northrop	63	Lafayette Jeff	49
Fort Wayne Northrop	59	Jeffersonville	56

8

Lebanon's Rick Mount typified Small Town-American Dream Image

Lebanon's Rick Mount would be the first choice almost every time if you had to pick one player as the ideal model for what Indiana high school basketball typifies in the minds of the sport's most avid followers all over the country.

A small town lad who had a dream and made it big, Mount is remembered for the countless shooting clinics he put on while he was a one-man wrecking crew at Lebanon High School from 1963 to 1966, and Rick still owns many of the Big 10 scoring records he set just a short hop down the road at Purdue University from 1967 to 1970.

Mount wasn't cut out for pro ball, and his career with the jet set ended much too soon after five years for reasons that probably had very little to do with basketball. But the 6-3 shooting phenom from Boone County left an indelible imprint on the high school and college front that endeared him to all who marveled at his picture-book form.

Pete Mount (Rick's father) owned all the Lebanon records before young Rick came along. Pete's high school team went all the way to the 1943 state championship game (losing 45–40 to Fort Wayne Central), and Rick's dad was such a talented player that he went right to the pros with Sheboygan.

Lebanon won the state championship three times as one of the true pioneers in the first eight years of the tournament. Glenn Curtis picked up the first of his four state titles as a first-year coach at Lebanon in 1918. Curtis put together three more state championship teams at Martinsville and occupies a special niche in the Hall of Fame, along with the other four-time winners—Marion Crawley and Everett Case.

Steve and Brian Walker also took another Lebanon team to the State Finals in 1975, where the Tigers lost to state-title-bound Marion in the afternoon, 73–65. Steve Walker was named Trester Award winner and he was voted to the Indiana All-Star team. One year later Brian Walker also wore an Indiana All-Star suit.

Jim Rosenstihl left a good basketball team in Bluffton to come to Lebanon as varsity coach in Rick Mount's freshman year—demonstrating that his timing as a coach was almost as good as Rick's timing as a pure outside shooter. Rosie had enjoyed much success at Bluffton with such players as Bob Purkhiser (Purkhiser still holds the Big 10 record for consecutive field goals with 18 set at Purdue in 1963) and big Chuck Bavis, and in 1963 decided to look into the job opening at Lebanon. Rosenstihl's home base was Zionsville in the same county with Lebanon, and Jim was one of Tony Hinkle's best disciples from a long list of Butler University greats.

Phil Buck was coaching Frankfort at the time, and Rosenstihl phoned Phil about the Lebanon job. Buck's Frankfort teams played Lebanon every year, and Rosie knew that Phil would have a pretty good working knowledge of the situation.

"Lebanon was a senior team, but there's a little blond kid in the eighth grade who can flat out shoot the ball—his name is Rick Mount," Rosenstihl was told.

Rosenstihl took the job and right away he was advised by such resident experts as Claude Wilson, Dick Perkins, and a few others that, sure enough, the young Mount kid might be good enough for a starting varsity role by the end of his freshman year.

Rosie arrived a bit early to see for himself, and in no time he could tell that the advance information on Mount was just a bit off target. Mount already was doing some unbelievable things as an eighth grader against many of the top high school players out of the very competitive Metropolitan Indianapolis league, picking up valuable experience on the outdoor courts in the summer.

"I could see that Rick was going to be in my starting lineup in his very first game as a freshman," said Coach Rosenstihl. "Rick was a little nervous in that first game against Brownsburg and scored 12 points. But one game under his belt was all he needed because the next game he got 24 against Crawfordsville and hit 11 of his 18 shots from the field."

It was the beginning of one of Indiana high school basketball's greatest careers because Rick went on to average 20.4 as a freshman, with a single game high of 30. He lifted that average to 23.6 his sophomore year and then hit 33.1 in each of his last two Lebanon seasons. He was a 48 percent shooter from the field and .808 at the foul line.

Mount's career total at Lebanon was 2,595 (averaging 27.3 for 94

As a member of the Indiana Pacers, Rick Mount was honorary chairman for membership of the Indiana Association for Retarded Children. Mount's teammate for this picture was Jimmy George from School 7 in Indianapolis. On the right, Rick is seen with All-Star coach Cleon Reynolds of Indianapolis Shortridge and Cathedral. Rick was to rewrite Big 10 recordbooks at Purdue, and he was Mr. Basketball in 1965.

games). Only one player in Hoosier Hysteria's long history ever scored more—Marion Pierce of tiny Lewisville had 3,019 in 1957–61.

Rick set a single game record for Lebanon with 57 points against Crawfordsville his senior year, tied the Semistate single game record with 47 against Logansport, and set a two-game record for the Semistate round with 76.

Mount now looks back on his high school days at Lebanon as being the best part of his outstanding basketball career. His biggest fans have only one regret: Rick didn't have a chance to show what he could do in a State Finals setting.

Mount did everything humanly possible to take his Lebanon ball club to the Final Four with a phenomenal 47-point blitz that erased a much-taller Logansport opponent, 65–64, and then came back with 29 at night in a heart-breaking 59–58 loss to East Chicago Washington in the Lafayette Semistate.

Mount caught fire in the fourth quarter against Logansport, which had rolled up a 36–27 half-time lead and increased that to 51–39 at the end of three quarters.

Tying the Semistate record set by Kokomo's Goose Ligon in 1962, the blond bomber from Lebanon drilled nine of his 13 shots in that incredible 20-point fourth quarter assault. In one bewildering stretch Rick connected on seven straight shots, the seventh putting Lebanon on top to stay, 58–57, with 3:19 to go.

Lebanon had outscored the startled Berries, 17–6, in less than five minutes, and Mount had done it all except for one drive-in shot by forward Jeff Tribbett.

Logansport blew a chance with only 11 seconds on the clock to deadlock the game, when the Berries missed the second of two free throw attempts and Lebanon was the winner, 65–64.

Mount, who took 38 of Lebanon's 55 shots in the game, totaled 19 field goals and nine free throws. Logan had better balance, led by Lee Whittington's 20 and Mike Alberts with 18, but it didn't matter. Mount had put on one of the most dazzling individual performances in state tourney history.

Mount, Tribbett, and Mike Caldwell showed the way as Lebanon built a 13-point lead over East Chicago Washington late in the third quarter of the Semistate final. But Mount developed leg cramps under a lot of defensive pressure late in the contest and the more physical Senators finished strong to record that one-point comeback decision.

Johnny Cousins and Drago Trifunovich combined for 33 points to provide most of the East Chicago scoring punch. Mount had to be rested during the fourth quarter, and the Senators took the lead at 55–53. East Chicago discarded its fast-breaking style in favor of the stall to protect that narrow lead.

Trifunovich's rebound basket on a missed free throw at the 17-second mark wrapped up the victory for the Senators. Lebanon was outrebounded 41–29 and, coupled with Mount's leg cramps, it was the deciding factor.

"If he had it to do over again, he'd play the Lebanon great the same way and just pray for better results," Corky Lamm of the *Indianapolis News* reported Logansport's coach Jim Jones as saying after Mount cut loose with his 47 in the Semistate opener. "Actually, I thought our defense was working well. It forced him out higher and wider on his shots. And we switched well almost every time. But they just kept going in. He was simply great.

"Our 6–5 guard, Steve Spangler, took Mount until he got in foul trouble. And then Neil Adams had him. Adams was in there when Mount got hot [in the fourth quarter]. Then we put Spangler back in.

"We didn't zone because I didn't think that would be any better—if as good—than the switching we were doing.

"I did think our own offense staggered a bit in the fourth period, and I suppose the only thing I could have done differently was to start holding the ball when we had a 12-point lead," the Logansport coach conceded.

Jones wasn't the only one impressed by Mount's eye-popping shooting clinic. Veteran *Hammond Times* sports editor John Whitaker, who had covered the Calumet's best for 37 years, seconded those thoughts. Said John, "I've seen a few great things in my time. I was there when Red Grange went wild against Michigan. I saw the famous Dempsey-Tunney long count title fight. I watched Babe Ruth call his home run shot. . . . And now this performance by Mount."

Rick set a Lebanon floor record his junior year with 43 one night against Indianapolis Crispus Attucks (the school that gave Hoosier Hysteria Oscar Robertson) and he broke it one week later with 50 against Danville. He set a 39-point single game record for the Lafayette Holiday Tourney the same year. Lebanon beat a great Michigan City team 82–81 in overtime and Mount's backdoor play was the clincher.

Mount hit his career high against Crawfordsville with 57 his senior year. It was the only time he took 40 shots in a game, and he was on target 24 times. He also converted nine of his 12 free tosses for the record-breaking total.

Mount's career low was 11 points so he had 94 straight varsity games in double figures. He was held to 11 his freshman year by West Lafayette.

Mount was named Indiana's Mr. Basketball for the two-game Blind Fund series against Kentucky in 1966, and once again the Lebanon townspeople rushed to the ticket windows to watch their most famous citizen at work.

Indiana encountered one of Kentucky's best All-Star teams in the series and lost both games, 104–77 and 77–67. A Kentucky lad named Gene Smith held Mount to 13 in the first game and 21 in the second.

Mount hit seven straight late in the return game at Indianapolis' Butler Fieldhouse, and the game was deadlocked at 67–67 with 1:30 remaining, but the Hoosiers couldn't pull it off. Rick was limited to just two points in the first half and regained his old shooting form in the second period with 19.

Lebanon fans shelled out $2,274.50 for tickets to the Louisville half of the series, and then the next week they sent game sponsors a check for $5,742.50. It guaranteed a capacity throng of 14,756 for Butler Fieldhouse.

Rick Mount was the first high school basketball player to have his picture on the cover of *Sports Illustrated* magazine, and Frank Deford wrote some incredible stuff about Indiana's most recruited player and his hometown.

"Sunshiny clover and chuckling ripples notwithstanding, Indiana is going to have a tall time holding onto Rick Mount, who may be as good a high school basketball player as there ever was. He has the moves of a cat . . . the eyes of a hawk, the presence of a king and he has visions of UCLA or Cincinnati or Miami or other faraway places. Coaches come clamoring to him. Not just the recruiters, but men like Vic Bubas of No. 1 Duke and old Adolph Rupp of No. 2 Kentucky and John Wooden of champion UCLA and Bruce Hale of Miami. . . .

"And like gun-slingers, the kids come from all over the state—the

Rick and his father Pete Mount had great fun reading about other Lebanon teams. Row after row of trophies and photos decorate the Lebanon school halls. Pete Mount played on a state runner-up team in 1943 and was the school's top hardwood talent until Rick came along. (Photo by Rich Clarkson, courtesy of Sports Illustrated.)

white farm boys and the Negroes from downtown Indianapolis—just for the chance to challenge him on the outdoor summer court in the Lebanon park."

Deford went on. "Comparisons are obligatory because Oscar Robertson played in high school just 26 miles away, down what is now the Interstate, in Indianapolis, and many people have seen them both. When Rick was just a sophomore Ray Crowe, Oscar's coach at Crispus Attucks High, said: 'At this stage, he's as good as Oscar was.' Most fans, like Pistol Sheets who runs the town pool hall, agree with this analysis. Pistol expresses the consensus this way: 'Rick is a better shooter than anyone you ever saw in high school, but Arsker—that's the way they pronounce Oscar in Lebanon—now Arsker, he had the better maneuverability.' "

The *Sports Illustrated* writer explained how teenage fame is not uncommon in Indiana and how it's the adults and not the crazy kids who are responsible for it.

"When Rick was playing in the fifth grade, crowds of a thousand or so would show up to watch him. Grown people, grandfathers and grandmothers. They travel 80 or 100 miles one way to see a game that does not even involve their own team. A bunch from Lebanon went that far to see a game in Cloverdale and ran into Tink Bennett from Rossville, and he had come 35 miles farther. Herbie West flagged a train once to get from Lebanon to a game in Shelbyville. He hitched a ride back with Ham Foster and Claude Wilson, and Ham says Herbie complained all the way home that the officiating had robbed the Tigers of victory, though Lebanon had lost by 45 points.

"These people go to fifth grade games, scouting the future for Rosenstihl. They cut work early to attend varsity practice . . ., get together for old game movies which they know by heart. Waiting lists for season tickets are impossibly long. Mayor and Mrs. Herb Ransdell have had the same seats at the Lebanon gym (capacity 2,200) since it was opened in 1931. Last year for the price of two tickets to the sectionals, Dick Perkins and Bob Staton were able to borrow a brand new $6,000 tractor so that they could get through a blizzard to rescue Daryl Kern at his farm. Daryl is a substitute."

So with this atmosphere it's understandable how the whole community got a little uptight when Rick Mount first announced that he would be playing his college ball for Bruce Hale at Miami. Kids of all ages from the Mayor right on down began a community drive to persuade Rick to second thoughts about his college choice. Miami Coach Hale spent one whole week in Lebanon camping on Mount's doorstep, and it has been suggested that Rick probably signed before he realized what he was doing just to get Hale out of town.

Many Purdue fans reside in Lebanon, which is just 35 miles away from this West Lafayette campus, and Coach George King held another little known trump. Assistant Coach Bob King, who did most of George's recruiting, was the nephew of the Lebanon mayor. A community-wide campaign was touched off, and the outcome was inevitable.

"Going to Indianapolis [a 30-minute ride] is a long trip for Rick, if you know Rick. So I don't really believe that he ever had any serious ideas about going all the way to Miami to play college ball. And there's just no way he could turn down all of those Lebanon fans who wanted to watch him play for Purdue because it was close to home," Bob King recalls.

Of course, Rick played before two sellout crowds as Indiana's Mr. Basketball in the All-Star series with Kentucky, then went on to have a fabulous career at Purdue where he joined up with 1965's Mr. Basketball Billy Keller, who had starred on Indianapolis Washington's 1965 state championship team.

Mount and Keller complemented each other so well in the Purdue backcourt that the Boilermakers went all the way to the NCAA championship game against UCLA in Rick's junior year. Rick hit the 20-footer in overtime against Marquette to put Purdue in the NCAA finals.

Purdue dedicated 14,123-seat Mackey Arena against UCLA in Rick's first varsity game as a sophomore. Mount scored 28, and the Boilers lost a 73–71 heartstopper to the national champs.

Above, Rick Mount, Indiana's Mr.
Basketball in 1966, with Lebanon coach Jim
Rosenstihl. Photo on right shows the classic
Mount style in free shooting.

Mount still owns the Big 10 records for most points in one game, with 61 against Iowa's conference champs [February 28, 1970], including a record-breaking 27 field goals. He owns the conference record with his scoring average of 39.4 for one year, as well as his average of 34.79 for a three-year career.

Rick bombed 27 of his 47 shots in that record-breaking 61-point assault against the Hawkeyes, connecting on 13 field goals in the first half and 14 in the second. But Iowa outlasted the Boilers in a 108–107 barn burner to nail down its first outright Big 10 title in 14 seasons.

Mount drove the lane hoping for a 3-point play that would send the game into overtime, but the Hawkeyes led 108–105 and they just gave Rick plenty of room to sink an uncontested layup as the final seconds ticked off the Mackey Arena clock.

Reflecting on his 61-point performance in 1970, Mount says the record could stand up for a long time considering all the ball-control basketball that is being played in the college ranks in recent years.

Mount also held the season record for several years with 1,461 points, but he played only three 14-game seasons. A short time later the freshman eligibility rule was adopted and Michigan's Mike McGee totaled 1,503 in four 18-game seasons.

Rick's 552 record for 14 games in one Big 10 season also was bettered by Terry Furlow with 558 in 18 games for Michigan State. His 2,323 career total still ranks second in the conference.

The two-time All-American had his finest year as a junior when he propelled the Boilers to a 23–5 mark, the Big 10 title, and the runnerup spot behind mighty UCLA in the NCAA tourney. Mount tallied 28 points in that 92–72 championship game loss to Johnny Wooden's Bruins.

Nobody was any happier than Iowa to see Rick move on to the pro ranks with the Indiana Pacers, because the Rocket averaged 45.1 in his six games against the Hawkeyes. He had 31 and 38 his sophomore season against Iowa, 45 and 43 as a junior, and then finished with 53 and 61 his senior year. He also made life miserable for Michigan, averaging 43 per game in four meetings with the Wolverines.

Mount closed out his college career with another outstanding 25-point performance in the East-West Classic played before a sellout crowd in Butler Fieldhouse. Mount led the East to a 116–102 win but the Star of Stars award was given to North Carolina's Charlie Scott. Rick hit 10 of his 15 shots in this game and was outscored only by Tiny Archibald of Texas-El Paso with 35 for the West.

Mount also led the East team to victory with a game high 24 as a college sophomore, but in that game the working press voted the MVP award to Louisiana State's Pistol Pete Maravich.

Mount's abbreviated career in the American Basketball Association included two years with the Indiana Pacers, two with the Kentucky Colonels, and one with Memphis and Utah. Rick left the sport and went home to Lebanon when the Utah franchise folded.

Many people thought Mount was nothing but a shooter, but Coach Rosenstihl and Purdue's Bob King were quick to refute those beliefs. "Rick was our best passer and also our best ball-handler at Lebanon," Rosenstihl said.

"Rick made a science out of shooting, and he helped a lot of other players on the Purdue team with their shot," King explained. "He had a good basketball mind and really knew the game. And he carried his load on defense in spite of what some said later critizing that part of his game.

"Mount not only wanted perfection—he made a point to do something about it. He had to work hard the first two years at Purdue, but he never asked for a thing. All he wanted to do was play basketball."

King said, "Rick Mount typifies what most people all over the

Rick always had time to talk basketball on some street corner in downtown Lebanon. Here he is cornered on the courthouse square by Claude Wilson and several other red-hot Lebanon rooters. (Photo by Rich Clarkson, courtesy of Sports Illustrated.)

country have heard about Indiana high school basketball. He came from a small town and had a dream about making it big someday in the basketball game he loved. This is the Indiana schoolboy image that people have come to know from coast to coast.

"Every good basketball player knew and admired Rick Mount. A lot of recruits on our trips from the Indianapolis Airport have seen those signboards posted along the Interstate—Lebanon, Home of Rick Mount. All good shooters belong to a special breed and every one of those kids who saw the signs had something good to say about Mount.

"It should also be remembered that we sold 1,000 season tickets in Lebanon for Rick's first year at Purdue, and that continued all the way through his college career."

Oscar Robertson and Jerry West were Mount's idols as a high school player in Lebanon. Of course, Mount's dad had much to do with Rick's development in the early years. "I'd go into the house crying because I couldn't beat him," Rick recalls.

But Pete Mount was a two-handed set shot artist from another era, and most of the credit for polishing Rick in high school goes to Rosenstihl. Purdue's Purkhiser also played a big role going one-on-one against Rick game after game on the practice courts in his Lebanon hometown. Purkhiser came to Lebanon as an assistant, and Mount became one of his personal projects.

Mount also has some flattering things to say about Billy Keller, who played next to him at Purdue. Keller was the best ball-handler

Rick Mount, seen at left, eyes a loose ball in the East-West College All-Star game at Indianapolis' Butler Fieldhouse in 1970. Marv Winkler of Southwest Louisiana, who played his high school ball at Indianapolis Washington, is at the left. The right photo shows Rick as he tries to stop a shot by Rick Ericson (University of Washington) in the East-West classic.

Mount ever saw, and Billy's talents were showcased best in their performances against UCLA's feared full-court press. "Billy had no difficulty at all breaking the UCLA press and then that left me wide open for a jump shot at the other end. We knew that Big Lew [Alcindor] would never come out on me from his position under the basket," Mount said. "This meant that Lew had to worry about stopping Chuck Bavis and me. And I got the 18-foot jumper just about any time I wanted it."

Unfortunately, Mount and Keller never had much of a chance to play together with the Indiana Pacers.

Mount and Indiana Pacers coach Bobby Leonard didn't hit it off real well, and Mount asked to be traded at the end of his second season. Mount was the No. 3 scorer in the league at Memphis before he suffered a shoulder injury and missed most of the year, and he was in the 20's three straight games before Utah folded. Other pro clubs beckoned with tryout offers, but Rick wasn't interested.

"I still loved the game of basketball, but I didn't enjoy all of the other things about the pro scene," Mount admits now. "Mike Storen was top-notch [Storen was the Indiana GM who signed Rick], and some of the others were okay. But pro ball is nothing like high school and college—it's a job and too much of a cutthroat proposition.

"Coach Rosenstihl recognized my talents and let me do what I could do best—shoot the ball. They tried to make a ball-handling guard out of me when I went to the pros. Now, none of your big scoring guards in the pros handle the ball, and that's the way it should be. They have shooting guards, and they have their ball handlers.

"Coach [Rosenstihl] was like a second father to me, and high school was the best part of my career. When I had problems in college later, he'd come up to Purdue to talk to me. He's that way with all his Lebanon players. What happened to me later on makes me appreciate Coach Rosenstihl and Lebanon even more."

That's where you'll find Rick Mount today, operating his own sports store in Lebanon and looking basketball-fit. His shooting eye is still 20–20.

Rick Mount at Lebanon

Year	Team Record	FG	PCT.	FT	PCT.	TP	AVG
1962–63	16–6	169	.438	111	.761	449	20.4
1963–64	20–5	223	.505	144	.766	590	23.6
1964–65	15–6	260	.505	176	.858	696	33.1
1965–66	21–6	344	.503	173	.828	861	33.1
Career	72–23	995	.488	605	.808	2,595	27.3

Rick Mount at Purdue

Year	FG	PCT.	FT	PCT.	TP	AVG
1967–68	259–593	.437	165–195	.846	683	28.4
1968–69	366–710	.515	200–236	.847	932	33.3
1969–70	285–582	.489	138–166	.831	708	35.4
Career	910–885	.484	503–597	.843	2,323	32.3

9

The Best of Bird

There was a time in the not-so-distant past when Larry Bird lived the life he probably enjoyed best. In long, hot summer days in the old ISU Arena, Bird would patiently shoot baskets alone—jump shots, layups, free throws. He was perfecting a craft which he would demonstrate in full public view in a short time. But in the summer of 1976, no one really knew Larry Bird. He practiced unencumbered by gawkers and curiosity-seekers, people who would later pay almost any price to associate themselves with this basketball player.

Life changed for Larry Bird. The Springs Valley High School graduate had left a stormy wake in his path to Indiana State. When he took his place as a Sycamore basketball player, no one could have predicted the lasting impact he would have on the school, the community, or on the game of basketball.

His rags-to-riches story seemed improbable during a time two years earlier when, as a senior at Springs Valley, he had established himself as an outstanding basketball player but remained painfully shy and backward. Many stories grow up around famous personages; it often is hard to separate the man from the myth, and the legend of Larry Bird is no exception. But the oft-told story about an airport visit gone awry during that senior year seems possible, at least, and most people who knew him in the early days would find it probable.

The story goes that Bird, who drew enough attention that year to earn a place on the Indiana All-Star team, was being recruited by a Florida university. In the course of recruiting, a coach suggested Bird visit the campus—a typical and quite legal recruiting technique. Apparently Bird made it to the Indianapolis airport and paused at a window to watch one of the mammoth jets take off. Seeing the fury of the takeoff at close hand for the first time frightened him so that he at once canceled the trip and any plans to attend school at any place an automobile could not carry him to.

Instead, he signed a letter-of-intent to attend Indiana State University. The unusual twists and turns of his career soon followed, stories which would haunt him most of his ISU career as he endeavored to play basketball and to deflect queries of a press he despised and feared.

Bird's story is significant in the annals of Indiana basketball not just because he is homegrown. He remains a basketball player of uncanny skill and style. At 6–9 and 220 pounds, he is an athlete whose smooth moves and accurate shooting at times wowed opponents. But he is most remembered by the fans of his college days as one of the most selfless players of modern times. Many people feel Bird and Michigan State's Earvin (Magic) Johnson influenced a national trend placing new emphasis on the pass and teamwork. If Bird could not always beat opponents with his feet, they could never seem to conquer his quick hands nor could they anticipate the next pass. He is gifted with extraordinary peripheral vision, permitting him to see oncoming teammates and feed their lay-ups with the flick of a wrist. Often described as having "floor presence," his style of play demonstrated basketball was still a team game in spite of an individual's remarkable ability.

He contrasted his incredible on-the-floor performance with marked reticence away from the floor during those painful early days at ISU. He shied away from strangers, was at odds with the press, and strained to protect his family and old friends from the glare of a spotlight moving more intensely on him. By the time he graduated from Indiana State, he had overcome many of those fears and learned to deflect questions and probing with grace. But, like overcoming the wariness of airplanes, change could only come with time.

Larry Joe Bird was born December 7, 1956. He spent his first 19 years—more or less—in French Lick, Indiana, a town previously known for its spas. It is a small town where big-city pleasures were neither known nor desired. He was one of six children, the fourth in the family, and soon demonstrated his adeptness as a basketball player. He describes those times when games were played with wadded paper tossed in a wastepaper basket. During a period between his junior and senior years he enjoyed a growth spurt of about four inches (from 6–3 to 6–7), giving him size to go along with his natural skills. And basketball was his life.

"He was a perfectionist," recalled Gary Holland, his B-team coach at Springs Valley. "I never saw a kid who played basketball so much. He didn't have a car or much money, so he spent his time at basketball."

Bird still holds nearly every record at the school. He scored 764 points as a senior, an average of 30.6 points per game. He had 516 rebounds that same season. The team went 21–4 and lost in the regional to Bedford, 58–55. He also has single-game records of 55 points (vs. Corydon) and 38 rebounds (vs. Bloomfield). He put back-to-back games of 42 points against West Washington and 55 against Corydon in the same weekend. This outstanding high school performance came after an inauspicious start—he broke his ankle in the first B-team game of his sophomore year. He played six games before the season ended. Holland soon lost him from the junior varsity roster as Jim Jones claimed him on the varsity team. And, despite the stellar perform-ances, his fans were still startled when he made all-state lists and the All-Star team. "They thought nobody from a small school could make all-state," Holland said.

The recruiting efforts followed that fine senior season, as did the All-Star stint. Still, as an All-Star he was mostly unrecognized, a shy kid with blond bangs and one who refused to enter one of the All-Star games when Coach Kirby Overman tried to use him in the waning seconds to mop up. Bird was not then and was never to be a mop-up boy. It may have been an All-Star game, but he still had his native southern Indiana pride.

Trouble lay over the horizon. His appearance at Indiana Universi-ty, where Bob Knight had recruited him, would be brief. The size of the campus, with its 30,000-plus students, overwhelmed him. Unable to adjust, he fled the campus in a matter of weeks and returned to more familiar ground. His basketball skills were relegated to playground performances. This was the fall of 1974 and Larry Bird's college aspirations—if, indeed, they could be called aspirations—were seemingly at an end. His personal crisis would increase with his father's suicide in early 1975. A marriage to a childhood sweetheart fizzled and divorce followed. He attended Northwood Institute at nearby West Baden, Indiana, briefly, but his skills were so clearly superior that he left there, too. And, so, Bird turned to work in his hometown, doing odd jobs like painting park benches and, in a job which would be noted so many times later in his life, collecting gar-bage. He would recall during his collegiate career, "It was the best job I ever had. . . . I told the guys, 'I'll be going up there to get a little education. Then I'll come back and be boss of you guys.' "

Bird was not particularly eager to leave the garbage truck and his buddies behind. New Indiana State Coach Bob King and his assistant, Bill Hodges, learned of Bird's basketball idleness. They were well aware of his skills and were eager to bring him to a smaller campus where his skills might lend aid to an ailing basketball program. Hodges encountered resistance and downright hostility. Larry's mother, Georgia, was not eager for new problems in the wake of the recent year's disasters, and Bird himself had all but given up on the notion of playing basketball anywhere but in the backyard. But Hodges, to his

Bird practicing with the Indiana All-Stars in 1975.

everlasting credit, remained persistent and, prior to the 1975–76 season, landed his quarry.

Due to his aborted stay at IU, Bird was required to sit out for a season, or "redshirt," under NCAA rules, but he was permitted to practice with the team. He was reducing the Sycamore starters to rubble in those workouts and establishing himself with his teammates. King was almost giddy. In the summer of '76 he privately boasted that Bird might turn around all of ISU's athletic fortunes.

Such a notion seemed unlikely, particularly to a wizened and cynical community which had heard promises before. Sycamore basketball had been a profitable enterprise in the late 1960s with outstanding teams in NCAA Division II competition. ISU was the runner-up in the Division II national tournament in 1968 and had utilized outstanding Hoosier high school players like Jerry Newsom, Rich Mason, and George Pillow to fashion several good seasons. The old ISU Arena, in which Bird would only practice, could seat 4,500 fans and sellouts were not uncommon in those days. Student ID cards were color-coded at the beginning of the year, and tickets were distributed on the basis of those colors for particular home games. Crowds even could become rowdy on occasion as paper throwing and expletive chanting were among the signs of a rebellious era.

With the move to Division I and the relocation to a fine new facility (Hulman Center—seating capacity 10,020), fortunes changed and interest waned. By the time King took over for Coach Gordon Stauffer, who incidentally had been among the coaches pursuing Bird as a high school senior, crowd averages hovered around 4,000 and thousands of empty seats were begging for customers.

There is little surprise, then, that the rumors about this Bird character hardly created a stampede at the ISU Athletic Ticket Office. His official debut came in late November of 1976 in a game against Chicago State University. A crowd of 3,000 saw the Sycamores win, 81-60. Bird started, of course, but suffered the jitters. His first trip down the floor produced a turnover—an errant pass which flew out of bounds. So much for rumors, huh? But he shook the jitters and finished the game with 31 points and 18 rebounds. In early December he made his maiden voyage before the big crowd and influential press at Purdue's Mackey Arena where 13,942 fans saw Bird and his teammates lose, 82-68, but left impressed by the "new guy." Bird scored 27 points and grabbed 15 boards.

Even after Christmas, with the Sycamores winning basketball games at an unusual pace, the Terre Haute crowds still weren't knocking down the gates. But 7,200 showed up for the Drake game over the holidays, the first game against a future Missouri Valley Conference rival (the Sycamores had been admitted to the league but were not scheduled into the title race). The game went two overtimes, Bird scored 25 points, had 15 rebounds, and the Sycamores won. Terre Haute sportswriter Carl Jones noted after that exciting performance that Terre Haute fans would soon come running. In a city which had been considered a "tough crowd" in Vaudeville days, interest was perking. It was attributable to one player.

For Illinois State later that season, more than 10,000 fans made an appearance to watch the Sycamores avenge their second defeat of the year handed them a week earlier by the talented Redbirds. Bird was sparkling, netting 40 points and confirming all rumors once and for all. The first sellout for an ISU home game since Hulman Center had opened in December 1973 greeted the Sycamores in the home season finale against Loyola of Chicago. Bird scored a phenomenal 45 points, had 17 rebounds and the legend was well on its way. More than 11,000 came to Evansville's Roberts Stadium to see him play a week later, and nearly 13,000 fans were at Hinkle Fieldhouse to see Bird's Indianapolis debut. The walk-up crowd was so large that thousands stood in line to buy tickets and saw only his second-half performance. Perhaps unconsciously wanting to entertain the late arrivals, Bird poured it on in the final 20 minutes and finished the game with a career-high 47 points and 19 rebounds. A makeup date with Valparaiso—a game which earlier had been postponed due to heavy snows—soon followed, and the Sycamores had finished the regular season with a 25-2 record. While the team and fans hoped for an NCAA at-large bid, they realized new kids on the block rarely get the nod from the powerful tournament committee. The NIT committee, however, recognized the ISU program and extended a bid, sending the Sycamores to a first-round game at the University of Houston.

A sellout crowd of 8,201 witnessed the game, but the Sycamores fell short. Bird scored 44 points and had 14 rebounds—leading the team in both categories for the 20th time in that season—but his twisting jump shot at the buzzer rimmed the flange and fell out. The season had ended, but fans who had been astonished by a 17-0 home record and the almost miraculous turnabout of ISU fortunes poured out at the Terre Haute airport to greet the returning team. Bird, still backward about crowds and fearful of microphones, cowered in the background on the truck bed where the team stood. They had arrived via an archaic DC-3 airplane, perhaps a transport which could have justified Bird's earlier aerial fears. But Bird, who was greeted by an enthusiastic ovation, muttered into the microphone with a grin, "Don't 'plaud, jus' send money." A voice called out from the crowd, "Wait two years," a remark which drew considerable applause.

For fears were growing that the greedy NBA, already aware of the ISU cage commodity, would lure Bird away before Sycamore fans could expend their funds and lungs to follow his career. Bird put the nix on that early, but no one really believed it would happen until he walked on the floor two years later to begin his senior season.

Bird's junior year would present new difficulties. It began with an appearance on the cover of *Sports Illustrated*'s college basketball preview edition with the headline, "College Basketball's Secret Weapon." Bird was still cautious about his press relations, partially due to his own shyness and partly from discomfort over his teammates getting ignored. Bird had been that way in high school, as Holland recalled, Bird coming to him and pleading for him to find ways to give publicity to teammates. Already the pundits were focusing on this atypical college athlete. Were there problems between Bird and the volatile Bobby Knight? No, Bird had never been to practice. And what of the suicide and the marriage and divorce and of the garbage truck days? Bird contended, and correctly so, that those were personal matters he did not like to discuss. He also was uncomfortable about his own speech, for he was a native southern Hoosier who, by his own admission, could occasionally butcher the King's English. He feared the

Bird in action at Indiana State (left). On the right, he is seen with Anderson's Tony Marshall and Coach Kirby Overman of New Albany during the Indiana All-Star workouts at Butler's Hinkle Fieldhouse in Indianapolis. Overman's New Albany were state champs in 1973, and Bird and company beat Kentucky convincingly in both ends of the home-and-home series.

big-time press would make light of him despite his demonstrated skills. He pleaded with one reporter late that first season, "I don't want to talk about personal things. Why don't they stick to me as a player? I'm just a guy." Or early in the junior season: "Why don't they ask me about basketball? That's my life." Indeed it was, but he was becoming a national celebrity. Wire services quit misspelling his name ("Byrd" was not uncommon that first season), and college basketball fans were interested in what was clearly an unusual story. By the middle of the second season he cut off the press completely, turning down all interviews. His coach endorsed the player's wishes and the media followers howled. The on-again, off-again relationship would continue the remainder of Bird's college career, but it was a career that would hang on the paraphrased assertion: I do my talking on the floor. And indeed he did.

Bird, who was performing on par in the classroom, was an accelerated Ph.D. on the basketball floor. Purdue paid a call at Hulman Center for the season's second game and a new routine began for ISU students. For hours prior to the game, students lined up outside Hulman Center to begin a mad rush for the seats reserved for their use at games. Students were admitted without charge upon the showing of an up-to-date ID card, but the seats were a first-come, first-served proposition, and the Larry Bird Show was too good to take the catbird seats. The large crowd was civil, but excited, and when the gates opened, damage occurred to a few of the doors in the stampede. Bob King made an early appearance on the floor to do a television interview and received a standing ovation more than an hour before game time from a large crowd of students already in its seats and waiting.

The game proved worth the wait for the ISU partisans. The Sycamores made short work out of a talented Boilermaker team, defeating Purdue, 91–63, in an astounding performance. Bird finished with 26 points and 17 rebounds and the sellout crowd was ecstatic. When Bird paid a courtesy call at the Ballyhoo, a local pub which had been a favorite college hangout for years, students literally danced on table tops. It was a rarified atmosphere previously unknown on the Terre Haute campus.

The season was not without its pitfalls. ISU won its first 13 games, including nonconference victories over talented Evansville (the weekend before the fatal airplane crash that killed team members and their coach), Ball State, Central Michigan, and Eastern Michigan. The initial MVC season also had a good start as the Sycamores won their first five games. But the dropoff was ahead. The day a *Sports Illustrated* profile appeared on newsstands, one to which Bird took pronounced exception, ISU fortunes tumbled. They lost five straight games, each fostered by its own unusual circumstances. Bird was angry because the SI writer, Larry Keith, had quoted Georgia Bird and had again brought up the bad news trio of suicide/divorce/garbage truck. Hence came his interview moratorium. They lost to Southern Illinois that night by three points. A long bus ride to Normal, Illinois, followed and the Sycamores lost to Illinois State, partly attributable to a technical foul whistled on Bird for dunking a dead ball near the end of the game. In the din of the Redbirds' hangarlike fieldhouse—where a sellout crowd, of course, was on hand—Bird never heard the whistle. The "tech" came down nevertheless and the frustrated Sycamores tussled with their opponents boxing-style—Bird not included—before the festivities ended in an 81–76 victory for Illinois State.

The next trip was a long one—a flight to Wichita which proved to be an up-and-down proposition for several hours. The team left Terre Haute a few hours before the famed Blizzard of '78 swept down on Indiana, and icing of the airlane had them making stops most of the night. They arrived in Wichita in the wee hours and played like it that night—losing an overtime bout with the Shockers, 74–70.

A blue-clad home crowd greeted the fading Sycamores on their return to Hulman Center a few nights later to face Creighton. A horrible second half unsaddled the Sycamores and they lost their fourth straight game.

After the Saturday night Creighton loss, the first and only home loss in Bird's career, the Sycamores traveled to Loyola of Chicago, where the crackerbox gym and waning fortunes handed them another defeat.

Even with the string of losses, the Sycamores could have won the MVC standings going into the post-season tournament had they been able to stop the Bluejays on that January night in Hulman Center. As it turned out, the Sycamores survived the opening rounds of the conference tournament, including a two-overtime semifinal game against New Mexico State at Terre Haute, before meeting Creighton in the conference title game. The 10th sellout crowd to see Bird that season—this time in Omaha's Civic Auditorium—cheered Creighton to the title, a narrow 54–52 victory won in the final second on a Rick Apke-jump shot. His brother, Tom, Creighton's coach, would lead the team to the NCAA tournament.

Once again the Sycamores would suffer a bridesmaid's fate, turning for post-season solace to the NIT. This time the Sycamores were awarded a home game as the selection committee knew a full-house would turn out in Terre Haute to watch Larry Bird shoot free throws. And the committee knew how to whip up a crowd, all right; they sent Illinois State to Hulman Center.

Few crowds have been more raucous, or more entertained. It was another classic battle as fans screamed much, tossed a few objects on the floor, and watched the coaches do a little confronting of their own at the scorer's table before the game was over. The Sycamores won this one, 73–71, to the delight of 10,150—more than capacity at the arena. A few days later, at Rutgers, ISU fell a win short of reaching New York City for the second straight year in a 57–56 loss at Piscataway, New Jersey. The season ended with a 23–9 record overall and 11–5 in the MVC. Larry Bird was no longer a secret weapon—more than a quarter of a million fans (268,223) had seen him play in person during the 1977–78 season.

Through it all, Bird was a most entertaining spectacle on the floor. He could dunk and rebound like a big man—he was, after all, 6-feet-9. Yet his jumper was clinic-perfect (he shot 53 percent for the season, hitting 403 of his 769 attempts). His crisp passing continued to wow the crowds. He had 125 assists that season, and though the records cannot show it, most of them made him appear as if he had eyes in the back of his head. There were times when even his teammates could not anticipate the ball was coming their way, but in time they learned to be on the lookout at all times. They were playing with a basketball magician, a man whose sleight-of-hand passes often were

Bird's talent on the hardwood made him the center of much media attention, despite his shy ways. Here NBC's Bryant Gumbel interviews him after an ISU game.

quicker than the eye, and nearly always quicker than the opposition. Favorite maneuvers were the fake shot and crouch, permitting the opponent, caught in mid-air with no place to go, to land on him for the obligatory foul. There was no mercy in his heart when he quickly thrust the ball behind a defender's head, causing the opponent to turn for an instant to see where the ball had been delivered and then having his heart sink upon discovering the ball had never left Bird's hands. In that instant of hand-turning, Bird had been given all the time he needed for an arching, and often successful, jump shot. The basketball world marveled at a player who had listened to that oft-repeated coaching direction to follow one's shot. Bird did so. His instinct for a bouncing ball directed him to the place where an errant shot would carom, often giving him the easy follow-up as the players around him stood flat-footed and astonished.

He declined enshrinement, of course, because he remained aloof. The city was then at his feet, no matter how many frustrating losses had been suffered that winter. And he proved he was a man of his word when the next season—his final college season—rolled around. There was a collective sigh of relief when he clearly and finally turned down overtures from the NBA. Boston had drafted him as its first choice in the June draft, taking a chance on signing him before the next draft would occur. Red Auerbach seemed content to wait. He had no choice. Larry Bird would fulfill his commitment to Indiana State.

Bird's reappearance was icing on the cake for the growing number of Indiana State fans. An ISU basketball ticket was a cherished possession. Contributions to the school's varsity club increased as patrons sought the best seats in the house.

No one could have predicted the season that was ahead. Bird had been remarkable for two years, true, but the previous season had not been the smooth path many fans had expected. There was no reason to believe the Sycamores would waltz through the upcoming Missouri Valley Conference season, either.

It is no great revelation to note, even before that final season is reviewed, that the Bird-led Sycamores finished the year as NCAA runners-up with a 33–1 record. Twenty-seven of the 34 games were sellouts and a record attendance (10,538) was set at Hulman Center as a new row of chairs was set up along a walkway at the top level of the arena. The Sycamores made their first-ever appearance on national television and drew sustained national attention. Terre Haute had never seen the likes of the emotion and fervor that season aroused.

Bird was surrounded by competent, steady teammates, though he remained the lone extraordinary talent on the club. Many of his teammates were Hoosier high school products, including starting guard Steve Reed (Warsaw), starting forward Brad Miley (who had played for the '76 state runner-up Rushville team), and sixth man Bob Heaton (Clay City). The other guard, Carl Nicks, a south side Chicago native, was a quick, if somewhat erratic, ballhandler and shooter. Alex Gilbert of East St. Louis, Illinois, was the other starter on the front line. It's not a group of names which will be indelibly etched on the minds of college basketball fans forever. But they played well as a group, sharing Bird's affection for the assist, indulging their coach's instructions to play dogged defense, and possessing a certain moxey that carried them through more than one ticklish spot as they sustained the undefeated record until the season-ending championship game against Michigan State.

The heart-and-soul of it all was Bird. His steely glances made occasionally lazy teammates cower, intimidated officials without a single word, and struck fear into opponents who knew that, one-on-one, Bird had few equals anywhere.

Still, as dreary fall became bitter winter, no one could predict an NCAA tourney outcome for the Sycamores. Few fans knew that Salt Lake City was the chosen site for the National Collegiate tournament finals. No one gave much thought about going there until, on an incredible St. Patrick's Day, the reality presented itself in an unforgettable game.

Bird dominated the season, beginning with early nonconference victories over Purdue and Evansville. The Purdue victory came at

Mackey Arena before a sellout. Bird scored 22 and had 15 rebounds to lead ISU to a 63–53 victory. Then the Sycamores could only squeak by a rebuilding Evansville team, 74–70, with Bird providing 40 points worth of firepower for the 12,488 Aces fans at Roberts Municipal Stadium. ISU turned around and had to sweat through another close game, this one a 78–76 victory over Illinois State.

It was a period of adjustment for the team, particularly since they were working for a new coach. Bob King had suffered a heart attack the previous summer and, while recovering and expecting to return to the bench, he suffered another setback in the form of a brain aneurysm. The corrective surgery occurred just as the season's practice was to begin, and King stepped aside in favor of assistant coach Bill Hodges. Hodges, himself a Hoosier native who had played for Jim Rosenstihl as a Zionsville High School player, hardly changed a King philosophy which concentrated on moving picks and passes on offense and intense, pressure defense. This was the style of play in which Bird best operated.

In the final nonconference game of the regular season against Morris Harvey, Bird set the all-time ISU career scoring mark, exceeding the record set by Jerry Newsom more than 10 years earlier. Newsom, the Columbus (Indiana) native who would graduate from player to referee status after hanging up the collegiate uniform, was on hand to congratulate Bird on the achievement.

Bird and Friends began a roll through the conference schedule in that January of 1979. Sellouts were to greet them—home and away—for the rest of the season. In that first month, no team had come close to stopping the Sycamores except for New Mexico State, a difficult opponent for ISU from the outset of their adversary relationship, which had lost by four points at Terre Haute. February arrived and the Sycamores were 18–0 overall and 8–0 in the league. Of course, the previous season had seen ISU win 13 straight only to begin that horrible skein of losses in the middle of the season. Someone was blowing up a big balloon and many fans wondered when too much air would force its way in; they crouched waiting for the bursting explosion.

Only a miracle saved the balloon, and Bird could not even claim credit. Nemesis New Mexico State was eager to welcome the Sycamores to its own arena where fans were eagerly cheering: "18–1, 18–1!" And, indeed, it appeared in the final seconds of that game that their wishes had come true. Bird had fouled out and was on the sidelines. The Aggies led by two points with three seconds remaining in the game and had their own Greg Webb at the free throw line with a one-and-one opportunity. A time-out gave the Aggie fans an extra minute of exultation. It was a short-lived party. Webb misfired, Miley

As a Boston Celtic, Bird is equally devastating. Here he is seen with the Phoenix Suns' Kyle Macy (Indiana's Mr. Basketball in 1975 from Peru) at the Boston Garden en route to a 105–92 victory. (UPI photo by Jim Daigle.)

grabbed the rebound and tossed an outlet pass to Bob Heaton who was waiting just short of the 10-second line. He released the shot from more than half the length of the floor and, to the amazement of television viewers in New Mexico and Indiana and to 13,684 fans, it banked home. Bird exploded from the bench to greet his roommate (Heaton and Bird shared a house on South Eleventh Street in Terre Haute that year) and urge his team on in what proved to be a saving overtime. The 91–89 victory gave the team an air of destiny. Never mind that two days later during a workout at the University of Tulsa, Heaton, at the urging of his teammates, tried repeatedly to fire home a like shot—and never even came close.

The juggernaut continued to roll up victories, playing very well at times and suffering poor games also. Bird's lone conference game without taking scoring honors for the team came at Bradley when the Braves decided to triple-team—that's right, they put three guys on Bird—in an effort to halt his 29-point scoring average. They kept him under double figures for the only time in his collegiate career, but it was a Pyrrhic victory. ISU won, 91–72, with Nicks scoring 31 to lead the Sycamores.

The regular season could close in splendid style against Wichita State. NBC brought its cameras to Hulman Center for the first time. A sellout crowd poured in despite a sudden and heavy snowstorm which struck that afternoon. The lines formed outside the arena as usual, and the students scrambled for the best seats. They were there early enough to greet NBC's Al McGuire, the former Marquette coach, who had articulately defended and supported the Sycamores on television all year. A sustained standing ovation greeted him and play-by-play announcer Jim Simpson. When a student presented McGuire with a powder-blue "Horrible Hanky" used by fans to demonstrate support for the team, McGuire promptly removed the handkerchief from his blazer pocket and replaced it with the Sycamore hanky. Again, the crowd was revved and it was still an hour before game time.

Only 9,759 saw it in person because of the snow, but what mattered to the ISU folks was that America was peering into its arena for the first time. Bird put on a marvelous show. He repeated the ball-over-the-opponent's-head fake and embarrassed a defender with a 25-foot jump shot. He turned, pivoted, fired, boarded, leaped, and stole the ball and the show. It was a 49-point, 19-rebound performance—his career-high and school record single-game scoring output—and the winning margin was 109–84.

The only news to come out of the MVC postseason tournament that would follow was a broken thumb to the star. Otherwise, it was three home games and three home victories, the latter and decisive one coming over New Mexico State (again) by 10 points.

Questions about the broken thumb were answered in the NCAA opener for the Sycamores at Lawrence, Kansas, the following Sunday. Bird scored 22 (so did Nicks) and a memorable Alex Gilbert dunk shot started a 20-point Sycamore offensive assault which took opponent Virginia Tech out of the tournament, 86–69. The Midwest Regional would follow at Cincinnati. The distance to Kansas had not intimidated some 3,000 Sycamore partisans, so the 3½-hour trip to Cincinnati was hardly a bother. Thousands of ISU backers crammed hotels, begged for tickets, and sat in pockets around the Riverfront Coliseum to watch more miracles in progress. ISU easily stopped Oklahoma, 93–72, on Thursday night to set up a meeting with the Sidney Moncrief-led Arkansas Razorbacks. What transpired on that electric afternoon in Cincinnati (March 27, 1979) was worthy of enshrinement. Bird parried, Moncrief answered, Bird rebounded, Moncrief drove for the basket. Their teammates complemented them—as always—and the handwringing throughout the arena would not stop until the game did. In the end, it came to one final chance, and the Sycamores had the ball. The game was tied, 71–71, and only 18 seconds remained. A Salt Lake City ticket hung in the balance. The ISU offense in the last play was hardly a precise display of X's and O's. The chief objective was to find—who else?—Bird, but the Razorbacks had him double teamed. There was no hope. Finally, Steve Reed hit Heaton a few steps in front of the basket. As the last seconds ticked away, Heaton reached over two defenders with his left hand and lofted the ball toward the basket. It bounced a full four times before coming down at the horn. Pandemonium! The floor filled with supporters and emotion. Bird was hugging one and all in sight, except for decking the fan who accidentally reached out and banged the tender thumb. The Arkansas fans were stunned and walked toward the exits in a daze. The remainder of the 17,162 fans on hand did what any self-respecting basketball fan would do after viewing a virtuoso performance by two outstanding teams—they stood and applauded for long minutes after the basket had scored. Many fans could not reach Salt Lake City for financial and time reasons, and perhaps that is why that spine-tingling moment at Cincinnati may have captured the best moment of ISU's best season of all time for them.

The NCAA was pressing hard to get Bird to open up and he was reluctantly doing more talking with the news media. Intensive lobbying efforts on Hodges, King, and Bird convinced them that Bird should be more accommodating at the national finals, and he was. As he reminded one writer that March, "I can handle the press, I can talk. But when they say something bad and put me down, it hurts my family. If I sit out, the press will talk to the other players. . . . Now they will get the publicity they deserve."

And so the headline writer's delight ("High-Flying Bird Leads Sycamores," "Sycamores Win on Bird's Wings," et al.) became a press wit at Salt Lake City. First he led the team in beating DePaul in the semifinals, 76–74, by scoring 35 points.

Then came the Sunday press conference giving Bird a chance to joust with more than 100 writers and commentators on the scene for the season finale. To one of the first questions, Bird demonstrated his economy of words. Question: "Larry, how's your thumb?" Bird leaned toward the microphone and unblinkingly replied, "Broke." No question could be asked again until considerable laughter had died down. Bird grinned. He knew exactly what he was doing. He seemed to enjoy the session, something one of the writers suggested near the end of the press conference. No, said Bird, he didn't enjoy news conferences, but they were something he was now obligated to do. Already he was preparing himself for the professional career that was moving ever closer.

The next night brought down the curtain on the season and the career, but not on the Legend of Larry Bird. He scored only 19 points in the loss to Michigan State (75–64) and the image of Bird sitting on the bench when it had ended, towel draped over his head, head in his hands, is hard for the thousands who saw it in the arena or at home (it set the television viewing record for an NCAA game at that time) to forget. He really had believed the Sycamores could win it all, despite the nay-sayers who had long ago been quieted by Bird and his buddies. He reverted to old form in the aftermath, refusing comment, and drawing verbal and printed ire in the next few days, but he had left his mark.

The community honored him that April with a huge banquet at

Hulman Center. Al McGuire, who had been honored in absentia in that arena all winter by a sign which read, "Al's Our Pal," was the guest speaker. The players wore tuxedoes provided by a local business, but Bird did all the dressing up he wanted to do in this life: nice slacks, blue blazer, red shirt, open collar. No one wears tuxedoes in French Lick.

He did unusual things after the season had ended. ISU baseball coach Bob Warn invited Bird to play baseball with the team, which he did. Nearly 2,000 fans showed up for the doubleheader against Kentucky Wesleyan to see Bird strike out his first time at bat and then stroke a two-run single in his second at-bat. The crowd went crazy—again. That summer Bird would break the index finger of his right hand while playing softball. It was not the first injury to that finger and surgery failed to relieve much of the pain and immobility the injury had inflicted. But he remained resilient, adjusting his shooting touch to deal with a finger that wouldn't work right again.

Big-time Eastern writers were aghast that Bird actually was doing his student teaching at West Vigo High School that spring. The tournament had delayed his official start there, so Bird stayed on after ISU's spring semester had ended (he was graduated that May) and served as assistant coach of the West Vigo baseball team. They found a uniform to fit his 6–9 frame and his critic teacher and WV baseball coach, Dick Ballinger, was heard to comment about his famous student teacher out cutting the grass in the outfield, "I've got the only three million dollar lawn mower in America."

Bird would sign a multi-million dollar package with the Boston Celtics, with the advice of attorney/agent Bob Woolf, a native Bostonian. Woolf had been selected through an unusual process in which Bird's Terre Haute friends familiar with the business world had interviewed agent candidates. Woolf was selected and when Bird moved to Boston the following summer, he conveniently located and purchased a home next-door to Woolf in suburban Brookline.

The legend remains in ISU's Hulman Center where pennants recall the legacy of Bird's career. Keepsakes are still kept by the faithful fans—from programs to 45-rpm records, "Indiana Has a New State Bird." His trips to Indianapolis with the Celtics always attract a large crowd and the standing ovation he nearly always receives is as much a credit to his current achievements in the NBA as to his past work at ISU. Boston broadcasts are carried by a Terre Haute radio station.

Bird repeated his magic in stuffy Boston, filling the aged Boston Garden and leading the team to a reclamation of its old and familiar NBA supremacy. Red Auerbach smoked a victory cigar in the locker room after Bird and teammates captured the 1981 NBA championship. Bird snatched the stogey away and enjoyed a few puffs himself. Auerbach didn't mind. He knew a legend when he saw one.

During the summer months, Bird returns to Indiana for a visit to family and friends and to conduct a basketball camp at French Lick. He does a commercial or two and spends idle hours fishing and playing golf. Wherever he walks, people stop. He gave up the privacy of those carefree days in 1976 when he could go to a store and not be recognized.

But the Legend lives on in Indiana because of his consummate skill and because he recognizes his roots. The best example came when the Celtics spent four days working out at Terre Haute North High School in the fall of 1980. It was a central location for three NBA preseason trips the Celtics would make, and the team preferred the quiet of Terre Haute. On the final day, the school's students quietly filed into the gymnasium to "watch professionals at work." As the students entered the gym the Celtics continued a lay-up drill. As Bird came toward the sidelines, he recognized a student whom he had taught in a West Vigo health class nearly two years earlier and who had transferred to North that fall. He caught her eye and greeted her by name. "Hello, Mr. Bird," she muttered. Her friends were stunned and impressed. Bird went about his basketball business, never thinking twice about the wave and greeting. But the story soon circulated. How had Larry Bird remembered a little Miss Nobody from a freshman health class after fame and fortune and achievement had rained down on him? That was easy, for the reason the legend lives on and will continue to live, no matter what he does, is that Larry Bird never forgot the roots of his life nor the people who had sent him on his way.

Larry Bird's High School Stats

	G	FG-FGA	FT-FTA	PTS	AVG	REB	A
Soph	2	3–4	2–3	8	4.0	8	5
Junior	22	137–279	79–105	353	16.0	217	136
Senior	25	305–606	154–205	764	30.6	516	107
Totals	49	445–889	235–313	1125	22.9	741	248

10

Marion Pierce—
The Henry County Hurricane

Ask almost anybody who knows anything about Indiana high school basketball to name the Hoosier state's all-time leading career scorer, and he is almost certain to give you Oscar Robertson, Rick Mount, Jimmy Rayl, Billy Shepherd, or George McGinnis.

Except for a few of us oldtimers, not many will remember that it is Marion Pierce, the 6-5 Henry County Hurricane, who put tiny Lewisville on the Hoosier Hysteria map from 1958 to 1961.

It has been written many times down through the years that the small schools are the real backbone of the hardwood sport in Indiana, and just a handful were smaller than Lewisville with its enrollment ranging from 78 to 84 in the upper four grades.

Pierce stole the thunder from all of his more-publicized big school challengers with the incredible four-year career record of 3,042 points in 94 games (comfortably ahead of Mount with 2,595 in second place), and 20 years later Marion still makes his home in Lewisville with his family.

Marion scored 454 points his freshman year for Coach Bob Scott's Lewisville Bears for a 20.2 average, and then the pride of Henry County led the state in scoring three straight seasons. Pierce had 797 points for a 34.6 average his sophomore year, 796 for a 36.4 average as a junior, and 995 for a 38.2 average in his senior season.

With Marion Pierce paving the way, Lewisville carved out a phenomenal 79-15 record, bagging its first sectional tourney since 1945 with a 56-49 win over mighty New Castle in the final and its sixth Henry County tourney crown with an 81-79 double overtime nod over an unbeaten Mooreland crew.

Pierce established a 140-point record for the New Castle Sectional which still stands (exploding twice for 43 against Middletown and Mt. Summit).

And he also recorded a game high 25 points the next week winding up his brilliant prep career in a 50–41 New Castle Regional loss to powerhouse Muncie Central. Lewisville missed its first nine shots in the third quarter after playing Muncie to a virtual 25–24 standoff in the first half.

It was during Marion's sophomore year that he bombarded his single game high of 64 in a 97–44 win over Union Township, piling up 50 points in a tremendous second half performance before Coach Scott decided to lift his superstar with four minutes remaining in the contest. He drilled 23 of his 35 field attempts against Union and 18 of 20 at the free throw line.

Pierce's 64 didn't break the Henry County record—Lee Bence rifled 76 way back in 1918 when New Castle walloped Noblesville by a staggering 112–0 score.

Pierce was voted all-sectional four straight years and had countless other big games for Lewisville.

Marion's scoring support wasn't always adequate, though, and on one memorable occasion he scored 56 his junior year in a disappointing 71–70 overtime loss to Spiceland. It was a bitter loss that broke the school's 45-game conference winning streak.

Lewisville's 72–70 sudden death double overtime win over Middletown in the 1961 New Castle Sectional is the one Pierce singles out as the most satisfying game he ever played—more satisfying even than the final game win over New Castle.

Marion got 43 points on 15 field goals and 13 free throws including the game-clinching jumper from 17 feet in the opening seconds of the second extra period.

Mike Peyton's two free throws for Lewisville had deadlocked the score at 70–70 in the last three seconds of the first overtime to keep the Bears alive.

Coach Scott, who succeeded Hall of Famer Jake Caskey as Indiana Deaf School athletic director in 1967, still felt the seven-point win over New Castle in the sectional windup was most important in his 11-year Lewisville career. It helped make up for a couple of double overtime losses to the Trojans in past sectionals.

Of course, he recalls vividly how a heavy snowstorm stranded many fans in the new 9,300-seat New Castle Fieldhouse Saturday night and forced postponement of the Lewisville-New Castle showdown until Monday.

Pierce was the big gun as usual with 27 points for Lewisville, but he ran into early foul trouble with 5:20 to go in the first half. Lewisville's early 21–8 lead was reduced quickly to only 25–23 at half-time with Pierce on the bench.

Marion returned in the third quarter to team up with Paul Mercer, Steve Hickman, and Larry Bussen and open up a 33–27 lead on the Trojans. Clutch 24–for–29 shooting at the foul line turned out to be a deciding factor.

One week later Pierce got very little scoring help in the Muncie game. Marion led both teams with 25 points but nobody else had more than 9, and that 13–5 Muncie spread in the third quarter proved to be too much of a hurdle.

Pierce still received some noteworthy plaudits from the big city writers. Bob Barnet wrote in the *Muncie Star*: "Marion Pierce, Lewisville's center who has been Indiana's leading scorer for the past three years, pitched 25 points into the hopper to lead his team and finish his four-year high school career with a total of 3,042 points.

"Refusing to quit and a serious threat until the final pistol shot, Lewisville led Central at the quarter, 14–11, and the Bearcats were on top by only a point at 25–24 at the end of the half. The Central margin had grown to nine points at 38–29 at the close of the third, but the Bearcats never really were able to shake off Bob Scott's persistent Bears and many brand-new gray hairs sprouted in the Central cheering section before it ended.

"The Bearcats had all kinds of trouble. They erred repeatedly and many times turned the ball over to their adversaries with mistakes that might have proved the difference."

Johnny Jordan penned the following tribute in the *New Castle Courier-Times*: "Because the admittedly bush league Pierce performed in does not provide top-notch competition, there's been considerable conjecture whether or not Marion could play in a stronger league. Several weeks ago Mt. Summit's Coach Gene Haynes said, 'That boy could play on any team in the state. For a big man he has an exceptional touch from the outside. He's not a selfish boy and he takes a lot with a wonderful attitude.' "

Jordan added: "In tournament play against North Central Conference members New Castle and Muncie Central, Pierce averaged 26.5 points a game during his career and dominated the boards as usual.

"For three consecutive campaigns Marion was individual scoring champion of all Indiana despite the most rigorous and at times unethical defensing. Opposing players hung on his arms, rode his back, vociferously and unkindly berated him—even drew blood. But the poker-faced, black-haired big guy never once, to his eternal credit, showed the slightest irritation or retaliation except with points."

Jordan went on to point out that Pierce never suffered a serious in-

Pierce enrolled at Lindsey Wilson Junior College and averaged 32 points with a single high game of 79, but he returned home after his freshman year. He's seen at left practicing for Wilson. On the right, Pierce drives on Middletown in the 1961 New Castle Sectional game. Pierce's 17-foot jumper was the clincher in sudden-death second overtime, 72–70.

jury or illness during his high school career, played in every game, and fouled out just once in 94 games for the Lewisville Bears.

After Pierce was named to the Indiana All-Star team for the annual Blind Fund series against Kentucky, Barnet praised his selection in this way: "You may add this reporter to the long list of folks who are happy to see the big Lewisville lad get the recognition he deserves.

"I am also happy that I do not have to execute one of those lightning flip-flops, on account of I never called Pierce just another good country ball player, as did several of my honored colleagues.

"I waited until I saw him in person for the first time in the 1961 New Castle Sectional and ventured the opinion that he was a great high school basketball player who belonged with big-timers. I'm happy that he will now get the opportunity to perform with big-timers."

Marion Pierce with trophy awarded him at Lewisville gym by Coach Bob Scott
culminating Marion Pierce Day, June 9, 1961.

Mr. and Mrs. G. W. Pierce of Lewisville had seven sons and two
daughters. Marion was the youngest of four brothers to play for Indiana State grad Bob Scott at the small Henry County school located
on U.S. Highway 40 just a short stone's throw from New Castle.

Beginning in 1951, Paul was the first, followed by Dale and Rex.
Scott's highly successful Lewisville teams put together seven straight
winning seasons for a 133–15 record including a 21–0 clean sweep in
1956–57 and a 20–1 mark in 1954–55.

Dale Pierce closed his career with 1,450 points in 1957—a Henry
County record at the time. Larry Johnson was another Lewisville
standout in 1958 and all had a tremendous influence on young Marion
Pierce.

Scott had no assistant at Lewisville so he coached all three
teams—junior high, reserve, and varsity. "Marion was in the fourth
grade when I first noticed him shooting baskets around town," Coach
Scott recalls. "I invited him to work out with the junior high team and
before the end of the season he was a starter. So beginning in the
fourth grade he played four or five years with the junior high."

Nobody could predict the big goals that Marion was going to realize, but according to Scott there was never any doubts about his determination.

"I knew he would be a tremendous shooter because of his dedication. He'd practice in the rain wearing a raincoat and shoot baskets at night using the headlights of an old car until the battery went dead. Marion's dad had a salvage yard in town so he would put one old car after another to good use lighting up the basket we installed at our community park. When the battery went dead he'd go get another car."

Pierce was described by his coach as being a shy young man who needed an outlet—basketball served as that outlet.

"Marion had complete control of his emotions, and I never saw him get upset to the point where it affected his performance," Scott added. "I remember in one sectional game I noticed at half-time he was bleeding on the shoulders, arms, and back. I asked him what happened and he said the other team was scratching him every time he went for the ball.

"I wanted to say something to the referee but he said, 'No. They're just trying to win—I'll just put a few more in the basket.' Most kids would have blown up under those conditions."

Scott also pointed out that Pierce had total confidence in his ability to score. "One time we were behind one point with only about 10 seconds to go, and I was trying to get a timeout," the Lewisville coach said. "We scored at the same split second, but one of the guards had asked for timeout and the refs erased what would have been the winning basket.

"I apologized to the team in the huddle and conceded that it might cost us the game. 'No, it won't,' Marion spoke up. 'Just give me the ball.' So I told the team to get the ball to Marion and sure enough he just turned and shot it through the net. I looked up but he was gone—as soon as the ball zipped through the basket Pierce took off for the shower."

Scott said he always tried to let the big guy get his 38-plus average, but there were a lot of games when he came out with six or seven minutes remaining. "And he didn't resent it at all, coming out with that much time on the clock.

"As a ballplayer he wasn't all that hungry, and he'd pass off frequently instead of taking the shot. He was our strongest rebounder and played a very respectable defense," Scott declared.

It also was an obvious fact that Pierce benefited greatly from playing alongside some very unselfish running mates. "We would have had a problem if they hadn't been so unselfish," Scott admits. "I think they realized without Marion we wouldn't have had much of a chance, but with him we could win. Some of the parents did resent the fact that their kids were scoring only seven or eight points and Marion was getting his 40.

"On one occasion Marion just didn't seem to be getting anywhere, and I called timeout to ask if he was feeling bad or something. He replied that he wasn't getting the ball, so I took him out of the game for a quarter and the other team caught up by half-time.

"I asked the other kids at the half if they thought it was best to leave Marion on the bench. I asked if they thought they could win without him, and they said they couldn't. So I put him back in the game in the second half, he scored 30 points the rest of the way and we won."

As a pure shooter, Marion might have been one of the very best, according to Scott. "He didn't have the moves or the quickness of Oscar Robertson and some of the other all-time greats, but as a pure shooter he was certainly among the very best. Game after game he'd shoot over 50 percent, and that was with two or three men hanging on him every night."

Scott remembers an amazing twist to Pierce's 64-point single game record against Union Township as a sophomore. "Marion only had 14 at the half and I told our student manager to punch me when he got his average. I didn't think any more about it until the manager gave me a poke and said Pierce had 60. I pulled him almost immediately with about 4 minutes to go and the whole crowd walked out."

Beating New Castle in the Sectional final was the most important game to Scott. New Castle had beaten Scott's Lewisville teams twice before in heartbreaking overtime barn burners. One year Lewisville led by six points with 40 seconds to play only to lose in a sudden death.

Scott believes it was the first time for a Lewisville team to upset the big county-seat school, although the recent Tri High consolidation of Lewisville, Spiceland, and Straughan produced a couple of sectional winners in succeeding years.

Lewisville needed a police escort to get safely past some troublemakers after that final game. A huge celebration with a bonfire and pep rally in the high school gym celebrated the school's first sectional title since 1945. (Beryl Bosstick coached that 1945 sectional champ and Principal Don Pfaff had been a member of the team.)

A decision to postpone the sectional final from Saturday to Monday because of a power failure and heavy snowstorm was a real lifesaver for Lewisville, in the opinion of Scott. "We beat Knightstown 76–70 in the second afternoon game and the power failure due to the heavy snow delayed it almost two hours," he explained. "The game

Driven by Rev. Art Tennies, Marion sits in an open convertible en route through town during Marion Pierce Day in 1961.

ended about 5:30 P.M. and we couldn't get out because of the weather."

New Castle was able to feed its team in the school cafeteria and wanted to go ahead with the final game at 8 P.M., but Gene Huddleston, who was on the Indiana High School Athletic Association's board at the time, said that wouldn't be fair.

"I don't think we would have been in any shape to play that same night. Many fans were stranded all night in the New Castle fieldhouse, and we had to spend the night in a New Castle hotel. All roads were closed, and several other tourneys around the state had to be postponed until Monday. Postponing the game until Monday probably won the sectional for us," Coach Scott conceded.

Muncie's win over Pierce and his underdog Lewisville teammates in the New Castle Regional windup the following week was anything but easy. In fact, Max Knight wrote in the *Richmond Palladium-Item,* "Few fans came to the New Castle Fieldhouse expecting to ever see the Muncie Bearcats stall to get a victory. But that is exactly what they did in the second half and it was a new role for Coach John Longfellow and his purpleclads.

"Lewisville, although finding itself fighting from behind the entire last half, never was out of the ball game until the final whirl of the clock.

"Muncie Central goes to Indianapolis next Saturday for the Semistate after beating Lewisville in regional action, 50–41. But a great majority of fans left the fieldhouse talking of the fabulous senior from Lewisville who had just ended a career that saw him hit 3,042 points."

Corky Lamm of the *Indianapolis News* added: "Central of Muncie's Bearcats have won 99 games, lost only 12, for Coach John Longfellow since he succeeded Jay McCreary four years ago. But Longfellow hopes No. 100 doesn't come quite as hard as No. 99 did Saturday night when his Bearcats had to scramble to beat the pride of Henry County—Lewisville's Bears—with a third quarter burst of buckets to win their 23d regional title and eighth in a row.

"As it happened, Lewisville clung to Muncie's heels, thanks to the Bears' 6–5 all-time scoring champ, Marion Pierce. It was Muncie by only 25–24 at half-time, Pierce having looped 15 of his game high 25 points in the first two quarters—despite a man to man proposition [Bill Dinwiddie] on the big Bear for the first quarter and a four-man zone box with a trailer on him for the next eight minutes.

"Richey Williams, Gerald Lanich and Dinwiddie took turns chasing Pierce—or fronting him, since Longfellow's strategy called for a defense that was supposed to keep the ball away from the big guy. It worked when you consider Pierce's 36-plus season average, but Longfellow had the sweats for a time."

Pierce outscored his highly-publicized Muncie counterpart Dinwiddie by a wide 25–11 margin, but Lewisville was outrebounded by the much taller Bearcats 45–25, and that proved to be the only difference.

Marion Pierce's limited playing time with the Indiana All-Stars was a disappointment, and his college career was shortlived although he scored 79 points in one game for Lindsey Wilson Junior College in Kentucky and averaged 32 points his first year.

Jay McCreary of Louisiana State, Guy Lewis of Houston, and Bruce Hale of Miami all had expressed a keen interest in the state scoring champ.

Pierce became disenchanted with college for personal reasons at the end of his freshman year, so he left school to return home where he joined his dad's successful wrecking yard business. Marion still resides in Lewisville, no more than a good jump shot from the site of his high school heroics.

Twenty years after his prime he was still playing amateur basketball in the New Castle area and pursuing his motorbike craze. Marion's motorbike trophies almost outnumber his basketball awards.

Lewisville lost its basketball identity with the school consolidation in 1969, but it will be a long time before oldtimers forget the Henry County Hurricane.

They retired old No. 52 on Marion Pierce Day in 1961 with a fire truck-high school band parade from the community park to the schoolhouse. All of Lewisville and many people from surrounding towns turned out to honor the Big Bear.

Thanks to Marion Pierce. Lewisville's identity lives on long after the little brick schoolhouse closed its doors.

Indiana's Finest

Career Scoring

Marion Pierce, Lewisville (1961)	3,042
Rick Mount, Lebanon (1966)	2,595
Billy Shepherd, Carmel (1968)	2,465
Mike Edwards, Greenfield (1969)	2,343
David Shepherd, Carmel (1970)	2,226
Kyle Macy, Peru (1975)	2,137
Dan Palombizio, Michigan City Rogers (1981)	2,092
George McGinnis, Indianapolis Washington (1969)	2,075
Ron Bonham, Muncie Central (1960)	2,023
Steve Collier, Southern (Hanover) (1974)	2,023
Pat Manahan, Delphi (1973)	2,003

One Season

Dave Shepherd, Carmel (1970)	1,079
George McGinnis, Indianapolis Washington (1969	1,019
Marion Pierce, Lewisville (1961)	995

High Average

Phil Wills, Grass Creek (1957)	42 ppg

11

New Castle Housewarming —Pavy 51, Rayl 49

"Two of the greatest shooters of our generation or any generation, for that matter, met head-on at New Castle Friday [February 20, 1959]. The result was an epic stand-off that will be described as long as Hoosiers maintain their reckless romance with basketball. New Castle won it, 92–81," Bob Collins wrote in the *Indianapolis Star*, "but the game was lost in the sheer beauty of watching two tremendous shooters practicing their trade as no two boys ever did before in one game.

"New Castle's Ray Pavy scored 51 points, Kokomo's Jimmy Rayl collected 49. . . . And Collins was not there, a fact he won't brood over for more than the next 10 or 15 years."

It was the most appropriate way to observe the last regular season game ever played in New Castle's legendary old Church Street gym. Steelwork already was up on the world's largest high school gymnasium (capacity 9,325).

Both Kokomo and New Castle teams ranked high in the state basketball polls. Both were chasing mighty Muncie Central in the North Central Conference race and then there was this extra bonus.

Rayl, best known around Hoosier Hysteria as the Splendid Splinter because of his slender physical build, led Pavy by just 10 points in their own personal season-long duel for the conference scoring championship.

"I never saw anything like it," all-time great Indianapolis referee Dee Williams recalls. "It was one of the easiest games I ever worked and that includes almost 30 years in the refereeing business. The thing I remember best is how fast the pace went from one end of the floor to the other—of course, there wasn't much rebounding. Rayl and Pavy were hitting almost every shot. At least it seemed that way."

Pavy drove the visiting Kokomo Kats goofy with his relentless thrusts inside. Ray burned the nets with 23 buckets in his 38 shots from the field, and he also converted five of his eight free throw attempts.

Rayl was equally hot from long range, bombing 18 of his 33 shots from the floor, and when Trojan defenses tried to put a tighter lid on the Splinter, he peeled off a deadly 13–of–15 performance at the foul stripe.

Both broke the old North Central Conference season record established by Rayl the preceding year and at one stage in the game Pavy was only one bucket behind the Kokomo phenom in their battle for the conference scoring championship.

Rayl repeated as NCC scoring champ with his 269 points in a 9-game conference season, and Pavy wound up only eight behind with 261. Both bettered the old conference record of 236 set by Rayl in his junior year.

Rayl also hit a new season high for Kokomo with 617 points, broke his own 48-point one game school record set the preceding week against Marion, became the first Kokomo player to score more than 600 points in 20 games and the first to average more than 30.

Two action photos of Jimmy Rayl against Muncie Central with all-time Bearcat great Ron Bonham (#30) and John Dampier (#50) on defense. Rayl scored 45 points in this game, and Kokomo upset Muncie.

Of course, Rayl took Coach Joe Platt's Kokomo crew all the way to the state runnerup spot against Indianapolis Crispus Attucks (Crispus Attucks 92, Kokomo 54) where he was named recipient of Indiana high school basketball's most coveted individual prize—the Trester Award. Later on he was Indiana's Mr. Basketball in the Blind Fund rivalry with Kentucky.

Jimmy's 61-game career record of 1,632 points was broken three years later by Jim (Goose) Ligon with 1,900 in 83 games. Ligon was a standout member of Kokomo's 1961 state title winner. But Rayl's 26.8 average still stands more than two decades later as the career high for all Howard County.

Pavy, the son of Baptist Church minister R. E. Pavy, became the first New Castle player to score 1,000 points. Ray's 51-point game against Kokomo, his 560 points for one season and three-year career total of 1,190 all were school records at the time.

Pavy's 1,190 still ranks high in the New Castle record books behind Kent Benson who established 55-point single game, 692-point one season and 1,496-point career marks in the 1973 campaign.

Ray still talks about how he missed five wide open lay-ups in the first quarter of the Kokomo game. Pavy scored just four points in that first period but he exploded for 47 in the last three quarters.

"We were running a simple clear out play where they'd just give me the ball and then clear out," Pavy explained. "Kokomo was playing me man-to-man, and we were playing Rayl the same way. Chuck Fawcett was guarding me (we roomed together for one semester at Indiana University), and John Lee was guarding Rayl.

"We started running a forward split, and Bill Fisher [a cancer specialist in Muncie now] said 'I think I can go up and sit in the crowd and Thurston [Kokomo's Roger Thurston] will come right up and sit along with me.' "

New Castle Coach Randy Lawson spoke up, "By gosh, let's try that."

"Fisher would come down, fake inside and then oftentimes stand clear out of bounds . . . and, sure enough Thurston would stand there right alongside. So I'd just take it right down the lane. . . . It wasn't a matter of great genius on our part. We just took what was open and used it as long as we could get it. I got all of the inside stuff and Jimmy bombed the eyes out of the basket outside—he was a great outside shooter. In fact, that was the best range I ever saw except maybe against Minnesota in college. We were at Indiana together, and he had great range that night too—scored 56 against Minnesota, set a Big 10 record and I believe we lost the game."

Pavy added, "Our Kokomo game was really an eight-point contest most of the way with Rayl scoring a lot of points against us in the last

Rayl as an Indiana Pacer against New Orleans' James Jones is seen on the left. On the right, Rayl goes up with the ball during his 40-point performance against Fort Wayne South in the Fort Wayne Semistate. Kokomo knocked off the defending state champs in a 92–90 barn burner, and Rayl hit the clincher with one second to go.

three minutes. They were behind and everything he shot was going in. At the end it was Jimmy bombing it through for Kokomo and John Lee hitting the free throws for us."

Pavy told how New Castle tried to pick Rayl up the minute he came on the floor: "Jimmy was very quick and had a great ability to dribble with his left hand. Not too many people gave him enough credit. He had a great move to his left, rocked you back on your heels going left and then he'd come back to his right. If he ever got you back on your heels, you couldn't stop him because he was too strong. He'd go up and stick it."

Pavy admitted the Kokomo game is the one he's remembered for most even though he turned in many other outstanding performances in his New Castle career. Ray rifled 34 one night against Indianapolis Tech when he drilled 13 of his 15 shots from the field in a bewildering first half. He scored 33 against Muncie Central when the Bearcats were 15–0 and No. 2 in the polls.

"You can hardly go anywhere 20 years later without somebody mentioning the 51–49 game against Rayl," Pavy asserts. "Interestingly enough, nobody seems to remember who won and that's why you really play the game. It's sort of *the* game that a lot of fans all over the state still talk about. When you talk to Rayl I'm sure he'll tell you neither one of us would have cared if we hadn't scored a point. It was an extremely important game for both of us, and I think in those days [before the Kokomo school split] there was more of a one town-against-another rivalry. No matter what you did, you represented the whole town."

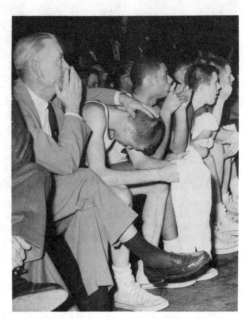

Jimmy Rayl, head bowed, next to Kokomo coach Joe Platt, set an all-time individual scoring record for the last four games of the state tourney in 1959 but his team lost the final game to Indianapolis Crispus Attucks, which took the trophy for the third time in five years.

One of Rayl's biggest thrills in high school was beating Muncie Central that year 72–70 when the mighty Bearcats ranked No. 1 in the polls—it was one of the biggest rivalries in the Hoosier state, and Jimmy got 45 before a capacity Kokomo crowd of 7,000.

Rayl outscored Tom Bolyard 40–38 in another classic when Kokomo took a 92–90 barn burner from Fort Wayne South in the Fort Wayne Semistate. South Side was defending state champ, and it was Rayl who canned the game clincher on a 25-foot jumper with only one tick remaining on the clock. Rayl's 40-point performance in that big Semistate showdown included an incredible 18–for–20 afternoon at the charity stripe.

But the Splendid Splinter's biggest game in high school was the 49-point blast against Pavy with the NCC scoring championship on the line. As Rayl says now, more than 20 years later, "It was the last game of the year, and it meant a lot. We had some pretty good players win that conference scoring title."

Rayl averaged 40 the last six games of his senior season, and he pumped in 48 against Marion the week preceding his 49 in the New Castle contest.

"Physically, I only weighed 138, and I didn't have that much ability in the way of strength," the former Kokomo standout concedes. "But I looked forward to Friday night's ball game so much that by game time I was ready to jump through a brick wall. I got by a lot on emotion.

"I'd be okay after the first two minutes but before that I was just a bundle of nerves. I never thought I loafed on the floor, always diving after loose balls and to me that's some form of defense. I never missed a game in my life because of injuries, and I'm talking about from the first time I ever played on a team in grade school. I might have missed one or two practices because of a cold or something but even then I think I was always around the gym."

Rayl's dad, who died when Jimmy was just 13, always thought basketball was a waste of time to some extent. Maybe he was right, in a way, because a lot of young kids wind up with broken hearts when they fail to make their school teams, Jimmy acknowledged.

Kokomo built one of the largest high school gyms in the country when Rayl was just a kid. Kokomo played before sellout crowds of 7,000 every game, and Jimmy credits those crowds for being a big influence on his dedication to the game.

"To a kid seven or eight years old, the gym looked twice that big, and it was always my goal just to make the high school team," Rayl said. "I'm sure a lot of my first inspiration came from those Kokomo crowds. We had only one high school in Kokomo at the time, and it was the big thing in town. Now it's kinda depressing to go to a high school game when you could shoot off a cannon sometimes and not hit anybody. When I was in school I'd put our crowds up against any high school in the whole country."

Rayl's Kokomo high school coach was Joe Platt, who took the Kats to their first state title two years later. According to Rayl, Platt was a special guy who treated everyone fairly. "Joe was a gentleman who had everybody's respect."

Jimmy also had a lot of praise for Chuck Fawcett who worked next to him in the Kokomo backcourt. Fawcett (a state long jump champ in track) was a good all-around ball player who was perfectly willing to let Rayl be Kokomo's top banana. "We never had any jealousies on our team, and I was fortunate to be playing next to a guy like Fawcett because he always passed me the ball," Rayl recalled. "I'm sure Rick Mount [Lebanon's all-time great] would say the same about Billy Keller when they played together at Purdue.

"I probably shot too much, but the best thing I could do was shoot. I sure wasn't going to go to college on my ball handling and defense. But I've had a lot of people tell me since that time that they enjoyed watching me play, so evidently I was giving em a little entertainment.

"A lot of nights you shoot when you don't have a decent shot, and you look bad when they don't go in, but I'm sure all good shooters go through the same thing."

Rayl also admitted that he was a little headstrong when he didn't break into the lineup at Indiana University as soon as he thought he should. "Maybe I was wrong but right then I decided I was going to shoot when I had the chance."

New Castle's Ray Pavy in action.

Pavy and Rayl went on to become close friends as Indiana University roommates in what seemed like something out of a storybook. They played together through their freshman and sophomore years in college with all the signs of even bigger things to come.

Then Pavy was struck down in a tragic auto accident just before he returned to school for his junior year at Indiana. Pavy suffered a paralyzing injury that would end his basketball playing career and a girl friend was killed in the collision on Road 41 in Northern Indiana.

Rayl went on to become Helms Foundation All-American and all-Big 10 twice, setting a school record with 56 against Minnesota in 1962 and equaling it with 56 against Michigan State the next year. Rayl's 56 still stands as a school record for one game, and Mount owns the Big 10 record with 61. Jimmy was second leading scorer in the old National Industrial League with Goodyear, and that was followed by a brief ABA career with the Indiana Pacers. He got 33 back-to-back in two games with the Pacers.

Rayl had been No. 3 draft pick with Cincinnati's Royals in 1963 when there were just eight teams in the NBA—by today's standards he would have been No. 1 with quite a few NBA franchises.

Pavy refused to let his paralysis keep him from becoming a successful high school coach in Henry County and after that assistant superintendent at New Castle High School.

Ray coached from his wheel chair at Shenandoah, Middletown, and Sulphur Springs high schools, and then he was New Castle assistant for three years before moving into the superintendent's office. One of Pavy's Shenandoah ball clubs compiled an outstanding 24–2 record.

"Pavy went beyond my own dedication as a player," Rayl said. "Ray was more into it than I was in some respects. He enjoyed watching any kind of a game. My main strategy was just hitting the basket. I've always thought Ray would have helped me a lot if we could have played those last two years together at IU. He had a lot of savvy and know-how. If it hadn't been for that accident there's no doubt in my mind he would have been a great playmaker."

Rayl still lives in his Kokomo hometown as a successful sales executive for the Xerox firm, and he still enjoys talking to people about basketball. "Every day I'm talking about basketball to somebody. I probably wouldn't even have gone to college if it wasn't for basketball. I got my job through a friend in college.

"You learn a lot from basketball or any other sport. Take Pavy for example, everybody has to face some adversity. You see people overcome things like Ray Pavy and how can you complain? You've gotta keep that in the back of your mind. You have to keep things in proper perspective and remember that others have it a lot worse.

"We're all winners, and I get a little upset from all this talk about

New Castle's fieldhouse, the world's largest (seating capacity: 9,325) opened in 1959, the year after the Rayl-Pavy duel.

somebody not being a winner. You overlook the benefits from things like physical conditioning, and you also learn how to lose once in a while. In my sales job the average is something like one sale out of maybe 20 calls. So you certainly hear a lot of 'no's.'

"You get so much recognition in high school and college sometimes you kinda take too much for granted. And then you get out of school, and it's not the same in the business world.

"Guys like Mount and myself got bitter over some of the things that happened to us later in the pro game. We've kinda shut ourselves off sometimes, but I still look forward to the Indiana state high school tournament—it's kinda special.

"We were overmatched against Crispus Attucks in the tournament. Basketball is a game of rebounding anyway, and you're not going to win with a high-scoring guard unless you have the big men up front. We didn't have anybody over 6–4, and we got by a lot on good luck, but we tried.

"It was quite a thrill for us just to get to that state championship game, I tell you that. . . . I still remember that night when we were walking up the ramp at Butler [Hinkle] Fieldhouse. It was just like a dream to me. You never ever dream of playing in a game like that, and I'm not kidding when I say, it was the biggest thing that ever happened to me."

12

Indiana-Kentucky All-Star Rivalry Works for the Blind

Indiana's All-Star basketball rivalry with Kentucky was started by the *Indianapolis Star* in 1940, and it has become perhaps the most successful and the best-known attraction of its kind anywhere.

It became a home-and-home series in 1955, and the game sponsors in both states earmarked the proceeds for sight-afflicted persons. Benefits from the Indianapolis game alone neared the $700,000 mark in 1982, and the Kentucky Lions Eye Research Institute was constructed in Louisville in 1969 assisted by All-Star game funds in that city.

Almost all of the best high school players and many of the most prominent coaches have been active participants in this All-Star series for the last 40 years. Other All-Star contests have come and gone, but the Indiana-Kentucky Blind Fund classic has long been recognized and blessed by the NCAA as well as the state high school associations as the granddaddy of all basketball benefits.

One reason for this unparalleled acceptance stems from attempts by the *Indianapolis Star* and the Kentucky Lions to work closely with the state coaches associations and the print and electronic media and to honor the ground rules set down by the state high school athletic associations.

Executive action by the Indiana High School Athletic Association in the early 1970s cleared the way for high school coaches to direct the Indiana Stars, and before that the use of IHSAA referees was approved.

Oscar Robertson, George McGinnis, Rick Mount, Jimmy Rayl, Hallie Bryant, Larry Bird, Bill Garrett, Ron Bonham, Tom and Dick VanArsdale, Billy and Dave Shepherd, George Crowe, Johnny

Wilson, Bob Masters, Dee Monroe, Joe Sexson, Bobby Plump, Larry Humes, Terry Dischinger, Dave Schellhase, Clyde Lovellette, and Louie Dampier are just a few of the all-time Hoosier greats who have worn the familiar red, white, and blue colors.

They have been opposed by such notable Kentucky superstars as Ralph Beard, Wah Wah Jones, Frank Ramsey, Cliff Hagen, Clem Haskins, Wesley Unseld, Darrell Griffith, Gene Rhodes, Jeff Mullins, Billy Ray Lickert, Johnny Cox, Larry Conley, Jimmy Dan Conner, Mike Casey, Darrell Carrier, Robert Carpenter, Butch Beard, Sonny Allen, and Kelly Coleman.

Hall of Famers Angus Nicoson of Indiana Central and Uncle Ed Diddle of Western Kentucky were coaching rivals in the early years of the colorful mid-summer rivalry. Ralph Carlisle, Gene Rhodes, and Joe Reibel were other well-known coaches who coached great Bluegrass All-Star clubs.

Doyal (Buck) Plunkitt and Tom Downey coached the first Indiana All-Star team in 1939 when the Stars defeated the Frankfort state champs, 31–21. Franklin's George Crowe was Indiana's first Mr. Basketball, and he wore the traditional No. 1 shirt.

Kentucky accepted the challenge the next year, and some of the coaching greats who worked with the Hoosiers in addition to Nicoson were Glenn Curtis, Tony Hinkle, Paul Lostutter, Bill Perigo, Ward Lambert, Wilbur Allen, Jay McCreary, Cleon Reynolds, Jerry Oliver, Kirby Overman, Bob Dille, Bill Green, Eric Clark, Bill Harrell, Bill Smith, Gunner Wyman, and Jack Edison. Nicoson coached the Indiana team from 1952–65 and then he returned in 1969 for three more years.

Indiana won 12 of the first 13 games in the Kentucky series when all games were played at Indianapolis' Butler Fieldhouse. Ralph Beard and Wah Wah Jones starred on the only Kentucky winner during that pioneer period with the Bluegrass lads defeating the Hoosiers by a 45–40 score in 1945.

Two things reduced Indiana's huge superiority beginning in 1955. All-Star authorities agreed to the home-and-home arrangement, playing two games each year instead of just one, and Kentucky dipped into the state's outstanding black talent for the first time. It's significant that Kentucky won three of the next six games under the new home-and-home format and 10 out of 13 in one stretch from 1961 through 1968. (Indiana still owned a wide 44-25 advantage in the series at the end of the 1982 games.)

Another change was introduced in 1976, adding still more interest to the All-Star production. Game Director Don Bates of the *Indianapolis Star* started an Indiana-Kentucky Girls All-Star counterpart the same year that Indiana held its first girls state tournament.

The first Boys-Girls doubleheader drew a sellout crowd of 17,490 to Market Square Arena.

Warsaw's Judi Warren who was the darling of the state tourney was Indiana's first Miss Basketball, and the All-Stars broke even in two games with Kentucky. In the series' first seven years the Kentucky girls led, 11 games to three.

Oscar Robertson was never better (and that's very good indeed) as he smashed the all-time scoring record with 34 points and won the coveted Star of Stars Award as the All-Star game's outstanding player in 1956. Indiana crushed the Kentuckians at Butler Fieldhouse, 92–78.

Robertson's advertised personal scoring duel with Kentucky's King Kelly Coleman never materialized, however. The youngster from Waveland, Kentucky, with the fantastic 46.7 average never had a chance against the Big O. Hoosier players were stung by Coleman's boast that he would score 50 points against them, and they threw a blanket over Kelley from the start. A little out of shape and completely befuddled, Coleman scored only three points in the first half and finished the game with 17.

Oscar, who had pocketed just about every honor obtainable for a high school player leading his Indianapolis Crispus Attucks High School teams to two straight state titles, also became the first to complete a Triple Slam. He was voted Mr. Basketball by sportswriters, elected captain by his teammates, and received the Star of Stars Award.

But anyone who sat in the stifling oven that was Butler Fieldhouse will tell you Oscar found the rainbow with the help of the finest and most unselfish group of All-Stars in the 16 years of the series.

The Hoosiers were a lightning-fast, cohesive unit. Each boy forgot his press clippings and personal glory, the *Indianapolis Star* pointed out.

The Hoosiers were on top 18–15 as the teams rolled into the second quarter. From there Frank Radovich and Bob Bradtke from Hammond, Lafayette's Ron Fisher, and Oscar gradually kept pushing the Hoosier advantage up until it hit 42–32 at the half.

Corky Withrow, called the best player on the floor for the Kentuckians, put on a one-man show that cut Indiana's 47–32 lead to 47–39 with 8:06 left in the third quarter. Seconds later Withrow committed his fifth foul. He took 13 points and all of Kentucky's fading hopes to the bench with him.

Paul Conwell, Ace Johnson, and Lavern Altemeyer got in their scoring kicks as the Hoosiers ran their three-quarter lead to 65–51.

Coleman finally came to life in the fourth quarter, and by 6:40 it was 67–62, with Indiana fans growing a bit uneasy. Then Bradtke hit two free throws, Radovich got a tip-in, and Oscar cracked two baskets to put the Hoosiers out of sight, 77–62.

Oscar got his 34 points with 12 baskets in 28 attempts and 10-of-15 free throws. Radovich added 12 points to the Hoosier total and Fisher 10. Bradtke scored nine points; Bob Hickman and Joe Simpson eight each.

"He's a pro playing with a bunch of high school boys," Kentucky coach Ted Hornback said later in the dressing room. Good as Oscar was in his 34-point first game effort, he was even better two nights later in Louisville.

Bob Collins of the *Star* marveled, "The greatest of all Indiana High School All-Star teams, its fantastic wonder boy bombing the nets for 41 points, ran the scoreboard out of numbers as it pulverized Kentucky, 102–77.

"If there is anyone who doubts now that Oscar Robertson is the best high school basketball player in the world, he is speaking in very faint tones. The lithe Crispus Attucks star, making his last appearance as a high school player, dropped 17 of 33 field attempts and seven of eight free throws.

"His 41 points cracked his own all-time All-Star game record of 34 set at Butler [two nights earlier]. It also broke the Louisville Armory mark of 30 set by Hallie Bryant, another Crispus Attucks All-Star in 1953.

"Naturally he was voted the Hoosiers' most valuable. Ed Smallwood who scored 29 points was given the Kentucky MVP award and he easily was the best Bluegrass player."

Big Frank Radovich came through with 22 points for Indiana, and Ronnie Fisher added 15 to the big Hoosier total. Kentucky led several times during the first half, and it was 47–46, Indiana, at the halfway mark.

With 6:40 to go in the third quarter, Corky Withrow connected to put Kentucky ahead for the last time.

Oscar's combined total for two nights' work was 75—a record that stood until Big George McGinnis of Indianapolis came along in the 1969 All-Star series. Big George set a 53-point one-game record and a 76-point two-game high that may outlast all of us. He had 53 points and 30 rebounds when Indiana bombed Kentucky, 114–83, in the return game June 29, 1969, at Louisville's Freedom Hall.

A record crowd of 17,875 was on hand to see that record-shattering performance by McGinnis, who wiped out the 42-point single game mark established by Kentucky's Jim McDaniels in 1967 and Robertson's 75-point record for two games.

McGinnis and 6–9 Washington running mate Steve Downing ruled the rebounds completely (74–47). Hammond Tech's Bootsy White thrilled the huge crowd with his incredible floor play, and Kentucky was handcuffed almost all the way by a hustling Hoosier defense.

But this one belonged to McGinnis, and Big George was named the game's outstanding player by unanimous vote of press, radio and TV. He rifled 20 of his 32 shots from the floor, 13-for-22 at the foul line, and he drew a big roar from the crowd when he split his right shoe in full flight during the closing seconds of the first half.

Joe Sutter, Marion's 6–7 Trester Award winner, who played a great game of his own, although troubled all week by shin splints, stood up in front of the Indiana bench and led the cheers when Big Mac left the floor in the closing minutes.

It was better than a three-ring circus and Kentucky's Joe Voskuhl, who had been quoted as saying that McGinnis "is overrated" earlier in the week after a 91–83 opening game win by the Hoosiers, was one of the first to shake McGinnis' hand at the end.

Downing was just as spectacular in his own way, scoring 17 points and adding 21 rebounds. Downing and McGinnis blocked numerous shots and the two combined to hold 7-footer Tom Payne to an incredible low number of just four points. Sutter scored 11 points, Greenfield's Mike Edwards 10, White and Scottsburgh's Billy James eight each for the Hoosiers.

The *Indianapolis Star*'s game sponsors sent that game ball to the Hall of Fame in Indianapolis, and the 1969 team still is recognized along with the Oscar Robertson team in 1956 as two of the strongest in All-Star history.

Robertson went on to instant fame in college at Cincinnati and in the pro ranks at Cincinnati and Milwaukee. McGinnis led the Big 10 in scoring and rebounding as a sophomore at Indiana University before turning pro. Downing played on an NCAA finalist at Indiana.

McGinnis' 148-point record for the last four games of the Indiana high school tournament still stands.

Indiana's 1981 All-Star team led by Mr. Basketball Dan Paolombizio of Michigan City Rogers, John Flowers of Fort Wayne South, Jeff Robinson of Indianapolis Broad Ripple and Rob Harden of Valparaiso also drew many rave notices after a 114–102 and 109–96 sweep against Kentucky.

The team was coached by Gunner Wyman of state champ Vincennes, who was assited by Anderson's Norm Held.

It closed a long and very successful coaching career for Wyman, who came to the Hoosier state from Kentucky and put four teams in the State Finals—one at Tell City in 1961 and three at Vincennes. Gunner's 1969 Vincennes team was unbeaten going into the Final Four.

Vincennes' 1981 state championship was the school's second, and there was a long wait between celebrations—Hall of Fame great John L. Adams coached the first Vincennes state champ in 1923.

Bob Dille who coached Fort Wayne Northrop to the 1974 state championship and Bill Green who coached three state titlists (Washington in 1969 and Marion in 1975–76) took the 1975 Indiana All-Star team on its historic 34-day trip through Europe and Russia. The AAU arranged the tour following Indiana's two-game win over Kentucky and it included stops in 10 different foreign countries.

The All-Stars flew out of New York to Lisbon, Portugal, and then to Madrid, Spain; Rome, Italy; Nice and Paris, France; Brussels, Belgium; Amsterdam, Holland; Vienna, Austria; Leningrad, Moscow, and Voroshilovgrad, Soviet Union; Warsaw, Poland; and then back to Amsterdam on the return trip to the U.S.

Sightseeing in places like the Vatican, Red Square, and the French Riviera created a problem for the coaches—it was hard to keep your mind on basketball, and the All-Stars split 14 games on the exhausting trip.

Indiana's All-Stars learned a lot about things like the much different lifestyles around the world and different eating habits. There was time for fun (five sun-soaking days on the Riviera and a night at the circus in Moscow) and an all-night train ride from Leningrad to Moscow was a special treat.

Some of the coaches of foreign teams drooled over our Indiana players, but the last two weeks were spent behind the Iron Curtain in Russia, and everybody was eager to board that return flight home.

There's no denying that it was a memorable experience for the entire group. Players on that trip were Bill Butcher of Loogootee, Sam Drummer of Muncie North, Val Martin and Glen Sudhop of South Bend Adams, Derrick Johnson of Indianapolis Manual, Kevin Pearson of Marion, Gary Raker of Beech Grove, Jerry Sichting of Martinsville, Rich Valavicius of Hammond, and Steve Walker of Lebanon.

Accompanying the team in addition to the coaches were Mrs. Bob Dille; Brad Osborne, team manager; Naz Servidio, an AAU referee from Erie, Pennsylvania; AAU Director Jim Fox; Don Bates, Tom Keating, and yours truly—all of the *Indianapolis Star.*

Indiana also accepted an invitation to play the Minnesota All-Stars in Minneapolis in 1979 and 1980, and the All-Stars met the touring Russians in separate years at Hinkle Fieldhouse, Richmond, Marion, and Washington.

Indiana Boys
All-Star Scores

1939—Indiana 31, Frankfort 21
1940—Indiana 31, Kentucky 29
1941—Indiana 52, Kentucky 41
1942—Indiana 41, Kentucky 40
1945—Kentucky 45, Indiana 40
1946—Indiana 62, Kentucky 55
1947—Indiana 86, Kentucky 50
1948—Indiana 70, Kentucky 47
1949—Indiana 66, Kentucky 61
1950—Indiana 70, Kentucky 57
1951—Indiana 68, Kentucky 57
1952—Indiana 86, Kentucky 82 (ot)
1953—Indiana 71, Kentucky 66
1954—Indiana 75, Kentucky 74
1955—Indiana 94, Kentucky 86
    Kentucky 86, Indiana 82 (ot)*
1956—Indiana 92, Kentucky 78
    Indiana 102, Kentucky 77*
1957—Kentucky 91, Indiana 71*
    Kentucky 77, Indiana 76
1958—Indiana 77, Kentucky 76
    Indiana 69, Kentucky 58*
1959—Kentucky 86, Indiana 81*
    Indiana 88, Kentucky 77
1960—Kentucky 95, Indiana 86
    Indiana 101, Kentucky 64*
1961—Indiana 82, Kentucky 71*
    Kentucky 78, Indiana 75
1962—Indiana 88, Kentucky 82*
    Kentucky 70, Indiana 68
1963—Kentucky 90, Indiana 86
    Indiana 90, Kentucky 75*
1964—Kentucky 68, Indiana 59*
    Indiana 68, Kentucky 54
1965—Kentucky 90, Indiana 80
    Kentucky 74, Indiana 69*

1966—Kentucky 104, Indiana 77*
    Kentucky 77, Indiana 67
1967—Kentucky 79, Indiana 67
    Indiana 78, Kentucky 76*
1968—Kentucky 59, Indiana 54*
    Kentucky 61, Indiana 56
1969—Indiana 91, Kentucky 83
    Indiana 114, Kentucky 83*
1970—Indiana 80, Kentucky 79*
    Indiana 108, Kentucky 97
1971—Indiana 115, Kentucky 99
    Kentucky 110, Indiana 91*
1972—Indiana 96, Kentucky 72*
    Indiana 115, Kentucky 86
1973—Kentucky 103, Indiana 82*
    Indiana 105, Kentucky 86
1974—Indiana 92, Kentucky 81*
    Indiana 110, Kentucky 91
1975—Indiana 95, Kentucky 91
    Indiana 94, Kentucky 85*
1976—Indiana 96, Kentucky 88*
    Indiana 77, Kentucky 71
1977—Kentucky 87, Indiana 84
    Kentucky 85, Indiana 84*
1978—Indiana 100, Kentucky 90*
    Indiana 98, Kentucky 78
1979—Kentucky 78, Indiana 59
    Kentucky 72, Indiana 69*
1980—Indiana 82, Kentucky 80*
    Kentucky 96, Indiana 93
1981—Indiana 114, Kentucky 102
    Indiana 109, Kentucky 96
1982—Indiana 96, Kentucky 94 (ot)*
    Kentucky 81, Indiana 80

* Louisville games

Indiana Girls
All-Star Scores

1976—Kentucky 59, Indiana 48*
    Indiana 68, Kentucky 55
1977—Kentucky 78, Indiana 69
    Kentucky 71, Indiana 54*
1978—Kentucky 64, Indiana 50*
    Kentucky 65, Indiana 55
1979—Kentucky 58, Indiana 57
    Kentucky 72, Indiana 54*

1980—Indiana 69, Kentucky 57*
    Kentucky 72, Indiana 64
1981—Indiana 64, Kentucky 59
    Kentucky 58, Indiana 54*
1982—Kentucky 72, Indiana 62*
    Kentucky 44, Indiana 41

* Louisville games

Miss Basketball

1976—Judi Warren, Warsaw
1977—Teri Rosinski, Norwell
1978—Chanda Kline, Warsaw
1979—LaTaunya Pollard, East Chicago Roosevelt
1980—Maria Stack, Columbus East
1981—Cheryl Cook, Indianapolis Washington
1982—Trena Keys, Marion

Indiana All-Stars
Mr. Basketball

1939—George Crowe, Franklin
1940—Ed Scheinbein, Southport
1941—John Bass, Greenwood
1942—Bud Brown, Muncie Burris
1945—Tom Schwartz, Kokomo
1946—Johnny Wilson, Anderson
1947—Bill Garrett, Shelbyville
1948—Bob Masters, Lafayette Jeff
1949—Dee Monroe, Madison
1950—Pat Klein, Marion
1951—Tom Harrold, Muncie Central
1952—Joe Sexson, Indianapolis Tech
1953—Hallie Bryant, Indianapolis Crispus Attucks
1954—Bobby Plump, Milan
1955—Wilson Eison, Gary Roosevelt
1956—Oscar Robertson, Indianapolis Crispus Attucks
1957—John Coalmon, South Bend Central
1958—Mike McCoy, Fort Wayne South

1959—Jimmy Rayl, Kokomo
1960—Ron Bonham, Muncie Central
1961—Dick and Tom VanArsdale, Indianapolis Manual
1962—Larry Humes, Madison
1963—Rick Jones, Muncie Central
1964—Dennis Brady, Lafayette Jeff
1965—Billy Keller, Indianapolis Washington
1966—Rick Mount, Lebanon
1967—Willie Long, Fort Wayne South
1968—Billy Shepherd, Carmel
1969—George McGinnis, Indianapolis Washington
1970—Dave Shepherd, Carmel
1971—Mike Flynn, Jeffersonville
1972—Phil Cox, Connersville
1973—Kent Benson, New Castle
1974—Steve Collier, Southwestern (Hanover) and
      Roy Taylor, Anderson
1975—Kyle Macy, Peru
1976—Dave Colescott, Marion
1977—Ray Tolbert, Anderson
1978—Dave Magley, South Bend LaSalle '
1979—Steve Bouchie, Washington
1980—Jim Master, Fort Wayne Harding
1981—Dan Palombizio, Michigan City Rogers
1982—Roger Harden, Valparaiso

Phil Wills, left, who played for tiny Grass Creek in Cass County and later for
Purdue, set a record for Hoosier preps with his one-season average of 42.4 in 1957.
Phil scored 849 points for Grass Creek, coached by Bud Jump, and hit a single-
game high of 60 against Medaryville. Wills' senior class at Grass Creek
(consolidated into Caston a short time later) had an enrollment of 17. Tom
VanArsdale, right, of Manual shoots and twin brother Dick (#30) watches from the
right during state championship game against Kokomo in 1961. Tom fouled out
late in the fourth period, and Kokomo won in overtime. Jim Ligon (#22) and Ron
Hughes are the Kokomo players under the bucket.

Dave Schellhase, Evansville North hot shot on the 1962 Indiana team, later the No. 1 scorer at Purdue, and now the Indiana State head coach.

Jim "Goose" Ligon of Kokomo (1962).

Bud Ritter with two Indiana All-Star selections—Buster Briley (left) and Larry Shingleton. They helped Ritter put together a 61-game regular-season winning streak at Madison in the early 1960s. Briley was Madison's career record-holder with 1,983 points.

Angus Nicoson of Indiana Central coached the Indiana All-Stars for 13 seasons and had a standout 19–12 record in the Blind Fund series with Kentucky. Billy Keller (left) of the 1965 state champ Indianapolis Washington squad was Indiana's Mr. Basketball in 1965, was a standout for Purdue and the Indiana Pacers, and then followed Nick as coach at Indiana Central, where he won 483 games.

Trester Award winner Eddie Bopp (left) and Mr. Basketball Billy Keller of Indianapolis Washington double team Fort Wayne North's Dave Moser in the 1965 state championship tilt. Both Keller and Moser were named to the Indiana All-Star team.

Bob Ford (left) carried Evansville North to a state championship his junior year and then went on to have an outstanding career at Purdue.

Trester Award winner and Indiana All-Star Jim Nelson gets off a hook shot against Vincennes in the 1968 State Finals. Nelson led Bo Mallard's Gary Roosevelt to the state championship, beating Indianapolis Shortridge 68–60 in the final game.

George McGinnis (#35) was Indiana's Mr. Basketball in 1969 and the Big 10 scoring and rebound champ as a sophomore at Indiana University. Here Big Mac is shown with Joby Wright (#44) and Steve Downing (far left) in a Big 10 game with Michigan. McGinnis and Downing were teammates on Indianapolis Washington's unbeaten state title winner in 1969.

Tom Abernathy, left, of South Bend St. Joseph (1972). On right, Kent Benson, Mr. Basketball in 1973 as New Castle superstar, then a standout at IU and the pros, during All-Star scrimmage.

The left photo shows Indiana All-Star Coach Jerry Oliver with Mr. Basketball Phil Cox of Connersville's 1972 state champs. Oliver coached Washington of Indianapolis to its first state title in 1965. On the right, George McGinnis (seen at left), who set 53-point and 30-rebound single-game records, is shown with 1969 Indiana All-Star teammates Joe Sutter of Marion and Mike Edwards of Greenfield (kneeling) and Steve Downing of Indianapolis Washington and Rick Risinger of Richmond (standing). McGinnis also set a two-game record with 76.

Kirby Overman coached New Albany to the 1973 state championship and later coached the Indiana All-Stars in 1974. Anderson's Tony Marshall (left) and Roy Taylor were two standouts on that All-Star squad. Taylor and Southwestern's Steve Collier were co-Mr. Basketball choices.

Dave Colescott, who led Marion to back-to-back state titles in 1975 and 1976, drives past Jeffersonville's Tres Sowder in the 1976 State Finals. Colescott later was named Indiana's Mr. Basketball and played for Dean Smith at North Carolina.

Indiana's 1975 All-Star team beat Kentucky twice and then left on a 34-day trip through Europe and Russia. Members of that team are shown here: front: Jerry Sichting of Martinsville, Derrick Johnson of Indianapolis Manual, Kyle Macy of Peru, Gary Raker of Beech Grove, Bill Butcher of Loogootee, and Rich Valavicius of Hammond; back row: Coach Bill Green of Marion, Steve Walker of Lebanon, Kevin Pearson of Marion, Glen Sudhop of South Bend Adams, Val Martin of South Bend Adams, Sammy Drummer of Muncie North and Coach Bob Dille of Fort Wayne Northrop.

Three of 1975's All-Stars: Sammy Drummer, Glen Sudhop and Rich Valavicius.

Hammond Noll's Thad Garner protects the ball during the 1978 All-Star game against Kentucky.

Landon Turner (#2) of Indianapolis Tech rebounds in the 1978
All-Star game. Turner helped
Indiana win its NCAA title in
1981 and then was involved in a
paralyzing auto accident that
ended his collegiate career.

Fighting Jack Moore (#11), a shifty 5–10 dynamo, led Muncie Central to its sixth
state championship in 1978. Moore led the All-Stars to a sweep in the Kentucky
series and then went on to become all-Big 8 at Nebraska.

Three of South Bend's finest:
1979 All-Stars Leroy Sutton of
Adams, Eric Williams of
Washington and Lynn Mitchem
of Adams.

Mr. Basketball Roger Harden
of Valparaiso with Coach Jack
Edison of 1982's state championship team Plymouth.

Judi Warren, Indiana's first Miss Basketball, cuts down the nets at Hinkle Fieldhouse after her Warsaw team won the first girls state championship.

Mr. Basketball of 1981 Dan Palombizio, Michigan City Rogers 1981 standout, is seen at left, and Big John Flowers of Fort Wayne South, who starred on the 1981 Indiana All-Star team that swept both games from Kentucky, is on the right.

Cheryl Cook (#1) was Indiana's talented Miss Basketball for the 1981 girls All-Star series. Cheryl was a standout guard for Indianapolis Washington.

13

Marion Crawley—734 Victories 4 State Championships

Hall of Famer Marion Crawley is remembered by his closest colleagues as a no-gimmicks coach who climbed to Hoosier Hysteria's loftiest heights using good common sense and keeping it simple. His record of 734 victories and four state championships was unmatched.

"Going up against one of Marion Crawley's Lafayette Jeff basketball teams was always a good barometer," said Assistant Commissioner Charlie Maas of the Indiana High School Athletic Association, who could speak from his own experience as Indianapolis Tech coach for eight years in the same North Central Conference. "He stressed the team concept, and it was a good lesson for the kids as well as for you as a coach," Maas pointed out.

"Crawley was looked on with so much respect by everyone connected with the game—you would have had the same feeling going up against Butler University's Tony Hinkle or Notre Dame's Knute Rockne. You always knew your team would be well-scouted and that Crawley's team would be well prepared."

Maas pointed out, "Because of his tremendous stature, people would listen to what Crawley had to say. No matter what the subject might be, you wouldn't be too smart if you didn't listen to what Crawley thought about it."

Crawley's 35-year coaching career began at Greencastle High School where he stayed for seven years. Marion moved on to Washington for the next four years and coached the famed Hatchets to back-to-back state championships with a 27–5 record in the 1940–41 season and 30–1 in the 1941–42 season.

Burl Friddle from the old Franklin Wonder Five coached Washington to its first state championship in 1930 and Crawley's

Washington's 1941 state champs. Front: Ivan Wininger, Calvin Thomas, James Riffey, Arthur Grove, Robert Donaldson, Charles Harmon; back row: Coach Marion Crawley, Leroy Mangin, Forrest Crane, John Dejernett William Harmon, Garland Raney, and Manager Boger.

1941–42 state championship team equaled the 30–1 record established by the 1930 state champs.

Crawley also compiled a standout 25–5 record in the 1939–40 season and except for an untimely attack of appendicitis that sidelined sophomore guard Art Grove in the Semistate, Washington's Hatchets might have won three straight state titles.

Grove was stricken between games, and Washington lost a one-point heartbreaker to Mitchell for the semistate title. Of course, Mitchell went on to the State Finals where it lost to Hammond Tech in the 33–21 state championship game one week later. On that same Washington team was Leo Klier—a two-time All-American later at Notre Dame.

Leroy (Hook) Mangin was the individual star for Washington in the 1940–41 State Finals, scoring 41 points in the two games played at Indianapolis. Mangin, who starred later at Indiana University, had 23 in the 48–32 afternoon win over Kokomo and 18 in the 39–33 state title win over Madison. Charley Harmon was the other forward, Jim Riffey the center, Bill Harmon and Grove the starting guards.

The next year Washington became just the fourth school in history to repeat when Riffey and John Dejernett led the Hatchets to a 24–18 final-game victory over Muncie Burris. Riffey scored a game high 10 points and Dejernett added seven more.

Dejernet tallied 14 and Charley Harmon nine in the afternoon when the Hatchets downed Frankfort, 42–32. Robert Donaldson and Grove were the Washington guards.

Evansville Central accounted for the only Washington defeat (32–31) during the regular season, and then the Hatchets reversed that loss with a 22–20 win over Central when the two met in the Semistate round at Vincennes.

Crawley wound up his four-year Washington stay with a brilliant 94–22 record and headed for Lafayette Jeff, where he coached for 25 years with an amazing record of 459 wins and only 147 losses while competing in the tough North Central Conference. He won two more state championships in 1948 and 1964, joining Frankfort's Everett Case and Martinsville's Glenn Curtis as Hoosier high school basketball's only four-time state title winners.

During his incredible 35-year career, Crawley outdistanced all Indiana high school coaches with his 734 victories against 231 losses. He won 32 sectionals (23 straight at Lafayette), 21 regionals, and 14 Semistates.

Crawley's Lafayette teams also finished in the state runner-up spot three times against Madison in 1950, Crispus Attucks in 1956, and Evansville North in 1967. Joe Heath took over when Crawley announced his coaching retirement after the 1967 tournament.

Mr. Basketball Bob Masters, Ernie Hall, and Joe Mottram were the leading scorers on the 1948 state championship outfit when Lafayette

The 1942 Washington state championship team: Coach Marion Crawley, Forrest Crane, Charles Harmon, Norman Harner, Merle Horrall, Robert Sum, James Riffey, Garland Raney, John Dejernett, Arthur Grove, Robert Donaldson, and Principal Wampler.

turned the tables in the final game on Evansville Central, 54–42. Mottram scored 12 points at one forward position, Hall tallied 11 at center, and Masters 10 in the backcourt. Charlie Vaughan and Dick Robinson completed the Broncho lineup. Jeff carved out an excellent 27–3 record on the way to the school's second state championship—first since 1916.

Evansville Central, featuring Trester Award winner Lee Hamilton had beaten Jeff during the regular season, 65–51.

Lafayette reached the state final game for the seventh time in history in 1964 and came through with a narrow 58–55 win over a strong Huntington team. Huntington had beaten a powerful Columbus ball club in the afternoon, 71–67.

Mr. Basketball Dennis Brady scored 17 points, Center Steve Ricks 13, and Terry Stillabower 10 for the Broncs in the state windup. Brady had 19 and Jack Walkey 16 in the afternoon when Jeff downed Evansville Rex Mundi, 74–61.

Trester Award winner Mike Weaver of Huntington ran into early foul trouble and a stubborn Jeff defense—he got just five points, and that was a deciding factor.

Before his death February 23, 1982, on vacation in Bradenton, Florida, the 73-year-old Crawley was persuaded to name the five best players he ever coached.

There were no big surprises in the opinion of those close to the

Crawley's 1948 state champs, Lafayette Jeff. Front: Jack Blosser, Ned Snyder, Bill Kiser, Dick Robinson, Earl Heninger, Switzer, Mottram; back row: Coach Marion Crawley, Bill Parker, Jim Lucus, Bob Masters, Ernest Hall, Dan Casey and Charles Vaughan.

master coach. Crawley named Mangin and Riffey from his two Washington state championship ball clubs, Hall and Masters from his 1948 Lafayette state title winner, and Brady who starred on his last state championship outfit in 1964.

Lafayette Jeff's 1964 state champs. Front: Coach Marion Crawley, Dan Walkey, Jack Walkey, John Henk, Jim Aldridge, Assistant Coach Sam Lyboult; back row: Wally Reeve, Dave Morrison, Terry Stillabower, Stewart Miller, Steve Ricks and Denny Brady.

Those who knew Crawley best at the end of his great career say that he rated his 1964 Lafayette team as the best he ever had. Of course, Brady and Masters were voted Mr. Basketball on the Indiana All-Star team for the traditional Blind Fund rivalry against Kentucky. Mangin and Riffey also were named to the Indiana All-Star honor roll by the state's sportswriters and sportscasters.

Only a few old-timers will remember that Crawley also coached football for 13 years with almost the same huge success he had in the hardwood sport. Indianapolis Cathedral's Joe Dezelan hadn't forgotten that Crawley owned a brilliant 93–24 record in his 13 seasons as football coach. Included in that record were five North Central Conference championships and a mythical state title in 1950.

"Crawley's football team was the only one to score on us in 1950," Dezelan recalled. "Crawley coached both football and basketball in addition to being athletic director for many years. His teams were always competitive, and we had a good rivalry going in football."

Crawley served for several terms as a member of the IHSAA's Board of Control and Athletic Council. He was the first executive director of the Indiana Basketball Coaches Association and a great believer in the Indiana Athletic Directors Association from the time it was founded.

And he was a long-time director and active worker in the Indiana Basketball Hall of Fame dating back to its very first year in 1962. He took personal charge of the hardwood shrine's scholarship program which benefits the Hoosier state's top student-athletes each year.

One of the highlights of his career was being named to the Hall of Fame along with Glenn Curtis, Murray Mendenhall, Jewell Young, and Haldane Griggs in 1964.

Richmond's Don McBride who was widely recognized as one of the state's top referees in the Crawley era, noted "just by his presence on

Crawley and Mr. Basketball Denny Brady on their way to the 1964 state championship.

the bench, Crawley was one of the game's biggest intimidators. He didn't have to say anything or do anything to get your attention."

For more than two decades Crawley produced the state's largest Coaches Clinic and Holiday Tourney at Lafayette each December. It was a must for coaches all over the Midwest because he attracted the top four teams in Indiana each year and brought in the best coaches to speak in lecture sessions.

Crawley devoted most of his time in the summer working with Taylor University's Don Odle to direct a Junior Basketball Camp on the Taylor campus.

It was the first and best-known camp of its kind for young boys and girls. Crawley touched thousands of young lives in those

Coach Crawley and Jack Walkey (#33) receive the state championship trophy in 1964 from IHSAA official.

memorable weeks at Taylor teaching the game of basketball he loved so much and the finer points of life itself.

Odle was closer to Crawley than most as a result and he often spoke warmly of his good friend's influence.

"Common sense is not a common thing and yet I believe that might have been Marion's biggest secret behind his great coaching success. He kept it simple and even though everyone generally knew what he was going to do, he would usually beat you because his teams were so well organized," Odle said.

"He had more influence on me than any man I ever met," said the Taylor University coach who has circled the globe many times coaching young Americans in the hardwood sport.

Sam Lyboult, Crawley's right-hand man for more than 20 years and later his successor in the Lafayette Jeff athletic office, called his boss "a great judge of character and athletic ability who always wanted to be remembered as a good friend of athletes and just plain students at Jeff.

"He was a wonderful friend," said Lyboult, a former Trester Award winner at Richmond and 1979 Hall of Fame inductee. "I knew him since he came to Jeff in 1942 and was his assistant coach until he

The traditional cutting down of the nets is here performed by Coach Crawley after his Lafayette Jeff team downed Huntington 58–55 for the 1964 championship.

retired. He really went after only two or three games each year and expected the players to win the rest on their own.

"He was a great football coach. In fact, he dominated the North Central Conference."

Walkey, who starred on Crawley's last state championship team in 1964, spoke on behalf of hundreds of former athletes who profited from the Hall of Fame coach's system. "Personally, I owe a lot to Crawley and especially benefited from his idea of the team concept. He geared his entire organization to go all the way every year.

"We were always booed when we went on the road. We knew many people wanted to see Crawley lose, but it just showed that he may have been bigger than the game.

"He could have been a great college coach because he never overcoached. People knew that Jeff would always play well in the state tourney, no matter what it did during the regular season."

Walkey said, "I remember in that final state championship game we were trailing by a few points, and Crawley calmly said we weren't playing well. He told us to just play ball the way we were capable of playing, and it worked."

West Lafayette's Bill Berberian, who coached against Crawley for so many years, was at the same time one of his biggest admirers.

"Obviously, he was one of Indiana's foremost high school coaches of all time. We had a great relationship all those years. We never had any problems because we both felt the same way about the game," Berberian explained. "Marion Crawley was truly one of the real pillars of Indiana high school basketball."

Herb Schwomeyer, sports promotion director at Butler University and the Hall of Fame's historian, observed that "Crawley's impact on individuals was the most important aspect of his life.

"As a coach, he always made sure his teams were fundamentally sound even though he seldom had standout players," Schwomeyer recalled.

Retired Lafayette sportswriter Dick Ham who covered Crawley's teams for more than 30 years told how "Crawley won many games before he ever sent his team out on the floor. People expected him to come up with something different every year. He won many times just by being Marion Crawley.

"His molding of young men is something I remember. The world didn't scare his players when they graduated from high school because he made men out of boys. He was a one-of-a-kind coach. And if they had football playoffs in those days, he would be just as famous for football as he was for basketball.

"I learned a lot from him, especially how to get along with coaches. Being a Westsider, it wasn't always easy for me to convince him it was important to talk to me. But through the years we became good friends," Ham wrote.

"Marion Crawley was a fine Christian person who always was doing something for kids that not many people knew anything about," said Commissioner Emeritus Phil Eskew of the IHSAA. Crawley and his wife Georgia were visiting the Eskews in Florida when he suffered a fatal heart attack.

"You know Crawley thought a lot of Indiana University's Bobby Knight, and Bobby thought a lot of Marion. In fact, Knight asked Crawley to speak to his basketball team at the time of the Indiana Classic tourney this past December," Eskew said.

Joe Heath, who starred on one of Crawley's State Finals teams in 1952 and stepped into his big shoes as Lafayette coach in 1967, reminded everyone how close the legendary figure was to Jeff's athletic program even after his 41-year career ended.

Now the school's athletic director, Heath said, "Crawley attended all of the Jeff athletic contests even after he left his job as coach and athletic director. I learned a lot about the psychology of coaching from him. He was a master coach who won many games that others couldn't have won.

"I had great respect for him as a coach, but those of us who knew

Marion Crawley best had a greater respect for his high qualities as a person. Crawley was proud of his coaching records, and he would want people to remember him as a great coach. But more than for his coaching, I really believe that he would want to be remembered for his character and integrity."

Gov. Otis Bowen recognized all those qualities in 1980 when he named Crawley Sagamore of the Wabash.

Washington

Season Record (27–5)
1940–41

Washington	37	Petersburg	19
Washington	15	Bedford	14
Washington	32	Bloomfield	24
Washington	15	Vincennes	24
Washington	33	Bicknell	34
Washington	21	Jeffersonville	16
Washington	41	Jasper	32
Washington	45	LaPorte	27
Washington	33	Huntingburg	32
Washington	34	Jasper	45
Washington	46	Delphi	21
Washington	24	Bedford	22
Washington	31	Mitchell	22
Washington	28	Jasper	26
Washington	38	Evansville Reitz	32
Washington	24	Evansville Central	26
Washington	49	New Albany	33
Washington	31	Vincennes	22
Washington	59	Fort Wayne Central	42
Washington	42	Martinsville	26
Washington	33	Greencastle	34
Washington	38	Bloomington	27

Sectional (Washington)

Washington	60	Odon	14
Washington	52	Plainville	35
Washington	36	Shoals	28
Washington	48	Loogootee	26

Regional (Washington)

Washington	52	Shelburn	34
Washington	54	Freelandville	43

Semifinal (Vincennes)

Washington	44	Evansville Bosse	27
Washington	44	Bedford	32

State Finals (Indianapolis, Butler Fieldhouse)

Washington	48	Kokomo	32
Washington	39	Madison	33

Season Record (30–1)
1941–42

Washington	46	Petersburg	31
Washington	25	Bedford	17
Washington	37	Jasper	29
Washington	37	Vincennes	21
Washington	41	Muncie Burris	30
Washington	46	Jeffersonville	16
Washington	38	Bicknell	18
Washington	33	Franklin	22
Washington	36	Delphi	18
Washington	34	Vincennes	26
Washington	34	Huntington	27
Washington	30	Bedford	26
Washington	53	Mitchell	20
Washington	39	Jasper	20
Washington	42	Evansville Reitz	28
Washington	31	Huntingburg	14
Washington	31	Evansville Central	32
Washington	44	New Albany	25
Washington	36	Vincennes	23
Washington	42	Martinsville	37
Washington	37	Greencastle	24
Washington	44	Bloomington	32

Sectional (Washington)

Washington	57	Loogootee	23
Washington	50	Montgomery (Barr Twp.)	30
Washington	55	Elnora	17

Regional (Washington)

Washington	53	Sullivan	29
Washington	27	Jasper	24

Semifinal (Vincennes)

Washington	22	Evansville Central	20
Washington	37	Bedford	20

State Finals (Indianapolis, Butler Fieldhouse)

Washington	42	Frankfort	32
Washington	24	Muncie Burris	18

Lafayette Jeff

Season Record (27–3)
1947–48

Lafayette Jeff	56	Delphi	23
Lafayette Jeff	37	Lebanon	34
Lafayette Jeff	46	Anderson	27
Lafayette Jeff	44	Shelbyville	20
Lafayette Jeff	43	Kokomo	21

Lafayette Jeff	37	Vincennes	34
Lafayette Jeff	31	Frankfort	27
Lafayette Jeff	36	South Bend Central	34
Lafayette Jeff	63	Columbus	54
Lafayette Jeff	51	Evansville Central	65
Lafayette Jeff	47	New Castle	31
Lafayette Jeff	50	Lebanon	27
Lafayette Jeff	51	Frankfort	41
Lafayette Jeff	44	Muncie Central	43
Lafayette Jeff	66	West Lafayette	30
Lafayette Jeff	43	Indianapolis Tech	47
Lafayette Jeff	50	Marion	31
Lafayette Jeff	39	Logansport	34
Lafayette Jeff	38	Crawfordsville	43
Lafayette Jeff	59	Richmond	55

Sectional (Lafayette)

Lafayette Jeff	67	Battle Ground	38
Lafayette Jeff	54	Buck Creek	16
Lafayette Jeff	51	West Side (Lafayette)	38
Lafayette Jeff	78	Klondike	37

Regional (Lafayette)

Lafayette Jeff	45	Lebanon	37
Lafayette Jeff	58	Rossville	46

Semifinal (Lafayette)

Lafayette Jeff	44	Hammond	39
Lafayette Jeff	60	Peru	46

State Finals (Indianapolis, Butler Fieldhouse)

Lafayette Jeff	60	Anderson	48
Lafayette Jeff	54	Evansville Central	42

Season Record (28–1)
1963–64

Lafayette Jeff	80	Attica	42
Lafayette Jeff	84	Rossville	57
Lafayette Jeff	57	Lebanon	44
Lafayette Jeff	79	Kokomo	71
Lafayette Jeff	72	Hammond	52
Lafayette Jeff	65	Anderson	63
Lafayette Jeff	75	Frankfort	54
Lafayette Jeff	81	West Lafayette	65
Lafayette Jeff	91	Valparaiso	81
Lafayette Jeff	67	Tipton	72
Lafayette Jeff	99	Crispus Attucks (Indianapolis)	68
Lafayette Jeff	85	Muncie Central	67
Lafayette Jeff	86	Monticello	53
Lafayette Jeff	113	Marion	78
Lafayette Jeff	81	Madison	56
Lafayette Jeff	76	Logansport	55
Lafayette Jeff	87	Crawfordsville	59
Lafayette Jeff	46	New Castle	45

| Lafayette Jeff | 92 | Richmond | 70 |
| Lafayette Jeff | 95 | Cathedral (Indianapolis) | 92 |

Sectional (Lafayette)

Lafayette Jeff	89	Lafayette Central Catholic	60
Lafayette Jeff	95	Southwestern	60
Lafayette Jeff	64	West Lafayette	59

Regional (Lafayette)

| Lafayette Jeff | 91 | Clinton Prairie | 73 |
| Lafayette Jeff | 89 | North White | 75 |

Semistate (Lafayette)

| Lafayette Jeff | 95 | Gary Tolleston | 64 |
| Lafayette Jeff | 73 | Valparaiso | 67 |

State Finals (Indianapolis, Butler Fieldhouse)

| Lafayette Jeff | 74 | Evansville Rex Mundi | 61 |
| Lafayette Jeff | 58 | Huntington | 55 |

14

Everett Case Puts Frankfort's Hot Dogs in Indiana Archives

Everett Case firmly planted Frankfort's Hot Dogs and his own name in the Indiana high school basketball recordbooks when he became the only coach to win four state championships at the same school.

Frankfort was recognized as one of the Hoosier state's strongest hardwood powers while the Grey Fox served as coach of the Hot Dogs for 17 years with an outstanding record of 385–99 from 1923 to 1942—interrupted by a brief fling with Anderson in 1933–34.

Everett won 15 sectionals, 14 regionals, and four state titles in the years of 1925, 1929, 1936, and 1939. His Frankfort teams swept 11 straight regional tournaments from 1921 to 1931, a record for Hoosier Hysteria which still stands.

Case's fourth state championship in 1939 equaled a coaching record set by Glenn Curtis at Martinsville in 1933. Curtis' first state championship came with Lebanon in 1918 and that was followed by three more at Martinsville in 1924, 1927, and 1933.

Marion Crawley came along later with back-to-back state titlists at Washington in 1941–42 and two more state champs at Lafayette Jeff in 1948–64.

Case's record in 20 years of high school coaching at Columbus, Smithfield, Anderson, and Frankfort was 726–75 (second only to Crawley's 734 wins). Everett was a key figure in forming the North Central Conference which his Frankfort teams won outright four times and shared a title with Muncie Central in 1937–38. All Hoosiers looked on the conference as the state's best, and Frankfort was a member for 40 years.

Case moved on to North Carolina State and the college ranks, where he won 379 games in 18 seasons with the Wolfpack. North Carolina State built the South's first basketball showplace; it was named after the Hoosier-bred coach, and his 10 conference championship ball clubs were heavily populated with Indiana kids.

"At North Carolina State, Case single-handedly lifted Atlantic Coast Conference basketball from something the lads did after milking cows or curing tobacco into a big time collegiate sport," sports editor Bob Collins wrote in the *Indianapolis Star.*

Everett was named ACC Coach of the Year three times from 1954–58. Case was honored by his home state with induction in the Indiana Basketball Hall of Fame in 1968 and his incredible 1,161–214 overall record (including a 56–5 hitch with DePauw Navy Pre-Flight) earned a much-belated nod from the Naismith Hall of Fame in 1982. Regrettably, both came a bit late for Casey, who died in 1965.

Old-timers insist that Coach Case has been charged unfairly for using undue influence to attract gifted transfers resulting in an IHSAA suspension during the first part of the 1928–29 season at Frankfort and the 1932–33 season at Anderson.

Case's reputation as a master coach impressed many parents who

Frankfort's 1925 state champs. Front: Ray Carman, Marvin Good, Doyal Plunkitt; second row: Milford Toney, Robert Spradling, Fred Coulter, John Ham; back row: Coach Everett Case, George Schultz, Wilbur Cummins, Rudolph Behr, and Manager Davis.

The 1929 Frankfort state champions. Front: Herbert Hollis, Roy Unroe, Evan Thompson, Robert Primmer; second row: Witsman, Edward Shaver, Charles Lawhead, Willis Unroe, Nate Hadley, Good; back row: Assistant Coach Pribble, Fred Armantrout, Manager Davis, Alvin McCreary and Coach Everett Case.

felt that playing for Everett would give their sons a much better chance to go to college.

"Case was more than one of Indiana's all-time coaching greats," said Bob Primmer, a member of Frankfort's 1929 state championship team who later became a highly successful coach in his own right at South Bend Central High School and Ball State University. "Everett was a great motivator of young men, and it was because of his tremendous influence that all of us went to college. He helped me get my first coaching job at Dunkirk, and I know that he did the same for many others.

"Case also was a very well-educated man, an excellent Latin and English teacher. He was a bachelor, and basketball was his whole life, although you know he didn't play basketball in high school at Anderson. He was a hurdler and also coached our track teams at Frankfort.

"I get a little tired of all the things that have been written down through the years about Case moving in players from everywhere to play for him at Frankfort. We did have some move-ins from Michigantown and Thorntown and Tipton and Flora and Amo, but it was the parents who wanted their kids to play for Everett, because he was the best.

"Not enough has been said about what Case did for his players all

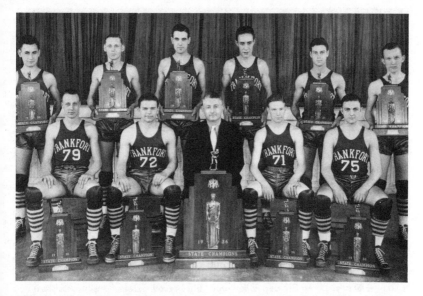

The Hot Dogs' 1936 state champs. Front: Loren Joseph, Ralph Vaughn, Coach Everett Case, Jay McCreary, James Miner; back row: Merlin Goodnight, Glenwood Witsman, Ralph Montgomery, John Slaven, Max Livezey and Ansel Street.

those years. He was a strict disciplinarian and a thorough fundamentalist. He made friends easily, he was an honorable man, and his word was law," Primmer said.

Case also had an enterprising side, owning a restaurant next to the high school in Frankfort and a root beer stand in Lafayette.

Everett was instrumental in starting the Indiana All-Star game in conjunction with the *Indianapolis Star* which has sponsored the Indiana-Kentucky series since 1939 with proceeds going to the blind.

Frankfort's state champs played the Indiana All-Stars in 1939 in a forerunner to the Kentucky rivalry. Buck Plunkitt, who starred on Case's first state championship ball club in 1925 and served as Everett's assistant for four years, teamed up with Tom Downey to coach that first Indiana All-Star team.

The All-Stars beat Frankfort, 31–21, and a short time later Commissioner Arthur L. Trester of the IHSAA ruled that the state champs would not be allowed to participate in future All-Star games.

Wilbur Cummins became one of the most prolific scorers in Frankfort hardwood history as a standout member of the school's first state title winner in 1925. The Hot Dogs beat Rut Walter and his Kokomo teammates in the 34–20 final game played in the old Indianapolis Exposition Building.

Cummins was a 3-year starter for Case, setting a 497-point single season record, which stood for 39 years, and a career high of 1,130,

The 1939 champion Frankfort team. Front: Lewis Cook, James Laughner, Charles Johnson, Coach Everett Case, Daniel Davis, Harold Pyle, Ernest McGill; back row: Manager Davis, Loren Brower, Ellis Good, Bill Wetzel, James Stinson, Assistant Coach Farrell.

which was finally broken by Doug Reid in 1961. Wilbur's 49-point single game record set against Owensville in 1923 still stands.

Cummins led both teams with 16 points the preceding year when Martinsville beat Frankfort in the 1924 state championship game, 36–30.

Robert Spradling was Frankfort's top scorer in the 1925 state title tilt with 13, Plunkitt had nine, and Cummins seven. Marvin Good and Fred Coulter started at guard for the Hot Dogs, who wound up with a brilliant 27–2 record.

Frankfort added its second state championship in 1929 with a 29–23 victory over Indianapolis Tech on the Hot Dogs' ninth straight trip to the state's final tournament. The tourney was played in Butler Fieldhouse for the second time, and all 13,798 seats were sold a week before the tourney.

Eddie Shaver led Frankfort's balanced scoring in the State Final with eight points, followed by Nate Hadley with six, Roy Unroe five, Willis Unroe and Charles Lawhead four each. Red Thompson also scored two in the final game.

Tech was the first Indianapolis school to reach the championship game, and Emmett Lowery was named winner of the Gimbel Medal. Frankfort had a 24–2 record, losing only to Muncie and New Castle on the road—both by one point.

Frankfort's 1936 state title winner thumped Fort Wayne Central by an impressive 50–24 margin in the final game and has been applauded frequently as one of Hoosierland's most talented state titleholders.

Jay McCreary went on to become an All-American with Branch McCracken's 1940 NCAA champs at Indiana University, and Ralph Vaughn was All-American at Southern Cal. McCreary later coached Muncie Central to a state high school championship in 1952—one of seven championships for the Bearcats.

Frankfort won its third state championship in the last year for the center jump (after each basket), and in the eighth game participated in what history books have recorded as the only tie. Frankfort and Indianapolis Tech battled to a 31–31 deadlock, and after two overtimes both Case and Tech Coach Bayne Freeman decided their ball clubs had labored long enough for one night. "At the end of the first overtime, Case and Freeman agreed that they would go one more period and then call it if the score still was tied," Plunkitt recalled. "I don't think either coach wanted to come away with a loss." It prompted the IHSAA to rule there would be no more tie games.

So Frankfort's state championship ball club ended the season with a 29–1–1 record, losing by a 21–16 score at Tipton.

Ralph (Monk) Montgomery, James Miner, Loren Joseph, Ansel Street, Merlin Goodnight, John Slaven, Max Livezey, Glenwood Witsman, McCreary, and Vaughn made up that formidable Hot Dog roster.

Vaughn rifled 12 points in the afternoon when Frankfort beat Anderson, 34–18, and then Montgomery set a tourney record with 19 against Fort Wayne in the final. Vaughn also had 14, McCreary and Miner six each. Paul (Curly) Armstrong and Gimbel Award winner Steve Sitko were the Fort Wayne big guns.

"A big, fast sturdy quintet coached by Everett Case—unquestionably one of the outstanding teams in tournament history—gave Frankfort its third state high school basketball championship by crushing Central of Fort Wayne in the final game," Al Bloemker wrote in the *Indianapolis Star*. "It was the worst rout in a titular contest since Wingate's 36–8 triumph over Anderson in 1914 and it is almost impossible to realize the amazing strength of the winners without taking into consideration Coach Murray Mendenhall's players never quit trying and appeared to be just as strong as some of the previous champions.

"Fort Wayne simply was up against one of the best combinations of individual brilliance and highly-polished team play that ever appeared in the Hoosier tournament.

"The Hot Dogs handled the ball well, passed fast and accurately, took care of their defensive assignments in almost flawless manner, worked the ball under the basket for almost all of their scoring attempts, made the most of their superior height, and above everything else played heads-up ball from start to finish."

Bloemker added that "Ralph Vaughn and Jay McCreary, serving as captain for the second straight year, performed brilliantly as forwards; Ralph Montgomery controlled the tip and used his exceptional height to bat nine field goals through the iron rim in the final game alone, and the two guards—James Miner and Loren Joseph—forced the opposition to shoot from far out most of the time."

Case's record-setting fourth state championship in a 36–22 win over Franklin brought together two legendary figures. Case became the first to win four titles at the same school and his coaching rival in the final game was Fuzzy Vandivier—an all-state player with Franklin's famed Wonder Five on three straight championship teams in 1920–22.

Franklin's George Crowe was the outstanding individual star in the championship game, but James Laughner matched Crowe's 13-point total for the Hot Dogs, and Laughner had a lot more support. Lewis Cook supported his running mate at forward with 11 points and Charles (Splinter) Johnson added eight at center. Harold Pyle and Daniel Davis were the starting guards.

Johnson scored nine points, Cook and Laughner seven each in the afternoon when Frankfort downed Evansville Bosse, 32–28. Franklin advanced to the championship game with a 31–25 win over Muncie Burris. Bosse's Jim Myers was named winner of the Gimbel Medal and several years later Jim coached Bosse to one of its three state titles in 1962.

"The Casemen passed over the heads of their rivals during most of the [championship] tilt and drove under the basket for points with express-train speed after reaching the final game with an impressive triumph over Bosse," one writer summed up.

"The Hot Dog team, definitely on the spot by virtue of its position as one of the heaviest tournament favorites in recent years, staggered through the first half of the matinee Bosse assignment before finishing strong for a 33–28 triumph.

"The championship battle, however, was a Frankfort parade all the way after an interesting first quarter which ended in a 5-all deadlock. The Casemen led at the intermission, 20–10, and they increased their margin as the game drew to a close to attain the coveted crown they visualized as early as January 1 following a victory over the South Side of Fort Wayne team which won the title last season.

"Frankfort's triumph also returned the crown to a member of the powerful 10-team North Central Conference for the ninth time in the last 12 years."

Case was surrounded by writers and photographers seconds after the final gun. "Of course, we're happy to win this fourth championship, but we won from a fine ball club coached by Fuzzy Vandivier."

Several of the Frankfort champs called Franklin's Crowe the toughest player they met all season, and Crowe was rewarded—he was named Indiana's first Mr. Basketball.

Everett Case won 20 or more games in 14 of his 17 seasons as Frankfort coach. His teams averaged 24 wins in nine years from 1922 to 1931, capturing nine straight sectionals and nine regional tournaments.

Case had an innovative basketball mind, and the best example of this took place during the 1927 season when the Hot Dogs defeated a powerful Logansport ball club in their famous 10–7 stall game. This historic battle unfolded in Frankfort's famous Howard Hall, and it didn't get under way until after midnight. Logansport's team bus got stuck in a snow drift at Michigantown, and the "B" team game was delayed several hours.

Logansport had a very strong ball club that had been beating everybody by 20–25 points, but Case vowed beforehand, "They're not going to beat Old Ev any 25 points because they're not going to have the ball."

Case was right, and his deep freeze led to the IHSAA's adoption of a 10-second midcourt line to prevent such stalling tactics in the backcourt. "Case always said it takes a great team to be able to hold the ball, and it takes a better team to take it away," Buck Plunkitt related.

Frankfort's stall upset Cliff Wells and the Logansport people so much that the return game was canceled.

Jay McCreary, who ended his coaching career at Louisiana State University, remembers the Frankfort Hall of Fame coach as a tough driver. "He drove himself and expected his players to give 100 percent," McCreary said.

"During our lay-up practices, he would sit in the middle of the floor with a big paddle. If you missed the lay-up, you would automatically run to his chair, assume the position and Case would smack you on the rear with that big paddle. And then he would say, 'Now that you're awake, make the *next* lay-up.' "

McCreary also recalls one sectional game against Michigantown in 1935. Ralph Vaughn faked and started his drive to the hoop. Ralph caught an elbow and lost two teeth. Case's only remark was, "Damn, Ralph, you lost some teeth. But go ahead and play—we've only got 12 minutes left in the game." Case was tough, but he was fair and he was basketball smart, McCreary concluded.

Old Howard Hall (named after Case's iron-fisted boss, Principal Katherine Howard) has been replaced by a much-bigger modern basketball arena, and numerous coaches, including Wilbur Commins, Marvin Cave, George Bradfield, Sam Ranzino, Phil Buck, Ray Green, and John Milholland, have worked in Case's shadow.

Frankfort still turns back the pages, and why not—they own a big chunk of vintage Hoosier Hysteria.

Everett Case's Frankfort Record:

Won 385, Lost 99

1923—Won 24, Lost 6
1924—Won 26, Lost 2
1925—Won 27, Lost 2 (state champ)
1926—Won 23, Lost 4
1927—Won 20, Lost 7
1928—Won 23, Lost 5
1929—Won 24, Lost 2 (state champ)
1930—Won 27, Lost 9
1931—Won 25, Lost 4
1935—Won 17, Lost 12
1936—Won 29, Lost 1, Tied 1 (state champ)
1937—Won 20, Lost 3
1938—Won 22, Lost 7
1939—Won 26, Lost 6 (state champ)
1940—Won 14, Lost 11
1941—Won 15, Lost 10
1942—Won 23, Lost 8

Frankfort

Season Record (27–2)
1924–25

Frankfort	59	Rossville	16
Frankfort	39	Martinsville	27
Frankfort	64	Greencastle	17
Frankfort	43	Rochester	33
Frankfort	35	Franklin	32
Frankfort	36	Columbus	26
Frankfort	2	Kokomo (Forfeit)	0
Frankfort	50	Indianapolis Manual	25
Frankfort	48	Richmond	19
Frankfort	47	Lebanon	17
Frankfort	33	Muncie Central	23
Frankfort	46	Gary Emerson	31
Frankfort	54	Lebanon	33
Frankfort	36	Vincennes	57
Frankfort	49	Bloomington	21
Frankfort	42	Franklin	34
Frankfort	43	Kokomo	35
Frankfort	41	Vincennes	40

Frankfort	29	Martinsville	31
Frankfort	33	Columbus	26

Sectional (Frankfort)

Frankfort	40	Colfax	4
Frankfort	46	Rossville	23
Frankfort	58	Michigantown	10

Regional (Frankfort)

Frankfort	49	Clinton	11
Frankfort	38	Clayton	12

State Finals (Indianapolis, Exposition Building)

Frankfort	25	Gary Froebel	23
Frankfort	24	Muncie Central	16
Frankfort	30	Washington	25
Frankfort	34	Kokomo	20

Season Record (25–2)
1928–29

Frankfort	38	Lebanon	26
Frankfort	39	Muncie Central	40
Frankfort	43	East Chicago Washington	28
Frankfort	36	Logansport	23
Frankfort	29	Indianapolis Tech	24
Frankfort	36	East Chicago Washington	25
Frankfort	33	Marion	27
Frankfort	38	Lebanon	23
Frankfort	43	Rochester	24
Frankfort	38	Martinsville	26
Frankfort	39	Kokomo	26
Frankfort	30	Logansport	23
Frankfort	23	New Castle	24
Frankfort	28	Columbus	26
Frankfort	47	Kokomo	29
Frankfort	45	Lafayette Jeff	20
Frankfort	41	Logansport	30

Sectional (Frankfort)

Frankfort	69	Sugar Creek Township	10
Frankfort	55	Mulberry	15
Frankfort	54	Michigantown	16

Regional (Lafayette)

Frankfort	51	Freeland Park	17
Frankfort	19	West Point	16

State Finals (Indianapolis, Butler Fieldhouse)

Frankfort	43	Columbia City	18
Frankfort	28	Columbus	21
Frankfort	22	Gary Horace Mann	17
Frankfort	29	Indianapolis Tech	23

Season Record (29-1-1)
1935-36

Frankfort	28	Dunkirk	19
Frankfort	16	Tipton	21
Frankfort	23	Anderson	17
Frankfort	49	Delphi	18
Frankfort	34	Muncie Central	23
Frankfort	21	Logansport	17
Frankfort	44	Lebanon	17
Frankfort	31	Indianapolis Tech	31
(Double Overtime—Tie Game)			
Frankfort	30	Kokomo	13
Frankfort	33	Martinsville	22
Frankfort	32	Connersville	28
Frankfort	33	Marion	14
Frankfort	46	Lafayette	18
Frankfort	37	New Castle	19
Frankfort	45	Lebanon	16
Frankfort	28	Kokomo	17
Frankfort	22	Anderson	18
Frankfort	33	Lafayette	24
Frankfort	31	Richmond	24
Frankfort	30	Muncie Central	24
Frankfort	25	Gary Horace Mann	22
Frankfort	34	Logansport	20

Sectional (Frankfort)

Frankfort	57	Scircleville	15
Frankfort	38	Michigantown	9
Frankfort	40	Rossville	13

Regional (Lafayette)

Frankfort	52	Lebanon	12
Frankfort	48	West Lafayette	12

Semifinal (Gary)

Frankfort	35	Froebel (Gary)	29
Frankfort	28	Logansport	27

State Finals (Indianapolis, Butler Fieldhouse)

Frankfort	34	Anderson	18
Frankfort	50	Fort Wayne Central	24

Season Record (26-6)
1938-39

Frankfort	42	Rossville	14
Frankfort	37	Tipton	33
Frankfort	29	Muncie Central	31
Frankfort	35	Logansport	37
Frankfort	43	Lebanon	25

Frankfort	40	Indianapolis Tech	29
Frankfort	30	Horace Mann (Gary)	88
Frankfort	25	Kokomo	28
Frankfort	44	Lafayette Jeff	36
Frankfort	31	Marion	23
Frankfort	36	New Castle	34
Frankfort	29	Lebanon	26
Frankfort	41	Kokomo	33
Frankfort	11	Anderson	6
Frankfort	49	Lafayette Jeff	26
Frankfort	27	Richmond	31
Frankfort	40	Jeffersonville	28
Frankfort	45	Vincennes	19
Frankfort	30	Elwood	26
Frankfort	49	Logansport	22
Frankfort	32	Hammond Clark	26
Frankfort	42	Fort Wayne South	40
Frankfort	25	Hammond	31

Sectional (Frankfort)

Frankfort	65	Sugar Creek Township	14
Frankfort	42	Jackson Township	18
Frankfort	57	Michigantown	25

Regional (Lafayette)

| Frankfort | 44 | Lafayette Jeff | 31 |
| Frankfort | 58 | Lebanon | 25 |

Semifinal (Hammond)

| Frankfort | 38 | LaPorte | 31 |
| Frankfort | 43 | Elkhart | 32 |

State Finals (Indianapolis Butler Fieldhouse)

| Frankfort | 32 | Evansville Bosse | 28 |
| Frankfort | 36 | Franklin | 22 |

15

Glenn Curtis, Johnny Wooden, and the Martinsville Dynasty

Glenn Curtis began his brilliant coaching career as a four-time state title winner with a 27–2 state championship ball club at Lebanon in 1918. It was Lebanon's second straight championship and third since 1912.

Curtis moved on to Rushville for one year and then headed for Martinsville where he built a hardwood dynasty that produced three more championships with a 22–7 record in 1924, a 26–3 record in 1927, and a 22–9 season in 1933. He had no background as a player himself, but he was a master coach.

Glenn became the first coach to win state chamionships at two different schools, and his record at Martinsville from 1920 to 1938 was 388–133–1. During that incredible stretch his Artesians had just two losing seasons—with an 11–13 record in 1932 and 9–17 in 1935.

Curtis took over the Lebanon job when state championship coach Alva Staggs answered a call from Anderson. Staggs had directed Lebanon to a 26–2 state championship season in 1917, and three starters from that ball club returned. So Lebanon was the state tourney favorite to repeat in 1918 under first-year coach Curtis.

Lebanon's defense in the state tourney was phenomenal, holding four opponents to just 33 points. Oddly enough, Lebanon's opponent in the championship game was Staggs and his Anderson outfit. Lebanon won in overtime, 24–20, led by Don White with 14 points.

Curtis turned out many excellent basketball players during his long career at Martinsville, and Johnny Wooden was destined to become the greatest coach in college basketball history with 10 NCAA titles at UCLA.

Wooden was a three-time All-American at Purdue University and coached South Bend Central High School for nine years with a 218–42 record and Indiana State for two seasons with a 47–14 record.

Wooden's 27-year record with UCLA included a record 88-game winning streak broken by Notre Dame in 1974 and 10 NCAA titles in his last 12 years before he retired from coaching in 1975. Johnny's 10 national championship teams compiled a dazzling record of 219–10 and four of those UCLA clubs were unbeaten.

Wooden's collegiate record was 667–161 for a winning percentage of .806. Eight months after his retirement in 1975, Johnny returned to his home state where many old high school and Purdue buddies along with 700 others, saluted him in a testimonial dinner at the Indianapolis Convention Center.

Governors, mayors, commissioners, university presidents, and even the President of the United States (who sent a telegram) took part in the Indianapolis testimonial. Wooden was one of five all-time greats to be installed in the Indiana Hall of Fame in its first year (1962). This was followed later by his induction into the Naismith National Hall of Fame.

Curtis recalled his first Martinsville state champion in 1924 for the *Indianapolis Star* Sunday magazine in an article that appeared almost 25 years later. It was perhaps his most satisfying year because nobody

Lebanon's 1918 state champs. Front: Gerald Gardner, Fred Adam, Merrill Gardner; middle row: Frank Martin, Clyde Grater, Don White, Henry Stevens, Basil Smith; back row: Coach Curtis, Manager Demaree.

Martinsville's 1924 state champs. Front: Clarence Poling and Walter Messmer; middle row: Darrell Wright, Robert Hines, Robert Schnaiter, Hugh Brown; back row: Stanley Byram, Coach Curtis, Principal Vandivier, Warren Schnaiter.

considered Martinsville a state title threat and the underdog Artesians battled from behind to down Frankfort in the 36–30 final.

"Martinsville was only one of 665 teams in sectional play that year, and while we beat Bloomington, Spencer, Paragon, and Monrovia in the sectionals, and won the regional by defeating Winslow, 30–18, nobody in his right mind was looking for much trouble from us in the semifinals," Curtis admitted.

"In those days, the bygone days of jumping center and guards who only guarded but rarely shot, the semifinals and finals were played on three consecutive days. In our first game as one of the Sweet Sixteen, Martinsville won over Liberty Center, 39–23, which was considered interesting but not very significant. Then we beat Connersville, 36–33.

"That was one upset that looked like an accident—one of those things that often happen to favorites like Connersville. After all, Martinsville had been beaten seven times that season, and you know how it is—beating Connersville made us slightly a villain of the piece.

"Nobody was hostile toward us, of course, but revenge was in the air, and Connersville's supporters found a lot of satisfaction in the fact that we had to play Bedford next. We had suffered two defeats at Bedford's hands earlier in the season—the second time in a wild overtime game.

"So you can imagine how high the feeling ran when Martinsville beat Bedford, 31–15, in that crucial game. The last act of the Great Hoosier Drama was coming up now, and it definitely had a hero and a villain. When the Frankfort team trotted out onto the floor that night in their blue and white uniforms, there was no doubt about who the hero was. The Coliseum was jammed with people, and when Frankfort came on they were crazy. My team and I stayed in the dressing room for five minutes before going out, and the din kept up all that time. It rattled the lockers.

"But when the game started," Curtis said, "it looked like that old physics puzzler—the irresistible force meeting the immovable body. Nobody was able to score for five minutes. Then Frankfort's Cummins got through for a field goal. Hugh Brown, Martinsville's center, tied that up right away with two free throws on a foul, but Cummins got through with another field goal. We closed the score to 4–3 on another free throw, and then things started to happen.

"Holz, Frankfort's forward, dropped in two of the prettiest field goals I've ever seen, and Cummins got another to make the score 10–3 against Martinsville. We brought it up to 10–5 and called time out, but when play was resumed Frankfort opened up on us with both barrels. Before we knew it, the score was 14–5 and it looked as if the villain was going to get his just deserts.

Martinsville's 1927 state champs. Front row: Charles Caldwell and William Neal; second row: Vince Bisesi, Arnold Suddith, Les Reynolds, John Wooden, Virgil David; back row: George Eubank, Bob Lockhart, Coach Glenn Curtis, Marshall Tackett.

Martinsville's own Johnny Wooden in a Purdue uniform, which he wore en route to All-American status. Later Wooden became perhaps the most famous basketball coach of all time at UCLA.

"I called out Darrell Wright, Martinsville forward, for instructions. I had had one of those hunches that keep coaches out of the Old Coaches Home. When Wright went back in that Martinsville team began to light up like a Christmas tree. The boys poured in points until we were within four points of Frankfort.

"Frankfort called for a time-out. As soon as play resumed, Wright dropped in a sensational field goal that made the score, 16–14. Frankfort was getting worried, of course. But Martinsville was still trailing, 16–14, at the half. A field goal and a free throw finally got us the lead after the intermission. We stayed out in front the rest of the way. The game ended with Martinsville as state champ, 36–30. And the villain, of course, in the best tradition of the annual Hoosier fairy tale, immediately became the hero.

"A lot of things win a ball game. One thing that broke the favorite, Frankfort, in that game 24 years ago was freeing Bob Schnaiter from guarding Petty, his Frankfort man, and thus turning him loose to concentrate on scoring. Those were the instructions Wright took into the

game with him at the start of the Martinsville rally. But behind that
was the fact that Schnaiter had been practicing angle shots an hour a
day for weeks beforehand.

"Then, too, Martinsville had what seemed like phenomenal luck in
getting the ball after center jumps. Brown, Martinsville center, had
perfected on his own a trick of deflecting the opposing center's hand
before it touched the ball, and flipping the ball into play with the back
of his own hand. It was the first time Brown had used the maneuver,
and he didn't disclose the secret of it until three or four years later."

Curtis explained, "Another thing that won for Martinsville was
Brown's shooting, which was deadly accurate. But there was
something behind that, too. He grew up on an Indiana farm where
basketball was unknown, but his father had seen a game and nailed a
wooden hoop to the barn door for him to practice on. His only basketball was a heavy, bulky cloth ball his mother made for him out of
some old dresses.

"When Hugh Brown got to high school in Martinsville, a regulation basketball was like a marble in his hands. And that's why I favor
the darkhorses in any tournament. You never know what's behind
them," the Martinsville coach pointed out.

Wooden, Les Reynolds, and Arnold Eugene (Sally) Suddith starred
on Martinsville teams that lost the 30–23 state championship game to
Marion in 1926, defeated Muncie Central 26–23 for the 1927 state
championship, and dropped a 13–12 heartstopper to Muncie the next
year in the state final tilt. Charlie Secrist's memorable shot from mid-

Johnny Wooden with two old Purdue teammates, Ray Eddy (left) and Charles
(Stretch) Murphy. They were teammates on the Big 10 championship teams in 1930
and 1932.

court in the closing seconds decided the latter and still is remembered as one of the most publicized shots in Hoosier Hysteria record books.

Wooden tallied 13 points in Martinsville's 26–23 victory over Muncie for the 1927 state championship. "In my day, Indiana was the cream of high school basketball," remembers Wooden. "No other area of the country produced as many outstanding players, and although some areas have now passed the state in terms of producing athletes, nobody has the same excitement associated with its state tournament."

Wooden added, "In those days you couldn't grow up in Indiana and not have a basketball touch you in some way. I can remember when it was the homeroom teacher's job to see that everyone in class had a season ticket. If a student was too poor to afford one, it was his teacher's responsibility to find a way to get him one.

"The size of our gyms astounded people from other parts of the country," Wooden said. "There were a dozen or more high school gyms in Indiana that were bigger than most college facilities at that time. Before I entered high school, Martinsville built a gym that seated 5,200 people. The whole town had only 4,800, but we always filled the gym."

Glenn Curtis Memorial Gym has since been remodeled and still stands as a museum full of old photos and other memorabilia honoring the three championship teams and other standout hardwood figures.

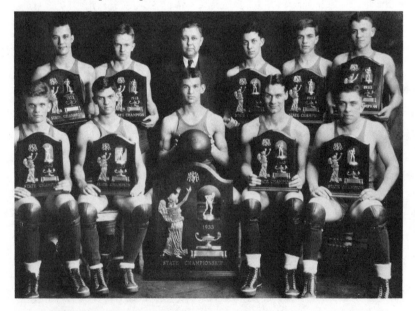

Martinsville's 1933 state champs. Front: Eugene Cramer, Wayne Garrison, Robert Norman, Clarence Coyle, Verl Beasley; back row: Hubert Scott, Kenneth Watson, Coach Glenn Curtis, Robert Dale, Kenneth Williams and Wendell Phillips.

Coach Glenn Curtis as he appeared in 1948.

A new school with complete modern athletic facilities was opened on the east side of town in recent years.

Wooden experienced only a few noteworthy setbacks in his own incredible career as player and coach, but the pageantry and glamor common to the Indiana high school tournament dealt him the loss that has stuck with him longest. David Minor of Gary Froebel hit a half-court shot at the buzzer that beat Wooden's South Bend Central team in the 1941 Hammond Semistate.

"It was an unbelievable shot, one you hear about all the time in the state tournament," Wooden said. "And it was the only time Froebel was ahead in the game. My team had a lot of talent, and I was certain we'd get to the Final Four. In all my years of coaching, I don't think I've ever been more disappointed."

Suddith made the starting lineup as a freshman forward in 1927 when Martinsville defeated Muncie, 26–3. The five starters played all the way without relief, with Wooden scoring a game high 10 points and Reynolds adding six for the Artesians.

Wooden and Suddith returned one year later when Martinsville suffered that electrifying 13–12 loss on Secrist's shot with just a few seconds on the clock. Martinsville got the ensuing tip at the center of the floor and managed to cut loose one last shot of its own, hoping to save the game at the wire, but it missed the mark.

Wooden and Bob Lockhart both had played for Martinsville in a state championship game three straight years. Wooden led the Artesians with five points and Marshall Tackett had four. Robert Yohler scored six and Secrist four for Muncie's champs.

Suddith played two more years with Martinsville losing a two-overtime thriller to Bedford in 1929 and then losing to eventual state champ Washington the next year. Sally went on to star for Everett Dean at Indiana University.

Reynolds captained the Martinsville teams that defeated Muncie in the 1927 state championship showdown and lost to Stretch Murphy and his Marion stablemates in 1926. He also was a sub on the 1924 state title winner. Les played four years at Indiana State and was voted All-America honorable mention in 1930.

Wooden and Reynolds were praised on all fronts as two of Hoosier high school basketball's greatest. Even in those days the press had trouble separating the two old Martinsville teammates. Dick Miller of the United Press wrote, "Lester Reynolds takes his place among such greats as Fuzzy Vandivier, Babe Wheeler, Don White and a few more outstanding candidates for Indiana's Hall of Fame. Johnny Wooden is one of the finest forwards ever to play at the [Indianapolis] Cow Barn or any other place for that matter."

Bob Gordon of the *Muncie Star* said, "Lester Reynolds was the one outstanding player at the cow barn. He was the brains of the team and every play centered on him. To Johnny Wooden goes the honor of being the fastest tumbling bug in the circus."

Bill Fox of the *Indianapolis News* added, "I salute Martinsville, salute Curtis, salute Reynolds and shake the hand of little Johnny Wooden."

At a community tribute to Martinsville's champions, Zora Clevenger, who was IU athletic director at the time, said, "Lester Reynolds is one of the greatest basketball players in the country, and Johnny Wooden is only a step behind him."

Of course, Curtis put both on his all-Martinsville team printed in Fox's " 'Shootin Em and Stopping Em' " column in 1955. Darrell Wright (1924), High Brown (1924), and George Eubank (1929) were the others placed on Glenn's first five.

On the second five he had Conrad Nash (1921), Dewey South (1920), William Sadler (1931), George Pearcy (1938), and Hugh Gibbs (1920). And he second-guessed himself a bit leaving off such standouts as Shanks Kriner, Claude Curtis, Mel Payton, Roger Adkins, Suddith, and the Schnaiter boys.

Claude Curtis was the first Gimbel Award winner in 1917.

Curtis landed his fourth state championship (third at Martinsville) with a 27–24 victory over Greencastle in 1933. It was Coach Curtis'

10th trip to the state tournament's Sweet Sixteen in his 13 years with the Artesians. Greencastle with all-state center Jess McAnally was making its fourth straight trip to the State Finals.

Butler University changed the Fieldhouse for the 1933 tournament to expand the seating capacity by 1,120 (increasing it to 15,000 for basketball), and the floor was shifted to run North and South instead of East and West.

Martinsville won the championship against a strong Greencastle ball club with an excellent team effort and good defense. Wayne Garrison led Martinsville scoring with eight points in the championship game, Robert Norman and Verl Beasley scored six each.

Jim Seward of Indianapolis Shortridge outscored the great McAnally in the afternoon (16–12), but Greencastle advanced to the final game in a 31–28 cliffhanger. Seward later received the Gimbel Award for his outstanding performance.

Martinsville's record in 1933 was 22–9, and it came on the heels of Curtis' first losing season. Glenn had another loser in 1935, but he came back with 23–5, 21–7, and 21–6 seasons in his last three years as a high school coach.

Curtis put together a phenomenal 388–133–1 coaching record. He left in 1938 to take the Indiana State job and then returned to Martinsville as school superintendent.

Glenn Curtis' Record
at Martinsville

1920—Won 26, Lost 5
1921—Won 24, Lost 6
1922—Won 27, Lost 6
1923—Won 15, Lost 10
1924—Won 22, Lost 7 (state champ)
1925—Won 22, Lost 5
1926—Won 25, Lost 4 (state runnerup)
1927—Won 26, Lost 3 (state champ)
1928—Won 24, Lost 5 (state runnerup)
1929—Won 18, Lost 11
1930—Won 21, Lost 7
1931—Won 13, Lost 10
1932—Won 11, Lost 13
1933—Won 22, Lost 9 (state champ)
1934—Won 13, Lost 7, Tied 1
1935—Won 9, Lost 17
1936—Won 23, Lost 5
1937—Won 21, Lost 7
1938—Won 21, Lost 6

Lebanon

Season Record (28–2)
1917–18

Lebanon	35	Anderson	26
Lebanon	25	Rockville	13
Lebanon	17	Muncie Central	8
Lebanon	30	Richmond	11
Lebanon	33	Martinsville	18
Lebanon	39	Thorntown	32
Lebanon	17	Lafayette Jeff	11
Lebanon	38	Richmond	5
Lebanon	36	Advance	25
Lebanon	40	Lizton	7
Lebanon	30	Thorntown	22
Lebanon	38	Frankfort	10
Lebanon	45	Advance	16
Lebanon	15	Lafayette Jeff	22
Lebanon	54	Crawfordsville	7
Lebanon	35	Anderson	21
Lebanon	39	Zionsville	10
Lebanon	37	Crawfordsvile	25
Lebanon	35	Frankfort	11
Lebanon	20	Rochester	24
Lebanon	34	Muncie Central	18
Lebanon	14	Martinsville	13

Sectional (Thorntown)

Lebanon	56	Kirklin	1
Lebanon	32	Advance	18
Lebanon	38	Colfax	10
Lebanon	43	Thorntown	14

State Finals (Indiana University)

Lebanon	15	Wingate	6
Lebanon	30	South Bend Central	3
Lebanon	17	Bloomington	4
Lebanon	24	Anderson (Overtime)	20

Martinsville

Season Record (22–7)
1923–24

Martinsville	61	Bainbridge	33
Martinsville	28	Crawfordsville	31
Martinsville	35	Bedford	31
Martinsville	29	Columbus	33
Martinsville	48	Lebanon	12
Martinsville	34	Greencastle	24
Martinsville	37	Franklin	35
Martinsville	29	Bloomington	24

Martinsville	44	Vincennes	30
Martinsville	37	Crawfordsville	15
Martinsville	28	Shelbyville	46
Martinsville	25	Vincennes	53
Martinsville	24	Bloomington	32
Martinsville	32	Franklin	27
Martinsville	48	Columbus	41
Martinsville	41	Greencastle	33
Martinsville	37	Lebanon	19
Martinsville	39	Bedford	40
Martinsville	42	Indianapolis Tech	34
Martinsville	41	Shelbyville	47

Sectional (Martinsville)

Martinsville	34	Bloomington	28
Martinsville	35	Spencer	17
Martinsville	30	Paragon	15
Martinsville	36	Monrovia	24

Regional (Bloomington)

Martinsville	30	Winslow	18

State Finals (Indianapolis Coliseum)

Martinsville	39	Liberty Center	23
Martinsville	36	Connersville	33
Martinsville	31	Bedford	15
Martinsville	36	Frankfort	30

Season Record (26–3)
1926–27

Martinsville	45	Mitchell	24
Martinsville	36	Washington	21
Martinsville	34	Bedford	35
Martinsville	42	Columbus	36
Martinsville	23	Washington	22
Martinsville	53	Franklin	34
Martinsville	57	Connersville	43
Martinsville	77	Kokomo	43
Martinsville	51	Shelbyville	34
Martinsville	27	Muncie Central	19
Martinsville	61	Linton	24
Martinsville	28	Franklin	22
Martinsville	28	Vincennes	33
Martinsville	70	Shortridge (Indianapolis)	11
Martinsville	53	Columbus	27
Martinsville	50	Marion	30
Martinsville	52	Shelbyville	27
Martinsville	36	Bedford	39
Martinsville	37	Kokomo	23
Martinsville	30	Vincennes	23

Sectional (Bloomington)

Martinsville	52	Morgantown	22
Martinsville	68	Eminence	27
Martinsville	25	Bloomington	21

Regional (Martinsville)

| Martinsville | 39 | Brownsburg | 14 |
| Martinsville | 40 | Spencer | 14 |

State Finals (Indianapolis, Exposition Building)

Martinsville	27	Logansport	14
Martinsville	26	Emerson (Gary)	14
Martinsville	32	Connersville	21
Martinsville	26	Muncie Central	23

Season Record (21–8)
1932–33

Martinsville	24	Washington	27
Martinsville	26	Logansport	22
Martinsville	28	Franklin	22
Martinsville	22	Bedford	24
Martinsville	20	Shelbyville	19
Martinsville	27	Dayton, Kentucky	15
Martinsville	36	Franklin	24
Martinsville	26	Bloomington	12
Martinsville	28	New Castle	19
Martinsville	21	Vincennes	24
Martinsville	22	Shortridge (Indianapolis)	25
Martinsville	21	Indianapolis Tech	24
Martinsville	40	Bloomington	20
Martinsville	29	Rushville	21
Martinsville	18	Shelbyville	21
Martinsville	29	Bedford	25
Martinsville	19	Logansport	22
Martinsville	20	Washington	30
Martinsville	21	Anderson	18
Martinsville	22	Vincennes	20

Sectional (Martinsville)

Martinsville	41	Smithville	7
Martinsville	22	Ellettsville	11
Martinsville	26	Bloomington	14

Regional (Bloomington)

| Martinsville | 33 | Brazil | 20 |
| Martinsville | 18 | Lyons | 11 |

State Finals (Indianapolis, Butler Fieldhouse)

Martinsville	23	Valparaiso	20
Martinsville	22	Bedford	18
Martinsville	23	Fort Wayne North	14
Martinsville	27	Greencastle	24

16

"SHARPIE"—
They Loved His Black Cats

When it comes to the subject of Coach Howard Sharpe, that controversial, noisy, competitive basketball wizard from central Indiana, there are few fence sitters. The loyal followers of his 42-year career in Hoosier basketball swore by him. His opponents and occasional enemies swore at him. His path for those years was the pursuit of a state championship—a goal which eluded him. After more than 700 high school basketball coaching victories, he still would trade them all for the golden spotlight of a state title.

Sharpe's reputation was permanently established during a string of extremely successful seasons during the 1950s when his Gerstmeyer Technical High School teams from Terre Haute achieved Final Four status on four occasions. Only once, in 1953, did the Black Cats reach the championship game and then lost in a controversial 42–41 decision to South Bend Central. Sharpe, at age 37, would have become one of the youngest coaches ever to coach a championship team. Instead, he was doomed to a career of frustration, knowing what it was like to stand on top of the world in Butler Fieldhouse and how it felt to walk away with only a silver ring.

When Gerstmeyer, a turn-of-the-century relic, closed in 1971, Sharpe moved his coaching operation to Terre Haute North Vigo High School, a consolidation of the former Gerstmeyer and Garfield high schools. In the early 1970s, Sharpe's teams again moved up the tournament ladder, but not far enough to satisfy his dreams.

Sharpe in action during a 1957 game.

Any narrative about Sharpe's career must constantly flash back to those glory days, and often his recollection is the only tool to open those dusty old trunks of memories. But the Sharpe of the early '70s really had not changed all that much. "I used to be a tiger and now they make me be a lamb," he once complained. Perhaps that was true, for Sharpe was a rebellious coach, an agitator of officials, and a particularly distasteful sight if your team preferences favored schools called Wiley or Glenn or Honey Creek. Fans, young and old, for all the years of Sharpe's career, would assail him from the bleachers: "Sit down, Sharpie!" It was a request akin to asking the earth to stand still. He roamed the sidelines, shouting instructions, coaching the bench (and often the people sitting behind the bench). He looked for an edge and then relished exploiting it. A new generation would add to the phrase for the 1973 sectional, holding aloft a sign which read, "Sit down, Sharpie, you redneck." Even though it was not intended to heap praise on him, Sharpe never minded the attention. "You see that? They're more worried about me than they are about the team," said Sharpe. He had them where he wanted them.

But to see the real Sharpe, to catch the essence of a man trained and driven to be a basketball coach, one needed only to witness one of those opening-day-of-practice talks which became a tradition. The older players would fight sleep during those opening minutes, for they had heard the routine before, but to the neophyte these ramblings were the first insight into a man for whom they would play three years.

Sharpe (and his printed handbook) always were full of truisms. "When the whistle blows during practice, everything stops except your ear." He demanded attention. "When the official hands you the ball, you are to say, 'Thank you.' " He demanded respect and he wanted the officials to whistle affectionately for his team. "We expect your hair to be cut and for you to be clean-shaven." He demanded pride and demeanor.

Of course, there were sidelights to this opening speech. He would describe a "bum" and then tell his players he didn't want bums. "This bum smells like a brewery, he hasn't taken a bath in weeks, there's a cigarette dangling from his mouth, he's got long hair and he hasn't shaved . . . you know, a bum." The players seated before him wouldn't have dreamed of appearing at a basketball game in quite that condition, but his message was clear. Sharpe would assert, "Not all people with long hair are bums, but all bums have long hair." The locks would have to be shorn above the ear. (Incidentally, he finally gave way in the late '70s and required only "neat haircuts," no longer specifying length.) He was a firm believer in the notion that participation on a basketball team was a privilege, not a right. And he always could fall back on the sincerely stated rationale that "we have found that players with shorter hair have fewer colds." This was in reference to the understanding the shorter hair dried more quickly, thus averting the dreaded combination of wet hair and cold winter winds. Howard Sharpe, self-proclaimed M.D., was hard at work on another season.

He could talk about the present and he could talk about the past. The glories of a previous day served to buoy him from time to time, for he was dismayed by the inattention a new generation had given sports. In those 1950s glory days, his team lived basketball 24 hours a day, or at least it seemed so. With cars and televisions and other school activities at hand, some of that former devotion was missing. Sharpe could recall his own playing days when he was a notorious scrapper. Among his college teammates was Ward E. Brown, later commissioner of the Indiana High School Athletic Association, and the student manager of the team was John Baratto, who would coach the 1960 state championship team from East Chicago Washington.

Those happy, raucous days seemed best characterized by an oft-told story about teammates and friend Wayne (Joe) Fox of Riley, Indiana. Fox was a benchwarmer on those Indiana State teams, but on a memorable night at Valparaiso in 1940, he was given an opportunity to start a game by Curtis. "Joe got out there," Sharpe recalled, "and the first time down the floor his man ran around him so fast he caught a cold in the breeze. Curtis took him out right then and never put him back. We got back to the old Lemke Hotel that night and Joe's standing there next to one of those great big four-poster beds in the room and he starts demonstrating how to defend a bed post. He's jumping around guarding a bed post in the hotel. And he's absolutely sober. When we stopped laughing, I finally told him, 'Joe, you know, you couldn't guard a bed post, either.' "

Basketball would bring laughter and tears for the remainder of his career and for a boy who once had nothing, it would bring him the respect and achievement for which he had longed.

Howard Lee Sharpe was born on January 5, 1916, in Vincennes. While still very young, he and his parents moved to Gary, Indiana, where he would spend most of his youth. Part of those opening day lectures of later years would recall those times when he grew up on the streets of Gary. He wasn't a gang member in the conventional sense, but he was a scrapper. He never was a big man, standing only 5-8, but he rarely balked at a challenge. "I didn't get my nose flattened and these scars on my arms from lookin' at the TV," he would say.

Somewhere in that youth the love of basketball took root. He played on his high school team at Lew Wallace High School, but difficult financial conditions imposed by the Depression prevented him from attending college immediately after high school. When he did leave for college, it was south to Terre Haute and to the former Indiana State Teachers College (now Indiana State University). Legend has it that Sharpe arrived in Terre Haute in 1936 via hitchhiking and without a penny in his pocket. He got a job as a dishwasher at a local restaurant and managed to get into ISTC. During his college career he also worked part-time as an usher at the Indiana Theatre.

He played for the Sycamores basketball team (he wore No. 57 one year) and played for Walter E. (Wally) Marks, a contemporary and former teammate of Tony Hinkle's, and Glenn Curtis, the legendary coach who had been John Wooden's mentor. The diminutive Sharpe bragged in later years that a yearbook photograph of that era revealed his great jumping ability. Perhaps the years inflated his vertical jump, but he clearly gave all of his energy on the court. He managed to survive in the classroom as well, failing to excel only in typewriting class where an understanding classmate with greater manual dexterity and speed managed to type both of their in-class assignments within the alloted time. He earned his baccalaureate degree in 1940 and began the job hunt.

The important first job came in 1940–41 at Clinton Township at Wanatah, Indiana, near LaPorte. The first season was a success as the team compiled a 15–7 record. Sharpe then spent two years at Monon where he compiled a 35–10 record and challenged for the sectional title when the school previously had enjoyed only limited success.

The 1942 Monon School yearbook records a particularly prescient assessment of the young coach's skills: "Mr. Sharpe first coached at Wanatah, Indiana. Here he enjoyed a successful season, winning 13 out of 20 games. This year at Monon is his second season of coaching and appears to be quite successful. He has proven to the students and to the people of Monon that he really knows his basketball, and we believe that he can stand toe-to-toe with any high school basketball coach in Indiana." Yet Monon would enjoy his services only two seasons.

The fourth coaching season was spent at Honey Creek High School in Vigo County. He finished the year 14–7. In April 1944, the spring after his first Honey Creek season, Sharpe was offered a teaching and coaching position at Gerstmeyer Technical High School. He accepted it and began a 27-year career at the school which ended only when the school closed in May 1971.

He would enjoy his greatest successes at Gerstmeyer. It was an oasis for him. He ran things pretty much his way and served as baseball coach during part of his tenure there. He also has coached football, tennis, and golf at various times during his career. He earned 509 baseball wins at Gerstmeyer and could claim one major leaguer for his efforts—the New York Yankees' Tommy John.

But his first love, and the main focus of community attention, came in the beloved Tech gym. It is a small place and, while the school was leveled after 1971, the gymnasium still stands and is used by a junior high school constructed on the site. Like many gyms of the era, it had a stage at one end and two tiers of seats. Noise resounded off the brick walls and reverberated to intimidate opponents. In the gym's projection booth, Sharpe would work each day at a desk in a makeshift office, working out the day's practice plan and keeping an eye on all of the activity below him. When school ended, he began molding basketball teams worthy of the state's highest honors.

The big year, the one which would thrill Sharpe and then haunt him in all of the years to follow, was 1953. No self-respecting Indiana basketball fan of the era could forget the playing trio with the lyrical identification: Harley, Arley, and Uncle Harold.

These were the Andrews boys. Arley and Harley were identical twins and Harold was, indeed, their uncle. Part of the mystery and controversy which would surround them was the fact that Arley wore #34 and Harley wore #43. And they were dead ringers. In the long years since that magical season, one that finished with a 31–4 record, Sharpe's enemies have accused him of switching jerseys in the locker room at halftime if one of the twins was hot and in foul trouble. How that would have achieved much is hard to imagine, for each was a talented player and, for Gerstmeyer to win, Sharpe needed them both on the floor. This would become painfully apparent in the season's finale. The Andrews boys and the team's guards, Jack Smith and Bill Bolk, were to reach the state championship game.

It was a period of great interest in basketball at Terre Haute. Other schools had excellent teams, but the Garfield and Wiley fans followed the Gerstmeyer fortunes once the Black Cats began to advance in the tournament. The school earned national attention that year when *Life* magazine sent photographers to the school for three days and captured for that publication not just basketball games, but cafeteria and classroom scenes as well. The new gymnasium, completed in January 1950, was being filled with as many bodies as school officials (and fire officials) could permit—somewhere between 1,500–1,600.

Sharpe had enjoyed previous successes at Tech, as the school also was known, most notably with a team led by future IU standout and Indiana Pacer coach Bobby Leonard in 1950. Leonard's senior season might have finished in the finals, according to Gerstmeyer fans, but an Ellettsville player hit a long shot at the horn of the regional title game that year and broke a tie to eliminate Gerstmeyer.

But the '53 unit was impressive, described by then Gerstmeyer athletic manager John J. Valle, as "very competitive" and as having "no selfishness." He points out that the Andrews twins were earning "80 percent" of the publicity, but the other players never complained. Harley Andrews would win the Trester Award that year, but the success of the twins was owing to Sharpe, a man who saw to it the boys ate at least one warm meal a day. "This was a poor family, but very honest," Valle recalls. The Andrews brothers were quite devoted to their family. Valle recalls that after the Semistate championship during their career, Arley and Harley went into the stands and brought their grandfather out to cut a piece of the victory net.

Among the legends—and a true one, at that—to come out of the '53 road to the finals was the halftime discussion during the Evansville Central game in the Semistate. The Black Cats were behind by 15 points and facing elimination. In the midst of the halftime talk, Harley spoke up: "Don't worry, Sharpie, it's only seven shots." It's not entirely clear whether Sharpe paled, fainted or used the assertion as a battle cry. John Valle, who was in the room, heard the words himself and then watched as the team rallied around Harley's boldness. Gerstmeyer hit approximately seven of its first nine shots, Valle recalls, and before the third quarter had ended the Black Cats

Arley Andrews (left) was No. 34 and his twin Harley was No. 43 when the official confused the two in the 1953 State Final, giving Arley, the team's best shooter, an extra foul in the second quarter. Arley eventually fouled out, and Gerstmeyer lost to South Bend Central. On the right is Sharpie in later life.

had caught and passed Central. Gerstmeyer won the game by 7 points, 78–71.

Thus Sharpe's first trip to the Final Four was assured. Gerstmeyer defeated Richmond in the afternoon, 48–40, to make the final game. The finale proved to be legendary because of the controversy which would evolve. The #43 and #34 confusion on the Andrews twins would work against Gerstmeyer. A foul whistled in the second quarter on Harley (official signal "four-three," "four-three") was marked in the scorebook as against Arley (official scorer interpretation "three-four," "three-four"). Sharpe caught the error almost immediately and pleaded with referee Don Polizotto to correct the mistake. No change occurred. Arley entered the fourth quarter with four fouls, three actual and one charged in error, and fouled out early in the period. Arley was perhaps the team's best shooter. Thus, Gerstmeyer would ever claim "we wuz robbed" with some reason. Sharpe later polled the 108 sportswriters and broadcasters on hand; his finding was unanimous favoring the Gerstmeyer position.

Still, the Black Cats hung close to South Bend Central until the end. Trailing, 42–41, Harley arched a two-hand set shot from the top of the key with three seconds remaining. If one watches the film carefully—an epic Sharpe kept in his locker the remainder of his career—a small man is standing in front of the Gerstmeyer bench. He watches the ball, leans with it, almost begging it to score. The shot hits the back of the flange and pops away. The man immediately throws his hands to his head. It is basketball agony at its most painful. The tragedy would be revealed in the later years when he knew that instant would be the closest he would reach to state championship glory. The man, of course, was Howard Sharpe. He cheerfully accepted his silver ring that night, but he rarely wore it. Somehow a second place ring didn't seem right.

The return to Terre Haute was glorious, however. It was in the old Tech gym that Sharpe made the assertion that he would bring a state championship to Terre Haute or die trying. While neither occurred, he would devote the remainder of his career to that goal. He was doomed to frustration.

Sharpe returned to the Final Four the next year and lost to Milan in the afternoon. He was back in '56 and '57, but fell in the afternoon games again. But that didn't alter the classic battles going on back on his home turf. Great games between rivals Gerstmeyer and Garfield, and thus between Sharpe and Willard Kehrt, drew huge crowds. Sharpe continued to be a master of the clinic speech and even tried his hand at invention.

The "Sharpie Goal" was a smaller rim attached to the backboard like a regular rim. The smaller rim would extend to a position away from the backboard equivalent to the exact center of a regular rim. In this way his teams could improve their shooting touch. McMillan's Sporting Goods of Terre Haute marketed the device, and Sharpe still collects royalty checks. Basketball coaches and carnival vendors all over the country have found use for the rim. Some of his innovations were less spectacular. Valle recalls the use of student managers holding aloft brooms to prepare Black Cat teams for taller opponents. The ploy was used again in the mid-70s, when Terre Haute North met Evansville Central's John Hollinden, a 7-4 shot swatter. And Sharpe's greatest skill—organization—still was in evidence in more modern times. He taught and supervised more than 300 student teachers in his career, and the first lesson they learned was the need for plans—practice plans and teaching plans. Practice always was mapped out well in advance, and each coach carried a copy of the day's plan. Drills were diagrammed and each minute of practice time was covered.

The modern-day Sharpe won great honors. He was inducted in the Indiana Basketball Hall of Fame in 1971, and it was an honor he greatly treasured. He was named National High School Basketball Coach of the Year in 1975, and he wore that ring with considerable pride. In December 1974, he won his 600th game, and another ring came his way to commemorate the occasion. IHSAA Commissioner Phil N.

Eskew was on hand to present the ring on behalf of North High School and praised Sharpe again as one of the hardest working coaches in the state.

But after 42 years times had changed. In the spring of 1982, the school board in Vigo County accepted the principal's recommendation not to reassign Sharpe to his basketball coaching position. The school community was divided over the matter, and that was evidence of Sharpe's ability to arouse controversy and emotion. Many of his former players came forward to fight for him, most of them from that '50s era. Sharpe was combative over the dismissal just like the games of old, making his parting from the basketball scene rather tragic. The career ended with 704 victories, 30 shy of Marion Crawley's state record 734. While Crawley coached fewer years than Sharpe, that did not deter Terre Haute's coaching legend from seeking the record for himself. Times had changed perhaps, but Howard Sharpe was still the scrapper of those days on the Gary streets.

So what of Howard Sharpe's coaching career can be remembered by his friends and foes? Perhaps the best portraits of Sharpe were in private moments, away from the crowds. He was at his happiest, it seemed, when teaching the youngsters during summer programs. He prowled the fields of Woodrow Wilson Junior High School teaching baseball for many summers. Former participants recall seeing Sharpe on the summer's hottest days wearing a safari hat with a handkerchief tied around his head to soak up perspiration. Yet he seemed tireless. The heat was equally taxing in the North High School gymnasium where Sharpe ran several programs a day for various age groups. The kids would bring him vegetables from the family garden, and Sharpe could not have been more thrilled with gold. Somehow the youngsters brought out his own youthfulness—for the world knows there is plenty of little boy left in any coach. He was relaxed, at ease, doing what he loved more than anything else: teaching the game of basketball.

Sharpe's career covered several eras. The two-hand set shot was no more by 1982. The center jump Sharpe had known as a player had long since been eliminated. He was known for longevity in a career that rarely keeps a man for many years. Sharpe claims the average coaching career lasts about seven years. He multiplied that number several times.

He is a proud, combative man—from the beginnings at Wanatah to the painful finish at Terre Haute he remained competitive. Even heart surgery in the spring of 1981 did not stop him; it only forced him to miss his first State Finals since the mid-1930s.

He was a coach of great devotion to his job and a man bent on achieving great things. He had grown up in tough times and tough territory. He had survived; he had beaten back the odds.

The best portrait of all is Sharpe at his desk, working over page after page of a legal pad. Each page is marked with X's and O's—hurriedly drawn foul lanes around which the X's and O's were to move. He was a general in the map room moving the troops. He was looking for an angle, a weakness. "There is an offense for every defense and a defense for every offense," he would say.

Thus, in the final analysis, friends and foes, teammates and opponents, would all concur the man left his mark on basketball. Howard Sharpe had a full career. He did not win the championship he wanted, but his greatest achievement may have been that he gave his all in its quest.

17

Some Other State-Championship Coaches

Cliff Wells (left) coached at Columbus, Bloomington and Logansport, winning the state championship with Bloomington in 1919 and at Logansport in 1934. Art Beckner (above) coached Muncie Central to the championship in 1951.

John Adams, the state championship Vincennes coach, whose teams won 38 straight—the longest streak until Crispus Attucks won 45 in 1955–56.

Orville Hooker (center), who coached New Castle's state champs in 1922, receives a plaque as the Hall of Fame's executive director in 1970 from Indianapolis Mayor Richard Lugar. Commissioner Phil Eskew of the IHSAA, Hall of Fame treasurer Nate Kaufman and historian Herb Schwomeyer received plaques at the same Indian Lake summer outing.

Herman Keller (right), newly appointed Indiana High School Athletic Association assistant commissioner, is being congratulated by Leo J. Costello (left), Loogootee, president of the Board of Control, and L. V. Phillips, commissioner of the IHSAA. Keller coached Bosse's state champs of 1944 and 1945.

On left, John Baratto (left), who won 484 games at East Chicago Washington, and top player Ron Divjak pick up the big IHSAA trophy after the 1960 state championship upset over Muncie Central. Two of Northern Indiana's greatest coaches got together before the 1966 state finals (right). John Baratto of East Chicago Washington and Doug Adams of Michigan City Elston, whose team won the 1966 State Finals.

Three of the best in action: Long-time Kokomo coaching great Joe Platt (left) shouts orders from the bench. He brought the Kats to a state championship in 1961. In the center is Louis (Bo) Mallard, who coached Gary Roosevelt to the Steel City's first state championship (1968). Jim Rausch (right) took the Bob Ford-led Evansville North team to a state title win over favored Lafayette Jeff in 1967.

Retiring Vincennes Coach Gunner Wyman had just won his last high school basketball game when this photo was shot—but it was a whopper. Wyman is shown hugging star scorer Doug Crook at the postgame celebration for the 1981 state champs.

Indianapolis Washington's Jerry Oliver gets a hug from his wife after winning the 1965 state title.

Coach Myron Dickerson (left) of Connersville's 1972 state champs with Mr. Basketball Phil Cox. On the right is seen Broad Ripple's Bill Smith (left) and Larry Liddle of Marion meeting Commissioner Ward Brown of the IHSAA (center) before their State Finals clash in 1980 won by Broad Ripple on a 57-foot shot as time expired. Broad Ripple went on to beat New Albany for the title.

18

Franklin's
Wonder Five—
1920–21–22

More than a half century ago Coach Ernest L. (Griz) Wagner and his Franklin Wonder Five clamped their stranglehold on three straight Indiana high school basketball championships. It established a record for Hoosier Hysteria that has withstood the assault of one super team after another down through the years.

Heading the famed Wonder Five in all three seasons from 1920 to 1922 was Robert P. (Fuzzy) Vandivier, still recognized by the best historians as one of the Hoosier state's all-time greats.

Fuzzy Vandivier and Coach Wagner were installed as charter members of the Indiana Hall of Fame in 1962, and in 1975 Fuzzy was named to his rightful spot in the Naismith national Hall of Fame at Springfield, Massachusetts.

Franklin compiled a spectacular 29–1 record in the 1920 season, mowing down Lafayette 31–13 in the state championship game played at Indiana University.

Vandivier was the only returning regular the next year, but Coach Wagner's mastery resulted in another standout 30–3 overall record defending the state title with a 35–22 triumph over Anderson in the 1921 tournament at the Indianapolis Coliseum.

Franklin was the pre-tourney favorite in 1922 with an all-veteran ball club, and sure enough the Wonder Five made it an incredible three straight state titles by whipping Terre Haute Garfield in the title bout, 26–15. It put the icing on a 30–4 season.

Wagner's unbelievable sweep to three straight championships set a phenomenal record that Hoosiers have labored to match for five

Franklin's 1920 Wonder Five: Burl Friddle, Ralph Hicks, Paul White, Fuzzy Vandivier, Sima Comer, John Gant, Harold Borden, Harvey Keeling, and Coach Ernest (Griz) Wagner.

decades—it still stands. And Fuzzy Vandivier was singled out for another special honor being named to the all-state tournament team all three years.

John Gant was the only other player to have a hand in all three Franklin state titles.

Coach Wagner moved his Wonder Five just a few feet south to Franklin College where the Grizzlies worked their magic on such big name powers as Notre Dame, Wisconsin, Marquette, and Purdue. Their only loss in a 17–1 freshman season was to Indiana.

They were even better as sophomores with 19–1 counting Wisconsin, Notre Dame, and Marquette on their casualty list. The Wonder Five trimmed Notre Dame twice, Wisconsin, Purdue, and the Michigan Aggies on the way to a 15–3 mark as juniors.

It wasn't until their senior year in college that injuries, ineligibilities, and sickness beset the Wonder Five, and their magic seemed to fade. Vandivier's unbelievable career was cut short by a serious back ailment. Fuzzy was named as the top player on the same all-Western team with Notre Dame's Noble Kizer and Michigan's Harry Kipke.

Indiana's greatest basketball player was walking to the shower room after his last game, *Indianapolis News* sports editor Bill Fox noted. More than 200 times he had done this. The path was victorious most of the time; occasionally defeat had been a visitor.

Now that it's all over, which part was the best part, Vandivier was asked. "The high school days," he answered unhesitatingly.

Vandivier went on to coach the Franklin High School team (1926–44), winning almost every sectional tourney until 1940, reaching the Semistate twice, and traveling all the way to the state championship game in 1939 before losing to Frankfort, 36–22.

He stayed on as athletic director for 18 years following his coaching retirement and didn't end his teaching career until 1968.

Burl Friddle, who starred on Franklin's 1920 state title winner,

The 1921 champs. Front: Robert (Fuzzy) Vandivier and Carlyle Friddle; second row: Harry King, Harold Borden, James Ross, Hubert Davis; back row: John Gant, Ike Ballard, Charlton Williams; Coach Griz Wagner stands in the back.

went on to coach state championship teams at Washington in 1930 and Fort Wayne South in 1938.

Members of Franklin's first state championship ball club in 1920, in addition to Vandivier and Burl Friddle, were Paul White, Harvey Keeling, Sima Comer, Ralph Hicks, Harold Borden, and Gant. Vandivier, Borden, and Gant were joined in 1921 by Carlyle Friddle (Burl Friddle's brother), James Ballard, Harry King, James Ross, Hubert Davis, and Charlton Williams. All but Borden returned in 1922 when

No, you're not seeing double. This is the 1922 Wonder Five. Front: Robert (Fuzzy) Vandivier and Carlyle Friddle; second row: John Gant and James Ross; back row: Harry King, Ike Ballard, Coach Griz Wagner, Charlton Williams and Hubert Davis.

they became prohibitive favorites to bag a third straight state championship.

It all began in 1920 when Franklin won 19 of its 20 regular season games and outscored opponents by a staggering 856–363 margin.

Martinsville was the only school to hold a victory over the state-title-bound Franklin crew. It came in a memorable Christmas Eve classic played on the Martinsville floor and the score was 24–18. Franklin later reversed that loss at home with a 41–32 overtime victory over the same Martinsville outfit.

Coach Wagner's Franklin ball club survived perhaps its toughest test in the state tourney semifinals when it had to battle overtime to slip past Anderson, 14–12.

Franklin owed its first state championship to a pair of standout forwards—White and Vandivier.

White led state tourney scoring with 66 points in the five games and Vandivier was just an eyelash behind with his 64. It was written that White combined headwork with speed, and he worked inside the foul line with deadly accuracy. Vandivier was steadiness itself and thrilled the capacity tourney crowds as a feeder for White.

With White out of the game on personal fouls and the score 12–11

Fuzzy Vandivier and John Gant—two key members of the old Franklin Wonder Five—are pictured in front of a store window decoration boosting another Franklin team on the way to the State Finals tournament in 1973.

in favor of Anderson, Vandivier was a lifesaver in the semifinal round with his game-tying free throw in the clutch. It sent the two state tourney powers into overtime where the incomparable Fuzzy came through once more with a game-deciding long shot.

Vandivier led Franklin scoring with 10 points in the Anderson overtime struggle even though he missed seven shots at the foul line—a rarity for him. He offset that with 17 points in the 31–13 state title win over Lafayette, including seven of nine free throws.

Franklin opened up a quick 14–4 lead on Lafayette in the final tilt with Vandivier and White scoring almost every point. It was 17–8 at half-time and Lafayette couldn't come closer than 18–10 in the second half. Franklin was in complete control with 53 shots from the field and handcuffed Lafayette with a defense that gave up just 30 in return.

Purdue's Piggy Lambert called Friddle the best high school player in the nation. Vandivier, White, and Friddle all were named first team all-state. Keeling was voted to the second team.

Vandivier was high point man one year later with 488 points when Franklin compiled a spectacular 30–3 record and outclassed Anderson for its second straight state title. Johnny Gant was No. 2 scorer with 274 points and Carlyle Friddle third with 167.

Fuzzy Vandivier led state tourney scoring with 44 points in four games. The Wonder Five defeated Martinsville, 27–24; Rochester,

Tony Hinkle's All-Time Dream Team (selected March 28, 1972). Front: Robert
(Fuzzy) Vandivier, Franklin; Tony Hinkle, Butler University; Bobby Plump, Milan;
John Townsend, Indianapolis Tech; back: George McGinnis, Indianapolis
Washington; Willie Gardner, Crispus Attucks; Oscar Robertson, Crispus Attucks;
Homer Stonebraker, Wingate; and Bob Ford, Evansville North.

19–18; Lafayette, 17–12, and finally Anderson by a more comfortable
35–22 margin in the windup.

Franklin led Anderson by a wide 21–20 margin at half-time paced
once more by Vandivier who had a game high 13 points. Gant and
Carlyle Friddle also contributed five field goals each.

A basket in the last 30 seconds by substitute forward Darby Davis
rescued Franklin in its one-point state tourney cliff hanger with
Rochester. Robbins, a standout floor guard, accounted for all 18
points scored by the Rochester team.

Franklin jumped off to a 10–0 lead on Martinsville but the Artesians rebounded stubbornly to deadlock the score in the closing
minutes.

The State Finals (16 teams) were moved from Indiana University to
the Indianapolis Fairgrounds Coliseum for the first time, and a standing room crowd of more than 7,200 was on hand.

Vandivier played the center position on Franklin's second state title
winner, and he was easily the class of the tourney. In the early state
tourney games when his forwards were not scoring too well, Vandivier carried the load despite the fact that he was a marked man.

Anderson concentrated its defense on Vandivier in the state championship game to such an extent that Friddle and Gant were able to penetrate for several easy shots underneath.

Vandivier's work following shots was uncanny at times and his dribbling, passing and timing made possible shot after shot for his teammates.

Heze Clark wrote in the old *Indianapolis Times*: "Team play of the most wonderful sort won for Franklin and the Lion's share of the honors must go to the wiry, quiet little man who sat on the bench and watched the machine he had built win the state championship. That man is Griz Wagner, coach of Franklin High School.

"Like flashes of lightning, Friddle, Gant, Ballard and Vandivier swept down the floor with the ball. The passing and handling of the ball was so fast and clever that the Anderson defense melted. . . ."

Clark added, "Four times Friddle slipped behind Anderson's McFarland for close-up baskets and once he caged the ball on a long shot. Five times Gant dropped the ball through the draperies, but it was the play of Vandivier, the best basketball player developed in many years in the high schools of the state, that stood out far above that of any man on the floor." Vandivier was named first team all-state and Gant was named to the second team.

Franklin closed the season with 1,206 points to only 589 for its opponents averaging 41 points per game while allowing the enemy just 17. It was a great testimonial to Wagner's masterful coaching, building another state champ around Vandivier—his only holdover starter from 1920.

Losing only Harold Borden by graduation, Franklin's path to a third state title in 1922 was much easier by comparison. Franklin carved out another phenomenal 30–4 record and beat most opponents on the tourney trail by 10 or more points.

Franklin mowed down Evansville, 27–16; Bedford, 32–15; Bloomington, 33–17, and Garfield of Terre Haute 26–15 for the title. The Wonder five shot .250 from the field for the four state tourney games.

Garfield led briefly 11–10 in the final before Vandivier and Gant took charge.

They showed the way for the Wonder Five and 10 straight points all but wrapped up the third straight title. Vandivier led state tourney scoring with 47 points, and Gant was just as outstanding with 45. Gant led everybody with 22 field goals in the tourney and a .393 shooting average. Vandivier was a unanimous choice for the all-state tourney team for the third straight time—a rare feat in Hoosier Hysteria records.

Burl Friddle was singled out later by Vandivier as one of the toughest competitors on the whole Wonder five squad. He started out at center and then moved back to guard. Of course, the backcourt players didn't shoot then the way they do now.

Gant, who stood only about 5-10, played forward and was an excellent shooter. He had a good head on his shoulders and made very few mistakes. He could score and was a good ballhandler, according to Fuzzy.

Coach Wagner was a fine Christian man and in the words of Vandivier "He'd make you want to die for him." The Wonder Five coach who died in 1934 preached ball control and the passing game long before Indiana University's Bobby Knight came to the Hoosier state.

"We played for the open man and always tried to get the ball inside," Vandivier explained. "On defense we had the zone and we also had a shifting man to man. We never even dreamed about all the pressing defenses that you see in high school and college ball today. Of course, you didn't see near as much scoring and people like scoring. The pros have been very influential in changing the game from our low-scoring offenses in the old days to the high scoring you see now."

Fuzzy talked about the small gyms that teams used in the old days. "Gyms were just like shoe boxes when we played, but I think playing in close quarters like that actually taught us to be good ballhandlers and it also led to better foot control," he remarked.

There has been much controversy in recent years revolving around the four-corner offense used by Bill Harrell to win two state championships at Muncie Central in 1978-79 and by many college coaches.

"It's nothing new," says Vandivier. "Everett Case had it when he won four state championships with Frankfort. Case would make you come out after the ball, and we always tried to protect a lead that way."

Vandivier believes the Franklin record of three straight state championships will be broken someday. "I'm surprised that it's held up this long, and it'll be broken one of these days. I really thought Muncie might do it because Harrell knows his stuff. He made good use of the small guard and that was the difference both times in 1978-79," he observed.

One of the highest honors to be paid any high school basketball player in the Hoosier state came many years after Fuzzy Vandivier's playing days had ended. Almost 50 years after the Wonder Five completed their sweep of three state championships, Fuzzy was named to Tony Hinkle's all-time Dream Team. Hinkle was one the nation's winningest coaches for 44 years at Butler University, and Vandivier was hand-picked on his Dream Team that also included Johnny Wooden and Oscar Robertson.

"Fuzzy had great hands and feet. I studied his fundamentals for a long time and it was very helpful in my own coaching," said Hinkle, who piled up more than 600 victories before retiring in 1970.

Homer Stonebraker, John Townsend, Willie Gardner, Bobby Plump, Bob Ford, George McGinnis, and James Bradley were the other all-time greats selected by Hinkle.

Franklin

Season Record (29–1)
1919–20

Franklin	60	Center Grove	8
Franklin	35	Anderson	28
Franklin	37	Spiceland	4
Franklin	34	Columbus	21
Franklin	35	Lebanon	13
Franklin	26	Shelbyville	14
Franklin	43	Rushville	7
Franklin	63	Hopewell	9
Franklin	18	Martinsville	24
Franklin	39	North Vernon	18
Franklin	57	Tipton	10
Franklin	22	Indianapolis Tech	14
Franklin	36	Shelbyville	19
Franklin	46	Indianapolis Shortridge	13
Franklin	41	Martinsville	32
Franklin	48	Columbus	7
Franklin	42	Scottsburg	13
Franklin	20	Bedford	17
Franklin	30	Anderson	24
Franklin	55	Rushville	7
Franklin	27	Spiceland	23

State Finals Sectional (Franklin College)

Franklin	57	Ninevah	14
Franklin	32	Shelbyville	5
Franklin	34	Hopewell	17
Franklin	49	Whiteland	14

State Finals (Indiana University)

Franklin	43	Young America	15
Franklin	30	Normal	8
Franklin	28	Bedford	12
Franklin	14	Anderson (Overtime)	12
Franklin	31	Lafayette	13

Season Record (30–3)
1920–21

Franklin	28	Whiteland	13
Franklin	45	Center Grove	19

Franklin	70	Greenwood	4
Franklin	59	Spiceland	3
Franklin	76	Hopewell	13
Franklin	41	Columbus	17
Franklin	33	Anderson	44
Franklin	26	Spiceland	11
Franklin	36	Indianapolis Tech	20
Franklin	19	Martinsville	11
Franklin	54	Columbus	8
Franklin	63	Tipton	14
Franklin	39	Crawfordsville	21
Franklin	45	Bloomington	31
Franklin	19	Shelbyville	25
Franklin	20	Bedford	16
Franklin	31	Anderson	27
Franklin	31	Lebanon	34
Franklin	29	Crawfordsville	25
Franklin	34	Shelbyville	17
Franklin	38	Bedford	18
Franklin	35	Bloomington (Overtime)	36
Franklin	42	Indianapolis Shortridge	8
Franklin	39	New Castle	11

State Finals Sectional (Franklin College)

Franklin	38	Waldron	5
Franklin	52	Center Grove	12
Franklin	38	Morristown	7
Franklin	26	Shelbyville	14

Regional (Indiana University)

Franklin	43	Sullivan	9

State Finals (Indianapolis–Coliseum)

Franklin	24	Martinsville	21
Franklin	19	Rochester	18
Franklin	17	Lafayette	12
Franklin	35	Anderson	22

Season Record (30–4)
1921–22

Franklin	57	Greensburg	7
Franklin	64	Fairland	7
Franklin	43	Center Grove	14
Franklin	50	Muncie Central	17
Franklin	38	Lebanon	21
Franklin	34	Shelbyville	26
Franklin	25	Anderson	21
Franklin	17	Martinsville	18
Franklin	44	Lebanon	20
Franklin	31	Columbus	29
Franklin	28	Indianapolis Shortridge	13
Franklin	25	Frankfort	17
Franklin	26	Muncie Central	21
Franklin	35	Newcastle	18
Franklin	39	Shelbyville	20

Franklin	29	Gary Froebel	17
Franklin	21	Gary Emerson	29
Franklin	29	Martinsville	16
Franklin	38	Indianapolis Manual	20
Franklin	24	Bedford	33
Franklin	26	Anderson	28
Franklin	26	Bloomington	24
Franklin	58	Indianapolis Tech	15
Franklin	52	Columbus	19
Franklin	46	Bedford	21
Franklin	36	Bloomington	30

State Finals Sectional (Franklin College)

Franklin	77	Geneva	9
Franklin	60	Waldron	6
Franklin	52	Whiteland	3
Franklin	33	Shelbyville	20

State Finals Regional (Indiana University)

| Franklin | 51 | Scottsburg | 6 |

State Finals (Indianapolis–Coliseum)

Franklin	27	Evansville Central	16
Franklin	32	Bedford	15
Franklin	33	Bloomington	17
Franklin	26	Terre Haute Garfield	15

19

David and Goliath— Milan's Magic Moment in 1954

Some say it was destiny, and some say it was magic—tiny Milan's miraculous, storybook 32–30 upset of mighty Muncie Central on Bobby Plump's legendary 15-foot jumper as time ticked away in the 1954 state championship classic.

Even Coach Marvin Wood who perfected Milan's much-discussed cat-and-mouse game (a forerunner of North Carolina's now famed four-corner offense) and his designated shooter agree nearly three decades later it was almost too good to be true.

How could Milan, one of the state's smallest schools with an enrollment of 162, put the handcuffs on perennial state tourney power Muncie Central—winner of four state championships at the time and three more since that incredible night? The only losses were to Frankfort and Aurora in a 28–2 season, and Aurora was beaten later in the regional.

It could happen only in Hoosier Hysteria, and every young man who's picked up a basketball with childhood dreams in the years that followed has heard the marvelous story. The players are approaching middle age, but Milan lives on in the hearts of all Indiana high school basketball fanatics.

"Now that I look back on it, I'm not so sure it wasn't destiny," says Wood, who just recently ended a long and successful career that took him to New Castle, North Central in Indianapolis, Shelbyville, and Mishawaka.

"Woody was a coach ahead of his time, at least in Southeastern Indiana," Plump believes. "He brought a disciplined offense to our part of the state which up to that time had been schooled mainly on freelance basketball."

Glen Butte, Roger Schroder and Gene White corner Bobby Plump in this alley ball game behind the Schroder family store in downtown Pierceville.

Coach Wood not only developed the ball-control offense in his two years at Milan, he also made good use of a trapping zone press defense, even though he had been a strict advocate of man-to-man defenses as a graduate of the Tony Hinkle system at Butler University.

Later Johnny Wooden relied on the same pressing defense to win a record-setting 10 NCAA championships at UCLA. Milan is said to be the third team to win the state tourney using a zone, following Bloomington in 1919 and Jasper in 1949.

Plump reminds everyone that the press produced two big turnovers late in the championship game against Muncie and one was converted into the basket that deadlocked the score.

Foul rules in those days also called for two penalty shots in the last three minutes, and that turned out to be another fringe benefit for Woody's cat-and-mouse offense. Milan sank 69 free throws in its last four state tournament games, becoming the first champion to hit more charity tosses than field goals.

"Our winning the state championship sure changed a lot of lives in Milan," Plump said. "Not just for the 10 kids on the team, either. It opened up college to Milan kids for the next eight to 10 years."

Ray Craft, Plump's running mate in the backcourt at Milan and later at Butler University, said "Any success I might have had in my lifetime after that has to do with us winning. I came from a large family that owned an 80-acre farm. I got a scholarship to Butler. I became a teacher, a coach, and an administrator. I appreciate it."

Craft now is the principal at Shelbyville High School, and Plump runs his own insurance agency in Indianapolis.

Plump was the winner of the Trester Award presented each year to an outstanding student-athlete in the state tourney and later was voted Mr. Basketball with the Indiana All-Star team for the traditional Blind Fund series against Kentucky's best seniors in June.

Bobby had been recruited heavily in his 2½ years as a starter but

Bobby Plump shoots over South Bend Central's Bob Scannell (#54) in the 1953 State Finals, and Jack Wiltrout (#55) waits under the basket. South Bend bested Milan this year and went on to beat Terre Haute Gerstmeyer 42–41 that night for the state championship. But Milan would be back.

winning the state championship rewarded the rest of the team with a chance to attend college. Nine of the 10 Milan players went on to college and eight finished.

Plump set single season and career scoring records at Butler and then he played four seasons with the Phillips 66 Oilers in the National

Bobby Plump drives under for this lay-up against Crispus Attucks in the 1954 Semistate. That's Oscar Robertson of Attucks watching Plump from the other side along with Gene White (#33). Oscar was a sophomore.

Industrial League. Phillips won the league in his second season on the team but lost out in the Olympic trials. A pretty fair team of collegians including Oscar Robertson, Terry Dischinger, John Havlicek, and Jerry West represented Uncle Sam in Rome.

Plump and three other members of that 1954 state championship ball club lived in Pierceville about three miles down the road from Milan in Ripley County. Roger Schroder is now coach at Marshall High School in Indianapolis, Gene White still teaches at Milan, and Glen Butte is athletic director at Batesville High School.

Rollin Cutter is in the Noblesville school system, Ron Truitt is a school principal in Houston, Bob Engel is in business at Kalamazoo, Bill Jordan became an actor in Hollywood, and Ken Wendleman still lives in Milan. Wood was inducted in the Indiana Hall of Fame in 1975, and Plump followed in his footsteps in 1981.

Bobby Plump held the ball at midcourt for more than four minutes in the famed 32–30 state championship game in 1954. Plump is guarded here by Muncie Central's Jimmy Barnes.

Milan's enrollment now doubles the school's size in 1954, and the town's population has grown somewhat from 1,150. Even in those days Milan was a metropolis next to Pierceville.

"I don't know the size of Pierceville, but I would say 45 people or maybe 50 at most," Plump likes to tell his audiences on frequent basketball banquet speaking engagements.

"We had a grocery store, a service station, and a post office, but they were all in the same building. Roger Schroder's dad ran the store, Gene White's father ran the feed store, and Butte's father drove trucks and farmed."

Plump swears that the Pierceville entrance and exit signs were fastened to the same post.

The Mighty Men of Milan, as they were affectionately tagged by different members of the press, still get together each Easter for their reunions and they probably do a lot of reminiscing.

You can still find old photos showing Plump and the others playing on some outdoor court in Pierceville. They hung a light bulb from a shovel handle with a tin reflector and played until midnight, according to Plump.

It was better than Roger Schroder's barn, where the upstairs loft

After the victory comes the net cutting, and it's Bobby Plump's honor to perform.

was equipped with a basketball goal, but it was precariously close to a door that opened up over a manure pile below.

"We had no telephone or indoor plumbing in those days, and I took the call telling me that I had been named Mr. Basketball over at Schroder's store," said Plump.

Marvin Wood came to Milan from French Lick at age 24 in 1952, after Herman Grinstead had been dismissed as coach in a dispute over ordering new basketball suits without the principal's okay.

Grinstead had elevated Plump and several other sophomores the previous year, following an especially embarrassing 85–40 loss to Osgood. Plump, Engel, and Truitt all had the flu, missed the sectional, and Batesville handed Milan a 10-point trimming.

Wood put in his disciplined offense and made several other revolutionary changes that were totally unfamiliar to the good folks of Milan and other Southeastern Indiana fans. They assured Marvin that he couldn't win with that stuff in much the same way that old Indiana University fans first received Bobby Knight's new look for the Hurryin' Hoosiers.

But Coach Wood and Knight came up with the same winning results, and by sectional time Woody had won over a lot of converts with his track record. "My junior and senior years, they would hold raffles to see who could buy a ticket for the county tourney and the sectionals," Plump recalled. It was the same in many basketball-nutty towns around the Hoosier state.

Wood also was a strict disciplinarian. Plump and Jim Wendelman found out the hard way before the county tourney in the 1953 season. They were suspended for one game for staying out past the 1 A.M. curfew on New Year's Eve.

"We had been fixing a flat tire in front of my house when Coach Wood drove up," Plump related. "My watch showed 1 o'clock but his read 1:05. I'll never forget it—he said we'd go by his watch, and I didn't dress for that first game in the county tourney." Plump and Wendelman hoped the game would be close and that they would be missed, but Milan won by 19.

Coach Wood had to do some adapting of his own, changing over from the man-to-man defense he preferred to the zone. He learned much about the zone from eighth grade coach Mark Combs.

"I had more trouble adjusting to the zone than the boys," Wood admitted later. "But I found out shortly that you can get some things done with a zone defense that you couldn't do with the man-to-man."

Milan became accustomed to Wood's coaching by the end of the season. The Indians won the sectional but had never won a game on several trips to the regional and that set up one of the most exciting chapters in the entire Milan story.

Milan trailed Morton Memorial by two points in that first regional

The Milan miracle makers of 1954. Front: Bobby Plump, Gene White, Ron Truitt, Bob Engel, Ray Craft; back row: Coach Marvin Wood, Rollin Cutter, Ken Wendelman, Glen Butte, Bill Jordan and Roger Schroder.

Small-town heroes Gene White, Bobby Plump and Ron Truitt are grilled by the younger generation on Milan school steps after the miracle.

game at Rushville when the clock stopped with less than one minute to go. It broke and was unplugged so there was a big controversy over the official time.

How much extra time ticked off was uncertain but Milan hit a pair of free throws with no time remaining. Then Plump sank two free throws in the sudden death second overtime and Milan went on to the Sweet 16.

"It was the first time Milan ever won a game in the regional, and they'd been there four or five times. I didn't know that, and there were a lot of other things we didn't know. It was probably best that we didn't because there wasn't any pressure.

"We beat Connersville that night in a cat-and-mouse game and then the whole state really got behind us," Plump said.

Milan's good luck continued the next week in the Indianapolis Semistate at Butler Fieldhouse when Milan defeated Attica in overtime and then walloped Shelbyville 43–21 in the Semistate title tilt, holding the Golden Bears to just two field goals. Shelbyville had already upset mighty Crispus Attucks of Indianapolis.

Going to the State Finals the next week was an incredible experience for Milan. The players had heard other state tourney games on the radio, but for most it was their first sight of the State Finals.

Plump scored 19 points but eventual state champ South Bend Central ended Milan's tournament bid in the afternoon round, 56–37. "I felt we were a team of destiny because we made it to the Final Four that first year, and we were terrible," said Coach Wood. "We shouldn't have been there in 1953. We beat teams that were better than we were because most of them had their poorest game against us.

"I was so upset that I even thought about going back to college as a graduate assistant because I felt I didn't have the background to do the boys justice. . . . But the next year we had some class. I felt we were destined or we wouldn't have had the chance to go back the second time."

It has been written that Wood laid the foundation for 1954 in the final game of the 1953 season against Osgood. Milan was scheduled to visit Osgood's small gym, and Coach Wood hoped to avert injury and save the team's strength by moving the ball from side to side in a time-consuming offense. The game site was moved to a bigger gym at Versailles, but the ball control plan would still be used.

Plump was positioned near the mid-court line, with two teammates spread to either side and parallel with the free-throw line. The other two players were stationed in the corners along the baseline. They would pass the ball or dribble, with Plump and Craft free to drive the middle. When the opportunity was there, somebody either drove down the lane or pulled up for the short jumper.

It was used by many coaches as a stall in succeeding years, but it

Mrs. Kohlerman gives her personal attention to Gene White in her composition class. Seated in the next row are Bobby Plump and Roger Schroder.

wasn't invented for that purpose by Wood. Plump pointed out that the Indians used it as a strategic offensive weapon, scoring 65 points against Crispus Attucks in the Semistate and 60 against Terre Haute Gerstmeyer in the State Finals leading up to the big showdown with Muncie Central for the title. Milan's 65–52 win over Attucks (Oscar Robertson's sophomore year) was the biggest margin ever over a Ray Crowe-coached team in tourney play.

Wood felt the cat-and-mouse was essential in some games because of Milan's lack of size. Milan's tallest was Ron Truitt at 6–2, but the center, Gene White, was 5–11—one inch taller than Plump. By comparison, Muncie's John Casterlow was 6–5, Jim Hinds was 6–4, and Gene Flowers 6–2.

So Milan went to the cat-and-mouse from the start against Muncie

Milan's Bobby Plump (seated, middle) was installed in the Indiana Basketball Hall of Fame in 1981 at the Downtown Convention Center in Indianapolis. He was snapped in this photo along with Commissioner Ward Brown of the IHSAA, Hall of Fame president Sam Scheivley and Hall of Famer Earl Townsend.

and as it turned out the strategy backfired at first. Rollin Cutter (a sophomore) replaced Bob Engel in the Milan lineup because Engel was having back problems.

"We still grabbed a quick 15–7 or 15–8 lead on Muncie in the opening minutes," Plump remembered. "But then for the first time since we first used it, the cat-and-mouse lost its effectiveness and Muncie caught up."

Milan led 25–17 at the half, but Muncie took the lead at 28–26 by holding Milan without a field goal in the third quarter.

"We felt that if we could hang in there toward the end of the game our experience would finally pay off," Coach Wood said. All Hoosier

Hysteria knows now that hanging in there meant for Plump to let the air out of the ball in the middle of Hinkle Fieldhouse with 15,000 screaming fans looking on in amazement.

Plump held the ball under one arm and then the other for four minutes and 14 seconds with Muncie holding a 28–26 lead. It was not the longest stall all year for Milan. They held the ball for six minutes against a high-ranking Connersville team in the regional.

The State Finals crowd was more bewildered than angered to think that Milan was holding the ball while trailing Muncie by two points.

"Everybody was going crazy wondering what the hell is going on out there. We're behind in the tournament and yet we're holding the ball," Plump explained. "I looked over at Coach Wood, and he's just sitting there nonchalantly rolling his ankle."

Wood told writers later that while the boys were holding the ball he was trying to think of something to do.

After a time-out, Plump moved in for a jump shot and missed. Muncie rebounded but threw the ball away against Milan's press. Craft tied the game with a jump shot a short time later, 28–28. Plump hit two free throws for a 30–28 Milan edge with 1:42 left, Craft missed what would have been a game-clinching lay-up with under a minute on the clock and Muncie tied it at 30–30. Somebody quipped that Plump might be back in Pierceville today pumping gas if Craft had made that layup. Plump held the ball once again until 18 seconds remained and Milan took another timeout.

Wood felt that Plump's quickness and savvy could beat his defender, Muncie's Jimmy Barnes. And although Plump had hit just two of 10 shots in the game, Wood knew that Bobby was the one to take the final shot.

Gene White suggested that the rest of the team clear out on one side to give Plump all the room he needed to maneuver.

Coach Wood diagrammed the play. "Pass the ball in to Plump. When Bobby crosses the line, everybody else clear to one side away from him. Bobby, with about 8 seconds to go, you start for the basket. Drive, shoot a jump shot, but don't shoot too early so they will have time to get another shot."

Plump almost spoiled the plan right away by taking the ball out of bounds himself. "I passed it to Craft and then he got the ball back to me. It wasn't exactly what Marvin wanted, but we never heard any complaints from him later," Plump declared.

The rest is part of Hoosier Hysteria folklore. Plump crossed midcourt, faked to the left and dribbled to his right. He stopped about 15 feet out and shot over Jimmy Barnes. The shot went "Plump" and it was Milan 32, Muncie 30.

"Yes, I knew," Plump agreed. "When you shoot, you usually know when it's good."

"The cows back home can milk themselves for a while now," said Coach Wood.

"I received a piece of mail later addressed 'Plump, Indiana,' " Bobby recalled.

Special permission was granted by the state athletic association for an extra set of jackets for the players, but other gifts were not permitted. One firm offered a three-week trip to Europe for the team.

Each week the Indians rode to the tournament in a more stylish automobile: Chevrolets in the sectional, Pontiacs in the regional, Buicks in the Semistate and Cadillacs for the State Finals. The champs made the 80-mile ride back home in Jaguars. Indianapolis policeman Pat Stark led the escort both years, and the Chris Volz agency in Milan provided the cars.

"I remember riding around Monument Circle in Indianapolis backwards with a police escort, and every community recognized us on the way back to Milan," Craft said.

"It started out as a fairy tale and ended an epic," Corky Lamm wrote in the *Indianapolis News.*

It was the improbability of small school Milan clobbering the establishment which endeared one of the smallest schools to the entire state. Not since Thorntown in 1915 had a school of such size won the title. And proponents of class basketball still use the Milan example to denote the inequities in Indiana's unique one-class tournament.

"Milan would not be Milan if we had class basketball in 1954," Craft offered.

"If Milan was the Class Two champ it wouldn't be near as significant," Plump agreed.

"There was talk about class basketball then and it gave impetus for a short period of time that really could shatter the myths that small schools can't compete with large schools. There is the opportunity for the small school to upset the larger school. That has made Hoosier Hysteria," he added.

Memories of Milan's Cinderella team have faded, along with all the old newspaper clippings saluting that incredible feat. None summed it up better than Tiny Hunt in the *Osgood Journal,* March 25, 1954:

"Indiana is still the best state in the USA for basketball and Milan made it a little better Saturday night."

Milan

Season Record (28–2)
1953–54

Milan	52	Rising Sun	36
Milan	65	Vevay	41
Milan	36	Osgood	31
Milan	61	Seymour	43
Milan	24	Brookville	20
Milan	67	Hanover	36
Milan	50	Lawrenceburg	41
Milan	39	Versailles	35
Milan	47	Frankfort	49
Milan	52	Columbus	49
Milan	74	Rising Sun	60

Versailles County Tourney

Milan	52	Versailles	46
Milan	36	Napoleon	30
Milan	40	Holton	30
Milan	58	Hanover	32
Milan	42	Sunman	36
Milan	61	Napoleon	29
Milan	49	Versailles	42
Milan	38	North Vernon	37
Milan	45	Aurora	54
Milan	38	Osgood	30

Sectional (Versailles)

Milan	83	Cross Plains	36
Milan	44	Osgood	32
Milan	57	Versailles	43

Regional (Rushville)

Milan	58	Rushville	34
Milan	46	Aurora	38

Semifinal (Indianapolis, Butler Fieldhouse)

Milan	44	Montezuma	34
Milan	65	Crispus Attucks (Indianapolis)	52

State Finals (Indianapolis, Butler Fieldhouse)

Milan	60	Terre Haute Gerstmeyer	48
Milan	32	Muncie Central	30

20

Wingate Had Stoney in 1913–14 —Enrollment of 12 Boys

Tiny Wingate had an enrollment of 12 boys in the first creative years of Hoosier Hysteria but one of the 12 was Homer Stonebraker. Stoney was the big Enforcer in his day when the small Montgomery County school turned back South Bend Central in five overtimes, 15–14, for the 1913 state championship and then came back the next year to repeat with a lop-sided 36–8 win over Anderson. Stonebraker went on to be named All-American three years in a row at nearby Wabash College.

"No game has changed as much over the years as basketball. It is the only sport in which stars of other eras readily admit they would have no place in the modern version," Bob Collins once proclaimed in the *Indianapolis Star.*

"Still, I remember conversations from back in the days when I made a living chasing basketball around Indiana. I would ask old-timers who had watched or played in the early years, if there were any players from that era who could cut it with the modern run-and-gun gang.

"Glad to oblige, they would rummage around in their memories and come up with a few names. The lists varied with the individuals, but three names usually tumbled out first. They were Homer Stonebraker, Fuzzy Vandivier [Franklin], and Johnny Wooden [Martinsville]."

Stonebraker, who died December 9, 1977, at the age of 82, starred for a Wingate team that captured the third and fourth state championships. As Collins pointed out, Stoney was present for the creation.

And at one time he was generally recognized as the finest basketball player in the nation.

During the 1912–13 season Wingate had a 16–4 record, losing twice to county seat Crawfordsville, 15–13 and 25–22; Lebanon, 44–25; and Thorntown, 23–22. Jesse A. Wood was the Wingate coach, and his seven-man squad included forwards Leland Olin and Forest Crane, Stonebraker at center, with Jesse Graves and John Blacker at guards. McKinley Murdock and Lee Sinclair were the subs.

They captured the two-day tourney played at Indiana University by downing Whiting, 24–12; Rochester, 19–17 in overtime; Indianapolis Manual, 16–11; Lafayette Jeff, 23–14; and then South Bend in the 5-overtime final.

"Our school had only about 60 students in 1913 and the town's population was between 400 and 500," recalls Coach Wood, who later moved to Shoals and became Martin County extension agent for 34 years.

"I still remember the sendoff the folks gave us when we decided to compete in the tourney. They followed us down to the taxi stand where we hired two Model-T cabs to take us to Crawfordsville. From there we rode the Monon train to Bloomington for the state tourney."

Wood said his team's uniforms consisted of baseball trousers, long

Homer Stonebraker (left) of Wingate's 1913–14 state champs and Coach Jesse Wood at the time of Wood's induction into the Hall of Fame in 1973.

socks, and sweat shirts. "We didn't have a gym at Wingate so we would go by buggy or Model-T six miles to New Richmond for practice and games," he explained.

Wingate had more than one tough game in the state finals that year, going an extra period against Rochester and then coming from behind to beat Manual of Indianapolis. Manual held an 11–5 lead at half-time and then Wingate shut out the Indianapolis ball club, 11–0, the rest of the way.

In those times the center jump rule still was in effect and one man usually shot all free throws.

Coach Wood told how the score in the championship game against South Bend was tied 13–13 at the end of regulation play and the referees ruled that the first team to make two points in overtime would be the winner. Four two-minute overtime periods followed without a point being registered by either team. In the fifth extra period, South Bend took the lead with a free throw, and then Stonebraker missed a chance to tie at the foul line. Crane came through a short time later with the field goal that won it for Wingate.

Stonebraker led Wingate scoring with nine points, and Crane got the other six. The small town of Wingate went bonkers after the victory, according to the coach. Twenty-five to 30 carloads of people met the team on its return, a parade celebrated the victory, and then everybody gathered for a victory dinner.

Wingate's 1913 state champions. Front: Leland Olin, Jesse Graves, Homer Stonebraker, John Blacker, Forest Crane; back row: Manager Sheaffer, McKinley Murdock, Lee Sinclair and Coach Wood.

Pete Thorn (left) was a member of the 1914 Wingate state championship ball club and went on to win 16 letters at Wabash—a record that still stands. Jesse Wood (right) coached Wingate to its state championship in 1913. He is pictured here as he was installed in the Hall of Fame in 1973.

Stonebraker returned in 1914 along with all but two of his 1913 state championship teammates. Pete Thorn and Paul Swank were the two newcomers to the Wingate roster. Leonard Lehman was the Wingate coach on its march to a second straight state championship with a 19–5 record.

Only 38 teams were entered in the 1913 tourney but the field jumped to 77 in 1914, and the unexpected large entry forced tourney officials to use four different gyms for the State Finals at Indiana University. Seventy-six games were played in two days. To win the championship, Stonebraker and his Wingate teammates played twice on Friday and four games on Saturday.

Wingate defeated Milan and Westport on Friday, and then prepared to meet its old Montgomery County rival Crawfordsville in the first game the next morning. Crawfordsville was no match for the veteran Wingate outfit this time, and the champs recorded a staggering 24–1 victory.

Stonebraker was the Wingate captain, and he had perhaps his finest state tourney game against Clinton. Wingate won a hard-fought decision 17–13 and Stonebraker scored all 17 for Wingate.

Of course, Wingate went on to nail down the 1914 trophy with a

Wingate's 1914 champs. Front: Leland Olin, John Blacker, Homer Stonebraker, Jesse Graves, Lee Sinclair; back: Coach Lehman, Pete Thorn, Manager Brown, Paul Swank and Principal Coons.

14–8 victory over Lebanon and a 36–8 romp over Anderson in the state windup. Stonebraker scored 18 points in that title tilt.

Wingate's two state championship teams have been singled out many times since as perhaps the first great state title winner. Stonebraker was the Oscar Robertson and the Larry Bird of his day.

Butler's Tony Hinkle, who had reason to know about such things, called Stonebraker one of Indiana's all-time greats. In fact, Stoney was one of the players named by Hinkle on his Dream Team a few years back. Two of Stoney's teammates on that select crew were Wooden and Robertson. Most of Wingate's firepower and much of the Wabash offense in the three years that followed was provided by Stonebraker.

"You've heard the old line about the player who could score from anywhere on the floor. Well, apparently, Stoney could do it. Of course, gyms were much smaller back then, but it was said that his shooting range began somewhere in the vicinity of the opponent's basket," Collins added.

"When he played at Wabash, Notre Dame defenders were instructed to not let him past the middle of the floor. They didn't—but he had seven baskets at the half.

"For a while Wingate practiced outdoors with the hoops nailed to posts. When the new gym was built, it had a low ceiling. So Stonebraker, who was tall for his era, perfected a shot with an unusually low trajectory, utilizing backspin.

Homer Stonebraker, one of
Indiana's all-time greats on two
straight Wingate state champs.
Stoney scored all 17 Wingate
points in one state tourney win
over Clinton.

"People who watched him play say it was uncanny. The ball
would—without arc—carry just over the top of the rim, hit the
backboard and plop into the basket."

Stonebraker worked for Uncle Sam in World War I, turned pro,
and had the same awesome results. He was a big man who had incredible moves around the basket, and yet he could also move outside and
shoot from some amazing distances.

Stoney was one of the first inducted in the Indiana Basketball Hall
of Fame in 1962—the year it was founded. He was installed along with
Fuzzy Vandivier, Johnny Wooden, Ward (Piggy) Lambert, and Griz
Wagner. Stonebraker also coached at Hartford City and twice was
elected sheriff of Cass County.

Wingate was gobbled up in Indiana's consolidation movement
nearly three decades ago—now part of the modern North Montgomery school system near Crawfordsville.

One of the last Wingate landmarks from the old days was advertised for auction in 1982, but the owner failed to find a buyer. From
the outside it looks like some old barn but the sign "Wingate Gymnasium" identifies the structure as the home floor for Wingate teams
from 1915 until the early 1950s.

Wingate's basketball program began in 1907, and because of the
two state championship teams the old barn carried a huge sentimental
value. Stonebraker's teams had no home floor so this gym was built as
sort of an afterthought in tribute to those outstanding teams. The gym
was heated by a couple of pot-bellied stoves tucked into the corners,
and there was a small section of bleacher seats on one side with room
for 187 fans, according to one old-timer. Showers came about 10 years

later. If players wanted to clean up, they jumped into a galvanized tub.

They say the barn (located in the middle of town) was used as a livery stable and later as an implement shed. Wingate rented it for basketball—paying $3 for practice and $6 for games.

The wooden playing floor had been removed several years ago. So were the antique coal and wood burning stoves that led sportswriters and sportscasters in those early days to coin the now popular phrase, "it was a real barn burner" as a way of describing any nip-and-tuck struggle.

Still part of the decor was an electric scoreboard—believed to be among the first such contraptions ever used in the Hoosier state—and one of the old backboards was in place. "The building was a credit to two great teams that were labeled "The Gymless Wonders," recounted another old-time Wingate rooter. Both the scoreboard and the backboard were destined to take their place in the Hall of Fame at Indianapolis, along with Stonebraker and Thorn.

Pete Thorn lettered three years in three sports at Wingate, and then at Wabash he won 16 letters in four sports—basketball, football, track, and baseball. It's a record that still stands for the Crawfordsville school. In 1940, the *Indianapolis News* named Thorn the greatest athlete in Wabash College history.

Pete was a guard with the 1922 Wabash team that won the national intercollegiate championship. Later, as a Navy company commander, he played for the Great Lakes Naval ball club. He went on to coach Warsaw High School teams and serve as the school's athletic director.

He was director of the Warsaw Boys Club for 37 years and guidance officer with the school system for 21 years.

Wingate and Crawfordsville both were under suspension for the 1920 season for using ineligible players and other reasons. Crawfordsville was cited in the IHSAA minutes for using undue influence in contacting Wingate's Alonzo Goldsberry.

So both former state champs were on the sidelines for the 1920 tournament, but they were busy. The two schools entered a U.S. Interscholastic tournament sponsored by the University of Chicago, met in the championship game, and Wingate was the winner, 22–16. On the way to the finals Wingate beat teams from Iowa, Ohio, and Illinois. Goldsberry was named captain of the All-American team named tournament's conclusion.

Coach Pete Vaughn of Wabash (earlier the great football ace at Notre Dame) called the Wingate team invincible with each player a star in his own position.

"It's a shame the whole United States could not have witnessed that demonstration . . . when the first news came of our victory," the *Wingate News* reported. "Bald headed men and gray-haired women, young folks and—well, they were all young, everybody forgot aches, pains and age to join the parade down to the school campus where a huge pile of boxes and baled straw had been collected. People five miles away saw the reflection of the fire, heard the shooting of the anvils and came bringing a noise of some kind.

"The celebration lasted until late in the night and some revelers visited nearby towns waiting to return until the wee hours."

Wingate's champs didn't return until the next day on the Monon at nearby Linden Station.

Forty car loads, including fathers and mothers of the players, gathered at the station, and the entire Linden High School student body turned out to welcome the team's arrival. On the way back to Wingate the caravan was stopped by another throng in front of the New Richmond school building.

On the steps of Wingate High School, the big parade ended and everybody got their first glimpse of the tourney trophy awarded by the University of Chicago. It proclaimed Wingate as Interscholastic High School Champion of the Middle Western states.

"Twice State Champions—now Champion U.S." the *Wingate News* boasted.

Wingate

Season Record (22–3)
1912–13

Wingate	72	Romney	14
Wingate	108	Hillsboro	8
Wingate	13	Crawfordsville	15
Wingate	22	Crawfordsville	25
Wingate	34	Linden	14
Wingate	25	Lebanon	44
Wingate	47	Odell	12
Wingate	21	Linden	11
Wingate	51	Breaks	21
Wingate	75	Waveland	7
Wingate	33	Odell	25
Wingate	49	Crawfordsville Seconds	4
Wingate	60	Covington	5
Wingate	39	Cayuga	23
Wingate	42	Roachdale	17
Wingate	49	Greencastle	15
Wingate	57	Colfax	17
Wingate	50	Waveland	28
Wingate	85	Cayuga	9
Wingate	22	Thornton	23

State Finals (Indiana University)

Wingate	24	Whiting	12
Wingate	19	Rochester (Overtime)	17
Wingate	16	Indianapolis Manual	11
Wingate	23	Lafayette Jeff	14
Wingate	15	South Bend Central (5 overtimes)	14

Season Record (19–5)
1913–14

Wingate	64	Williamsport	17
Wingate	35	Cutler	28
Wingate	50	Advance	12
Wingate	25	Rockville	17
Wingate	42	Waveland	13
Wingate	23	Advance	12
Wingate	33	Kokomo	13
Wingate	22	Lebanon	26
Wingate	15	Thorntown	16
Wingate	18	Bloomington	21
Wingate	21	Anderson	23
Wingate	23	Clinton	12
Wingate	64	Veedersburg	7
Wingate	41	Rockville	10
Wingate	64	Pendleton	13
Wingate	34	Bluffton	37
Wingate	43	Swayzee	25
Wingate	76	Waynetown	10

State Finals (Indiana University)

Wingate	44	Milan	14
Wingate	44	Westport	12
Wingate	24	Crawfordsville	1
Wingate	17	Clinton	13
Wingate	16	Lebanon	8
Wingate	36	Anderson	8

21

Carmel's Football All-Staters Put on a Basketball Crown

"In 1966, we won the sectional for the first time in 41 years," recalls Billy Shepherd. "That kind of started it all off."

That championship laid the pavement on a long road for the Carmel basketball program; from Carmel Lumber Yard to Market Square Arena, from small country school status to state champions.

It was in 1916 that Carmel first started playing basketball inside—in the Carmel Lumber Yard.

The members of that team were so thrilled to be playing inside that they nicknamed themselves the Carmel Lumberjacks.

By the mid-1920s, the Carmel Lumberjacks had become the Carmel Greyhounds. When Carmel moved its games to the wooden floor at the new high school, it apparently helped the players run faster. So much faster, in fact, that they looked like greyhounds.

It was March 7, 1925, that Carmel nipped Tipton, 19–18, in the sectional championship game at Noblesville. One week after Carmel won the sectional, the Greyhounds won the regional at Anderson.

It would be, however, the final sectional championship until 1966 and the final regional championship until 1970.

In the 1925 regional, a crowd of 5,000 watched Carmel beat New Castle, 26–24, and Muncie beat Shortridge, 37–19, in the two championship games. In those days, before the Semistate concept was introduced, two teams from each regional advanced to the 16-team State Finals at Indianapolis.

For the next 41 years, Carmel teams spent most of March watching, not playing, basketball. During the 1930s, '40s, '50s, and early '60s, the Greyhounds lost each year in the sectional, despite produc-

Teaming with Steve York (center) are sophomore Dave Shepherd (left) and senior
brother Billy Shepherd. They made up a formidable backcourt combo. Billy was
Mr. Basketball in 1968, and his brother won the same high honor two years later.
Billy scored 2,465 career points in four seasons, and David 2,226 in three years.

ing some excellent individual players. Among these were Bob Jeffries,
Dick Stratton, Pete Adams, Dale Cox, Larry Isley, Scott McKinney,
Greg Ferrin, and a 5-11 center named Eric Clark.

It was Clark who in 1953 almost single-handedly knocked off
mighty Sheridan in the sectional, scoring nearly half the team's points
in a 58–56 loss to the Blackhawks.

"We practiced a 2–2–1 press all year, but we never used it until that
sectional game against Sheridan," recalls Clark.

"Joe Hobbs [an all-stater from Sheridan] was the one who scared
everybody but we got him to foul out in the third quarter. We were
ahead much of the way. But we just couldn't beat them.

"Carmel at that time was sort of like Noblesville and some of the
other county schools are now. We didn't have the tradition, we were a
smaller school, and we were playing the team which won the sectional
almost every year. If we had the tradition of winning, we might have
done it then."

The drought finally ended in 1966, when a 5-7, 130-pound sophomore named Billy Shepherd dramatically gave Carmel its first sectional crown since 1925. The Greyhounds, at that time, were coached
by Billy's father, Bill Shepherd.

"It happened years ago but it seems like just last night," says

Shepherd, the coach. "Billy brought it across the time line with about 30 seconds to go and he just kept dribbling the ball in and out with two guys on him.

"Then he looked up at the clock with seven or eight seconds left, made his move, and hit a 20-foot shot just as the gun went off. When the ball went through, you would have thought we won the state tourney.

"That was the game that turned around our program. When we won that game, it gave our school the idea that we could really win."

"Yes, that kind of started it all off," says Billy proudly. "My junior year we were 18–6, and my senior year we were 21–3 and got beat by Marion in the regional. My high point game was 70 points against Brownsburg. I took about 50–51 shots and hit 8 of 12 free throws. I had 46 in the second half. And this was before they had girls' basketball, so we didn't play the girls' team that night, either. It was just one of those nights."

Billy was selected to the *Indianapolis News'* All-State team in 1967 and in 1968 and was Indiana's leading scorer for high school players from 1966 through 1968. He's also Carmel's all-time leading scorer with 2,465 points, one-game record-holder with 70 points, and all-

Billy Shepherd turns the corner on his way to the basket during his senior year at Carmel as shown in the picture on the left. Billy ended a long sectional famine for the Greyhounds and became one of the Hoosier state's top scorers. On the right, brother Dave (left) and Dean Ransom look disconsolate as they hold the state runner-up trophy after their loss to unbeaten East Chicago Roosevelt in 1970. Dave set a 40-point championship-game record in the losing effort and also set a one-season record for Hoosier preps with 1,079 points.

Dave Shepherd on his way
toward record 40-point
championship effort against
East Chicago Roosevelt in
1970. But Carmel lost to
Roosevelt anyway. In the
bottom photo, Shepherd is
being guarded by Cavanaugh
Gary.

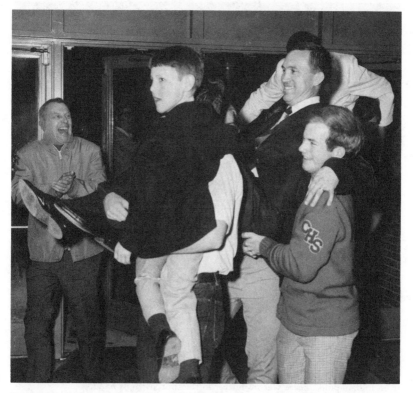

Coach Bill Shepherd is carried into the Carmel gym by young Greyhound fans after a long bus-ride home from the Fort Wayne Semistate. Carmel was going to the Final Four, and the entire town turned out well after midnight to cheer their heroes.

time assist leader. He was a standout later at Butler University and played for three teams in the ABA pro circuit.

"We [the team] were packing the place," recollects Billy. "That was a great era for Carmel basketball traditions. We were playing a good schedule, and being named Mr. Basketball was the highest honor an Indiana high school basketball player could attain. But after I left they didn't miss me much—they went undefeated the next year."

Although Billy finished his four-year career with 2,465 points, among the top four in all-time Hoosier scoring, it took younger brother David to lead Carmel into the State Finals in 1970.

Ironically, Carmel wasn't even supposed to win its sectional that season. Tipton, with former Indiana Pacer Darrell Elston, beat Carmel early in the season, but in the sectional championship game David poured in 33 points as the Greyhounds beat the Blue Devils, 81–74. It was like that throughout the tournament.

"We were the underdogs in every tournament game," remembers

Coach Shepherd is welcomed home from Fort Wayne by a sleepy-eyed sportswriter from Indianapolis. There was no buzzer in the sportswriter's hand.

David. "We were a come-from-behind team. Tipton was picked to win the sectional. We were the underdog in the Semistate, and we were the underdog in the State Finals.

Anderson Madison Heights was supposed to win the regional, but Carmel beat the Pirates in the afternoon and Blackford that night for the trip to Fort Wayne. Shepherd scored a record 88 points in the two regional contests.

Fort Wayne North and its 6–10 center Doug Brown were Semistate favorites, but Shepherd's 25-footer at the gun gave Carmel a 61–59 afternoon victory.

That night, with its Mr. Basketball candidate barely able to walk because of a knee injury in the regional, Carmel knocked off Plymouth by one point.

In the first game of the State Finals, Loogootee fell 71–62 as the Greyhounds won their 17th consecutive game. It was to be their last.

Jim Bradley, who later played for the American Basketball Association Kentucky Colonels, and his East Chicago Roosevelt teammates ended Carmel's dream with a 76–62 championship victory at Hinkle Fieldhouse.

The unbeaten Rough Riders led at halftime by just three points,

32–29, and it was just a four-point game until the final three minutes.

When it was all over, David had scored an all-time Indiana record 1,079 points during his senior year with 2,226 for his 3-year career. Those 1,079 were 65 points more than George McGinnis popped in one year earlier. Among that total were 66 points in one game against Frankfort, coming on 26-of-49 shooting from the field. David also set the championship game scoring mark totaling 40 points against East Chicago Roosevelt. Both Shepherds followed their father to the In-

Columbus East's Ted Rutan (right) grabs the arm of Carmel's Mark Herrmann in a desperation foul, hoping to jar the ball loose with two minutes left on the clock in the afternoon game of the finals. Carmel went on to win 71–60.

diana All-Stars, one of Hoosierland's best-known basketball families.

Oscar Robertson scored 39 in Crispus Attucks' 79–57 win over Lafayette Jeff in 1956.

And then it was on to 1977 and what has to be considered Carmel's strangest season.

Let's face it. When one thinks of a state championship basketball team in Indiana, it is easy to conjure thoughts of a ballclub with two or three all-state basketball players and perhaps a Mr. Basketball candidate.

Carmel had the all-state players, all right, all of them in football. All were standouts on Carmel's state runnerup football powerhouse in the 1975 playoffs.

"Wouldn't it be ironic if we won a basketball state championship after missing in football," said Bart Burrell a couple of days before the State Finals.

Burrell, Mark Herrmann, and Jon Ogle all were headed to college on football scholarships.

"I remember in seventh grade, basketball was the important sport for all of us, and we just played football for the fun of it.

"Then we got to high school and all of that changed. I didn't even know if I wanted to play football in high school at first but all of a sudden football got to be the important sport and basketball was just a fun sport. So, it sure would be ironic if we won a basketball championship."

Only twice since 1950 had a ballclub lost as many as seven games during the regular season and still won it all. New Albany did it with a 21–7 record in 1973 and now the Greyhounds pulled it off with a 22–7 mark.

Coach Arlan Lickliter and his North Cenral Panthers whipped Carmel, 75–62, on November 27 and again in the championship game of the Carmel Holiday tourney December 29, North Central repeated its dominance over the Greyhounds with a 60–46 lashing.

And when Ben Davis crushed Carmel, 80–66, in the final regular season game, well, the sectional, not to mention the state champion-

Carmel Coach and Vice Principal Eric Clark with Greg Jones of Plainfield.

ship, seemed out of the question. However, three games later, the Carmel Greyhounds were suddenly and easily in the Anderson Regional.

In sectional action, Carmel rolled up its second highest point total of the season burying Westfield, 88–56, and then eased past Hamilton Heights, 77–64, before Herrmann and Brian (Mongo) Greene teamed to help beat Noblesville in the title game, 59–40.

"I was surprised we won with that much ease," conceded Coach Clark. "I think coming out of those three games like that made us realize we were better than people thought. I don't suppose many of the kids were thinking state championship at that time, but it got us on our way."

Next stop: Anderson. Five times Clark had gone to Anderson with a sectional winner and five times the Greyhounds had come away empty-handed. That changed in 1977.

Wes-Del was Carmel's first opponent, and after a relatively close first half, the Greyhounds blew them out, 75–51. The bench scored 50 of the 75 points that afternoon, including 24 from Greene, who was unstoppable along the baseline.

Then came Kokomo. The Kats jumped to a 12–2 lead and hung on to beat Anderson in the second afternoon game.

With the Kats' 1-2 punch of Willie and Ricky Myles effectively in check, the Greyhounds broke from a three-point second quarter deficit, increased the lead to 10 early in the final quarter, and sailed into the Fort Wayne Semistate with a 57–50 victory.

The Fort Wayne Semistate was another storybook tournament for the Greyhounds.

Carmel's Mark Herrmann is fouled by East Chicago Washington's Curtis Lewis (behind Herrmann) as he grabs a rebound during the 1977 State Final. On the right, Carmel's Bart Burrell (#43) moves to the basket and releases his shot over East Chicago's Darryl Bridgeman (#45) in the Finals.

Carmel's 1977 state champs. Front: Manager Scott Reynolds, Rick Cox, Tim Wiley, Bart Burrell, Steve Shepherd, Dave Bauer, John Salz, Manager Jim Kline; second row: Assistant Coach Gregg Ferrin, Trainer Greg Gossard, Jon Ogle, Rick Sharp, Paul Hensel, John Lake, Mark Herrmann, Brian Greene, Assistant Coach Tom Wiley and Coach Eric Clark.

Fifty-four seconds remained in the championship game. Carmel had the ball, the game with Fort Wayne South was tied at 41, and suddenly Herrmann zipped a pass to Burrell across the middle of the key.

On its flight, the ball deflected off two arms and a leg and bounced to Burrell. Bart spun toward the basket, South's Travis Magee stepped in front of him, they collided, the ball banked off the glass and in, and Magee was whistled for a foul. Burrell completed the three-point play, and a near-disaster had turned into the winning play for Carmel. The Greyhounds were on their way to the State Finals for the first time since Mr. Basketball David Shepherd took them there seven seasons earlier.

When the 1976–77 season began, the Carmel Greyhounds were ranked No. 7 in the Associated Press poll. Between that time and March 1, they lost seven games.

When the state's sportswriters and sportscasters picked the eventual state champions on the eve of the State Finals, Carmel was third and joined Hensel for rebounding honors with 11. So there it was.

In the opener before 17,490 at Market Square Arena, Terre Haute South's Braves put up barely more than a whimper in losing to East Chicago, 66–45. The Senators' zone defense, blazing fast break, and 37 points from all-state candidate Drake Morris blew out the youthful Braves in the second half.

The second game looked like a Carmel-Plymouth rematch all over again. With Herrmann, Burrell, and Paul Hensel leading the way,

Carmel grabbed a 32–16 lead over Columbus East midway through the second quarter. But the Greyhounds didn't shake the opposition until late in the game. The Olympians rallied to whittle the Greyhounds' lead to 34–29 early in the second half.

Time after time, the Olympians cut the Carmel lead to six points but each time, Herrmann, Burrell, Hensel, Ogle, or Tim Wiley would help get it back to 10. Hermann topped the Greyhounds with 22 points and joined Hensel in rebounding honors with 11. So there it was. Carmel versus East Chicago Washington for the state championship.

That night, when the Senators bombed in seven of their first 11 shots to grab a 15–10 lead, it looked like all the experts who picked East Chicago were right. Anyway, what was a team full of football players doing playing for the state championship in basketball?

The answer to that question might have something to do with desire. For instance, when Burrell's driving lay-up put Carmel ahead for the first time, 25–24, he never left the game. Yet every time he stepped to the free throw line, he had to keep massaging his legs because of cramps in his right calf.

By the time the fourth quarter began, Carmel had a 48–40 lead and moments later it was ahead by 10 points. But this East Chicago ball club refused to quit and Morris and 6-6 teammate Clem Murrell brought the Senators back within one point with less than a minute to go.

Jim Bradley of East Chicago Washington takes a jump shot against Carmel in the 1977 State Finals, won by Carmel 53–52.

Ahead 51–50, Carmel had a chance to go up by three points with :34 seconds remaining on a Hensel lay-up. But Murrell blocked Hensel's effort, and the Senators had the ball with just a point disadvantage.

With 5–9 Ezell Foster calmly running the offense, the Senators played the clock. All East Chicago wanted was a pass to Morris, and it came with :12 remaining.

Foster found Morris as did Carmel's Ogle, who fouled the all-stater. Morris hit two free throws for a 52–51 Senators' lead with :11 left.

Five seconds later, Carmel's dream apparently had come to a conclusion. Troubled by East Chicago's press, a jump ball resulted between Morris and Herrmann.

However, as Morris tried to tip the ball to Foster, Burrell stole the ball in mid-air, headed down the court, and threw a football-type pass to Ogle, who had got free of his man. Ogle put the ball in the basket with four seconds remaining. On the Senators' inbounds pass, Foster found Morris, who fired a 26-footer with one second to go. It was too long and bounced off the backboard.

Thus it was all over. This incredible adventure to the school's first basketball state championship, led by three football players and a coach who had been criticized all year.

Carmel

Season Record (22–7)
1976–77

Carmel	72	Brebeuf	68
Carmel	62	North Central	75
Carmel	49	Madison Heights	51
Carmel	66	Zionsville	47
Carmel	41	Noblesville	37
Carmel	59	Pike	51
Carmel	84	Tipton	60
Carmel	68	Terre Haute North	45
Carmel	46	North Central	60
Carmel	63	Huntington North	76
Carmel	68	Lebanon	52
Carmel	67	Greenfield Central	51
Carmel	62	Kokomo Haworth	61
Carmel	63	Warren Central	54
Carmel	63	Anderson	64
Carmel	78	Crawfordsville	58
Carmel	57	Muncie North	64

Carmel	96	Muncie South	74
Carmel	74	Lawrence Central	63
Carmel	70	Ben Davis	86

Sectional (Carmel)

Carmel	88	Westfield	56
Carmel	77	Hamilton Heights	64
Carmel	59	Noblesville	40

Regional (Anderson)

| Carmel | 75 | Wes-Del | 51 |
| Carmel | 57 | Kokomo | 50 |

Semistate (Fort Wayne)

| Carmel | 58 | Plymouth | 54 |
| Carmel | 47 | Fort Wayne South | 43 |

State Finals (Market Square Arena)

| Carmel | 71 | Columbus East | 60 |
| Carmel | 53 | East Chicago Washington | 52 |

22

Jasper's 1949 State Champs' Most Unpredictable Saga

Bill Litchfield had to hail a taxi to reach Indianapolis' Butler Fieldhouse in time for the opening tip-off.

Jasper's electrifying 62–61 victory over hot-shooting Dee Monroe and his Madison Cub teammates in the 1949 state championship game was a fitting windup to one of the most unpredictable chapters in Indiana's hardwood hoopla.

Cabby O'Neill's Jasper ball club had gone into the state tournament's sectional round with an unheralded 11–9 record, and losing the last two games of the regular season to Muncie Burris and Vincennes.

Only one other state champion going all the way back to the first tournament in 1911 lost nine times during the regular season. Anderson's 1935 state champs lost nine.

It might also be added that Jasper did very little in the early stages of the 1949 state tournament to convince forecasters that they had overlooked the Wildcats. Game after game Jasper had to scramble from behind in the second half and sometimes in the final minutes to move on to the next tournament test.

Litchfield, the lad who somehow missed Jasper's police-escorted caravan from the Indianapolis Athletic Club where the team was housed to Butler Fieldhouse on the night of the championship battle, hit the shot with 15 seconds to go in the Semistate that whipped a tough Bloomington ball club 50–49 and put Cabby's unsung Wildcats in the Final Four.

Big Jim Schooley and his highly regarded Auburn crew led Jasper by a 42–36 score early in the fourth quarter of the second State Finals game, but once again the Wildcats got their act together in the stretch and yanked it out of the fire, 53–48.

Jerome (Dimp) Stenftenagel, No. 1 scorer in Jasper's well-balanced offense with a season total of 338 points, and Paul (Buzz) Rumbach sank the go-ahead buckets wiping out a 45–44 Auburn lead. Tom Schutz and Litchfield teamed up for the valuable insurance that put Jasper ahead, 51–46, with less than one minute on the clock. Auburn lost for just the third time in 29 games in spite of an outstanding game high 21 points by Schooley. Bob White, a 5–6 stick of dynamite in the Jasper backcourt, had 17 and Stenftenagel 15 for the Wildcats.

Jasper's championship struggle with a Madison ball club that returned one year later to collect a crown of its own, was tight for all but the opening minutes.

Dee Monroe exploded for a state tourney record 36 points in the game, and after Jasper seized a shocking 15–4 lead at the outset, it was Monroe's blistering 18-point flurry in the second quarter that shot Madison back into a threatening position. Jasper's big lead was cut to 31–28 at half-time.

White and Schutz cracked two buckets each as Jasper opened up a more comfortable 41–31 lead early in the second half, but the Cubs refused to fold and deadlocked the game for the first time at 45–45.

White's shot from long range regained the lead for Jasper but Monroe, who hit 14 of his 26 field attempts in the contest, knotted the score again at 55–55. This time Stenftenagel came through with a key go-ahead basket, Johnny Berg shook loose on a 3-point play and a short time later White connected again from the outside.

Jasper led 62–59 with 47 seconds to go and except for one last lay-up by Monroe following a steal, the much-underrated Wildcats stalled out the closing seconds.

White led Jasper scoring with 20 points in the title tilt, Stenftenagel had 15, and Schutz 10. White, Monroe, and Schooley all were voted to the Indiana All-Star team for its Blind Fund battle against Kentucky in June. Schooley was named winner of the state tournament's Trester Award in post-game ceremonies.

Jack Rumbach, sports editor of Jasper's *Daily Herald* at the time, recalled that following an overwhelming 56–26 sectional win over the Dubois Jeeps the Wildcats were subjected to eight straight comeback struggles. "They either overcame halftime deficits, third quarter leads or, in at least one case, turned the tide in the waning seconds," Rumbach explained.

Holland's Dutchmen, using a slowdown game perfected by Coach Lowell McGlothin, led Jasper by a 20–19 score in the third quarter before the Cats surged ahead to win, 36–28.

Jasper's next opponent in the sectional semifinals would be old rival Huntingburg, the Southern Indiana Conference champ with a classy 17–3 regular season record. It was a typical Huntingburg-Jasper

Jasper's Jerome Stenftenagel (left) and Bob White watch girl friends do a quick repair job on White's letter sweater before the trip to Indianapolis. White scored 20 and Stenftenagel 15 in the 62–61 final game win over Madison.

head knocker, with Huntingburg holding a slim 12–6 lead at the quarter and the Wildcats on top 22–16 at halftime.

Huntingburg regained a 29–27 lead at the end of three quarters and clung to a 34–31 margin early in the final period. But Jasper bounced back with time running out and escaped with a 44–35 win over the Hunters.

"The Winslow Eskimoes, led by the redoubtable (Indiana University Hall of Famer) Dick Farley, were favored to take the sectional that year," Rumbach added. "I recall that when the halftime gun went off with the Pike Countians ahead by 10 points, 24–14, it was as ominous as a death knell. But for the Cats, that half-time bulge was a clarion call—they ran the Eskimoes into the floor with a third quarter fast break that left Jasper on top, 35–32. The Wildcats won it, 48–39."

Going to the regional wasn't a new experience for Cabby O'Neill's teams who had been there seven times before, but according to the Jasper sports editor it was a redeemer for these unsung Cats and there still was not much talk about state titles.

Jasper met two small school teams—Shelburn and Monroe City—in the regional, and both demonstrated that it was no accident that they had won sectionals the preceding week. Jasper had to overcome a 30–28 halftime deficit to turn back Shelburn, 61–52, and Monroe City held a 53–50 lead midway in the fourth quarter before the comeback Cats rebounded for a narrow 57–55 verdict.

Bedford also led Jasper, 26–24, at the halfway mark one week later in the Bloomington Semistate, which was played in the old IU Fieldhouse. Once again Jasper scrambled from behind for a 41–33 victory and faced Bloomington's Panthers at night.

Litchfield's bucket with just 15 seconds on the clock was the Jasper clincher in the 50–49 Semistate final which sent the Wildcats to the Final Four for the first time since 1934. It was a real nail-biter with the lead changing hands 10 times and the score deadlocked on six other occasions.

"All of a sudden sports scribes from all over the state were quizzing us—who are these Jasper Wildcats? What're their credentials? How'd they get to the State Finals?" Rumbach said. "Most [writers] were of the impression that Auburn's Red Devils would be a cinch to get into the final game against Madison or South Bend Central.

"After five consecutive games in which they trailed at the half, Jasper held a seven-point lead this time, 32–25. But not for long. Auburn squeezed to a 38–36 three-quarter mark lead and was still ahead by one at the official time-out [midway in the fourth quarter]. The Cats then hit three times to one for the Devils and were out front to stay. Final score was 53–48."

Jasper had advanced to the state championship game for the first time in the school's history. In 1934, the Wildcats lost to ultimate state title winner Logansport in the afternoon round.

"By this time the 49ers were battle-hardened and smelling gold," Rumbach added. "The Cats couldn't afford to let Madison get in front like eight of their nine previous tourney opponents had done. They pounced early and came up with an 11-point lead. It was up to the Ohio River Cubs to play catch-up ball.

Stenftenagel rebounds against Bloomington in a 50–49 Semistate thriller. Tom Schutz (#8) and Bob White (#4) are watching in the backcourt.

"Dee Monroe almost did it single-handedly, but Jasper's balanced attack prevailed. Monroe scored 36 points to set a record but it was the Jasper Wildcats who picked up all the marbles at the end, 62–61."

And 15,000 people by police estimate jammed the Public Square the next afternoon (March 20, 1949) to welcome home the conquering Jasper heroes. Dan Scism wrote about Cabby O'Neill and his wonderful Jasper state champs in his Evansville sports columns. "someone with the gift should write a story of the Jasper Wildcats of 1949. If he could dig deep enough and find out just when and how this team became great; how it acquired that fierce competitiveness and gained that deadly determination to win, he would have a great story."

"Cabby O'Neill can throw off more misinformation than a horse trainer," Scism pointed out.

"When Cabby said his Jasper Wildcats were plumb lucky to win the sectional and regional championships, I didn't question his opinion. Unconsciously, I accepted it, and when the Wildcats whipped a real good Bloomington team, 50–49, in the semi-final tournament title

Jerome (Dimp) Stenftenagel and Bill Litchfield lost the ball briefly in Jasper's State Finals clash against Auburn.

game, I thought the luck of the Irish was really riding with Cabby this year.

"However, every time one of those retrospective moods came along, I became skeptical of the part Mr. Luck was playing in the title drive of the Wildcats. Luck is fickle. It comes and goes without warning.

"This Jasper team had shown remarkable consistency in rising to the greatness needed to turn defeat into victory when the finish line came into view. It had come from behind to whip such clubs as Huntingburg, Winslow, Shelburn, Monroe City, Bedford and Bloomington.

The Jasper 1949 state champs. Front: Student Manager Bohwert, Bill Byrd, Sam Allen, John Berg, Paul Rumbach, Ed Stenftenagel, Tom Schutz; back row: Coach O'Neill, Assistant Coach Wuchner, Bob White, Bill Litchfield, Dave Krodel, Jerome Stenftenagel and Principal Miller.

"And when I saw it defeat Auburn's big Red Devils, the team with the most physical ammunition in the State Finals, and then beat Madison's Cubs, a smart, sharp, fast-striking team, in probably the greatest championship game ever played in this state, I knew I had the answer."

Scism agreed, "Jasper had the same kind of luck that Man O' War had when he could run faster than his rivals; the same kind of luck that Bobby Jones had when he won every major golf title in 1930 by producing the best shots under the same conditions, and the same luck that enabled Joe Louis to stand out supreme during his long reign as heavyweight champion.

"Don't compare it with other Jasper teams or any team which missed the state championship. Those teams can't carry the 1949 state champions' shoes. Only this Jasper team of the 769 entered in the state tournament knew how to win every game. And the field was one of the best balanced in the 39-year-old history of the IHSAA.

"Understand, I belong to that large army of people who underrated the Wildcats. They were rated in the pre-tournament dope on their season record of 11–9. And after watching them play in the Bloomington semifinal, I didn't see their championship greatness. Frankly, when I saw them line up against Auburn's giants in the second game, I thought they would lose. However, after a few minutes of play, I remarked that Auburn wasn't smart enough to beat Jasper.

"Jim Mitchell of Kokomo and Ben Tenny of Fort Wayne who were at my elbows, looked at me and shook their heads.

" 'This Auburn team,' said Jim, 'will explode in a minute and blow Jasper out of this place.' "

Scism didn't reply but he could see how the Wildcats were taking advantage of every opening and capitalizing on every Auburn mistake. When Auburn cut loose with a scoring burst and jumped to a 42–36 lead early in the fourth quarter, Mitchell and Tenny nodded that "Jasper is through."

Scism knew that Jasper wasn't through, that the Wildcats would fight until the last second and hit their hardest in the closing minutes. Jasper's spectacular finish left Scism's press box pals dazed. "The trouble is," Tenny confessed, "Jasper didn't know it was beaten."

The Wildcats whipped that Auburn team good in the last two minutes," Scism remembered. "In that tense stretch, Auburn, when behind, kept possession of the ball 38 seconds without shooting. The Red Devils were in a mental stew. They knew they had met their master.

"Madison's Cubs, however, were not beaten until the final gun. They kept coming and coming, but they couldn't crack the composure or even dent the will to win in the Wildcats.

"This Jasper team knew it was in for the fight of its life when it squared off against Madison. Every Wildcat was alert and ready for his best effort. They didn't fool around. They struck like lightning right at the start to race into a 8–2 lead. They knew they couldn't play along with this team and come from behind to win as they had so many times. So they just broke on top and were never headed, although twice Madison pulled even.

"The Wildcats had on their gold uniforms and there was a flash of gold rising into the air on each rebound and a streak of gold darting on every loose ball.

"Every outstanding basketball team must have a brain, and little Bob White was the pilot for the Wildcats. They missed him when he had to leave the game near the end of the third quarter. They hit their old stride when he came back into the game in the final quarter.

"I'm hard-headed but I was convinced Saturday afternoon and night that the Jasper Wildcats of 1949 are one of the greatest teams this basketball state has ever produced. I know now that if they were to play this tournament over and someone would say, 'Your life is at stake. Name the winner,' I wouldn't hesitate a split second in saying Jasper.

"You can't beat a team that won't be beaten," Scism declared.

Schutz, a land developer in the Indianapolis area since 1960, was an all-state selection on Jasper's state championship outfit. He reminds all that there was a good reason for that unimpressive 11–9 record going into the tournament.

"We were handicapped by all sorts of injuries and illness during the regular season, and Cabby didn't really have our full team together until a short time before the sectional. Late in the year we upset New Albany when it was ranked No. 1 by the pollsters and then we lost our last two games.

"Cabby brought in a lot of the strong teams from the north for us to play but Jasper was not a comfortable place for their blacks, so teams like East Chicago Washington usually stayed overnight in a Washington motel.

"Stenftenagel was our leading scorer, averaging about 14 points a

Jasper's Cabby O'Neill, a member of the IHSAA's Board of Control, presented the Trester Award to Eddie Bopp of 1965 state champ Indianapolis Washington after the State Final.

game, but we had good balance and we were about seven deep. We had been together since our early grade school days and knew each other like a book."

Schutz compared Coach O'Neill to a tough Marine sergeant, and his Jasper teams were always well-drilled. "No matter where they went to college (and Cabby always helped his players with their college contacts), his Jasper players were known for strong fundamentals.

"I was recruited originally by Wisconsin but that was too far from home for a country boy like me, so after my freshman year I transferred to Western Kentucky and played for Coach [Ed] Diddle for two years. I was so well-schooled by Cabby in fundamentals that Diddle asked me to set up some drills for Western. It was like a traveling circus in those days and we played some outstanding teams like Seton Hall, LaSalle, and Cincinnati.

"I played with Gene Rhodes at Western and Detroit baseball great

Harvey Kuenn was a sophomore at Wisconsin when I enrolled up there. Following two years of basketball at Western, I decided that I needed to get an education. So I began work on a degree in engineering at Purdue," Schutz added.

Jasper was the first team to win an Indiana state championship using a zone defense.

"We played a 2–3 zone most of the time and that's how we started out against Madison in the state championship game. But when Dee Monroe got 21 points in the first half, Cabby switched to a box-and-chaser the rest of the way, and I was the chaser," Schutz related.

"Monroe was a tremendous shooter and he seemed to know where the ball was going to come off every time a shot was missed. I held him to nine points until I fouled out with about three minutes to go. I don't remember much else except that I was awful tired."

Jasper sports editor Jerry Birge wrote that few individuals had greater impact on Southern Indiana sports than Cabby O'Neill did, as a player, coach, and athletic director in a career that covered nearly half a century.

"When a young, smiling Irishman arrived on the scene in Jasper in the fall of 1939, few Jasper basketball fans realized what was ahead," Birge observed.

"In the 13 basketball seasons which followed, the O'Neill-coached Wildcats won an incredible 247 games, lost only 76 for a .765 percentage, won nine sectionals (eight in a row), won five regionals, one semi-final title, and of course the coveted IHSAA state championship.

"Leo Cavanaugh O'Neill started his career in sneakers at St. Simon's Grade School in Washington shortly after the armistice was signed in France . . . From the grade school ranks he moved up to the high school level at St. Simon's, acquiring the nickname of Cabby along the way, and eventually led the Cardinals to the Indiana State Catholic championship in 1925.

"A football and basketball career at Franklin College ended in its first year when the young athlete suffered a shoulder injury on the gridiron. O'Neill moved south to the University of Alabama where he starred for the Crimson tide varsity basketball team for three years, serving as team captain his senior year and leading the Tide to an undefeated season and Southeastern Conference championship in 1930.

"O'Neill stepped into the coaching ranks in 1930 at little [school enrollment 85] Epsom High School in Daviess County. His first team at Epsom won the Daviess-Martin County tournament.

"Three years later Cabby's Epsom team went undefeated into the finals of the prestigious Wabash Valley Tourney."

Birge tells how Montgomery lured O'Neill away from Epsom in

1934 and his first Viking team defeated the former state champs from Washington in the Washington Sectional as well as former state titlist Vincennes in the Vincennes Regional, advancing to the 16-team State Finals at Indianapolis' Butler Fieldhouse.

Cabby moved on to Jasper in the fall of 1939 and has been a sports fixture there for more than 40 years. Louis (Nip) Wuchner was his devoted right-hand man for most of that time.

He built one of Southern Indiana's finest sports programs as

Jasper's Tom Schutz in action against Augurn's Kenneth McInturf.

athletic director at Jasper before he stepped down in 1971, expanding the athletic department to include eight sports. He was a moving force in the construction of Alumni Stadium for football and track as well as the refurbishing of old Recreation Field for baseball. Cabby also found time to serve on the IHSAA's powerful Board of Control and its Athletic Council. He was active as a director with the Indiana Hall of Fame.

Cabby's home is packed with trophies, plaques, photos, and other souvenirs. Included among his top awards is the Joe Boland Award presented in 1949 by the Indiana Sportscasters and Sportswriters Association. It's presented each year by the media for contributions to youth in the Hoosier state.

Cabby O'Neill's outstanding coaching record and Jasper's historic ride to that 1949 state championship received the ultimate tribute 20 years later in 1969 when Cabby was installed in the Indiana Basketball Hall of Fame.

Much about the game has changed and Hoosier Hysteria itself has taken on a much different look through consolidations across the state, but Jasper's Impossible Dream is not forgotten.

As Schutz concluded with a satisfying grin, "We shocked 'em all."

Jasper

Season Record (21–9)
1948–49

Jasper	41	Loogootee	38
Jasper	64	Washington Catholic	47
Jasper	37	Bloomington	47
Jasper	44	Seymour	33
Jasper	52	Bedford	41
Jasper	39	Huntingburg	42
Jasper	58	Washington	27
Jasper	51	Evansville Reitz	60
Jasper	62	Princeton	43
Jasper	37	New Albany	54
Jasper	59	Columbus	31
Jasper	61	Bicknell	32
Jasper	51	Vincennes	49
Jasper	50	Huntingburg	53
Jasper	54	Evansville Bosse	33
Jasper	49	Evansville Central	57
Jasper	43	Washington	44
Jasper	57	New Albany	56
Jasper	41	Muncie Burris	58
Jasper	55	Vincennes	57

Sectional (Jasper)

Jasper	56	DuBois	26
Jasper	36	Holland	28
Jasper	44	Huntingburg	35
Jasper	48	Winslow	39

Regional (Vincennes)

Jasper	61	Shelburn	52
Jasper	57	Monroe City	55

Semifinal (Indiana University)

Jasper	41	Bedford	33
Jasper	50	Bloomington	49

State Finals (Indianapolis, Butler Fieldhouse)

Jasper	53	Auburn	48
Jasper	62	Madison	61

23

Argos—The Spirit of 76

Tiny Argos put its name in the Hoosier Hysteria record books on January 16, 1981, when the Dragons bettered the state's longest regular-season winning streak of 61 straight established by Madison from 1960 to 1962.

It happened on Coach Phil Weybright's 35th birthday, and Argos went on to extend that record for Indiana high school basketball to 76 straight before it came to an end at the hands of Glenn's Falcons almost a year later on December 17, 1981.

"Today you will find some gloom and maybe a few tears in Argos. But the Spirit of 76 will live forever in southern Marshall County," wrote Forrest Miller in the *South Bend Tribune* after Glenn's 58–50 win ended the phenomenal Argos string in the first round of the Culver Holiday Tourney. "Weybright never lost his composure when he knew the outcome was inevitable. He knows that this Argos team isn't as talented as those of recent years."

Before the loss to Glenn, Argos' last regular season defeat was a 67–65 overtime loss to Triton on the road February 3, 1978. The streak began the next night with a 58–57 win over LaVille.

During this record-smashing streak, Argos compiled an incredible 93–4 record with four sectional titles and a spectacular trip to the 1979 State Finals where the Dragons lost to Anderson in the afternoon.

Argos took a 28–0 perfect record to the State Finals at Indianapolis' Market Square Arena. The 12 members of that team were Doug Jennings, Don O'Dell, Bill O'Dell, Mark Malone, Dave Calhoun, Mike Sheetz, Rich Tuttle, Chuck Evans, Tim Montgomery, Kevin Heuer, Bob Daughtery, and Steve Davis. Jennings and Bill O'Dell both averaged 17-ppg on the state tournament squad. Thirty players had a hand in putting together that 76-game regular season streak, and the

On the left are Doug Jennings (left) and Coach Phil Weybright. Jennings was Argos' top player in 1979 when the Dragons went to the Final Four. Weybright-led Argos established the state record for regular-season straight wins at 76. The sign on the right speaks for itself.

school would display an appropriate plaque honoring all of those Dragon team members.

Included along with those state-tournament team members were Bruce Grossman, Tim Castle, Mike Malone, Dale Prochno, Terry Davis, Scott Friar, Brad Rowe, Robin Roberts, Kip Edmonds, Kim Edmonds, Scott Jennings, Adam Malcolm, Mike McCay, Boyd Hollabaugh, Jon Eby, Gary Eby, Bob Powell, and Dave Tuttle.

Argos won the hearts of the entire state in the 1979 Elkhart Regional, knocking off 1978 State Finalist Elkhart Central by a staggering 84–68 score with a blistering 65 percent shooting average from the floor.

Outsized by almost every favored opponent along the way, the Dragons followed that up the next week with a 66–64 win over Fort Wayne Harding and an 84–83 victory over high-ranking Marion in the Fort Wayne Semistate.

Two free throws by Mark Malone with only seven seconds to go sewed up Argos' two-point win over Harding, and then Billy O'Dell's last second rebound basket bumped Marion out of the state title chase at night.

Coach Weybright's magic finally came to an end in the State Finals against a much taller and much quicker Anderson ball club which took an early lead and refused to let the People's Choice entry gain any kind

Holding the Bi-County Basketball championship trophy for 1981 are Coach Phil Weybright, players Mike Scheetz and Rich Tuttle, and Argos Principal Stephen Keith.

of momentum. The final score was 74–64, but the Dragons played well enough to convince a sellout crowd of more than 17,000 that they were not out of place. Anderson in turn lost a 64–60 heartstopper to old North Central Conference neighbor Muncie Central for the title.

All the television coverage from all over Indiana (and from Chicago) and the frequent visits from writers became almost old hat for the small town of Argos with its population of 1,500 and the school with an enrollment of 247.

Several metropolitan dailies and even *Sports Illustrated* sent their writers and photographers to record one of the most unbelievable chapters in Hoosier Hysteria since Milan's Cinderella team upset mighty Muncie Central in the 1954 state championship classic. Community billboards proclaimed the Argos record but the small town and the student body took all the excitement in stride.

Coach Weybright and Principal Stephen Keith told how adult fans appeared to get a lot more worked up over the long winning streak than the youngsters. "Our student body has been taking everything in stride and I'm not sure the kids fully understand what's being done—you know most of 'em have never seen us lose a regular-season game," the Argos principal explained.

Weybright felt the outstanding community support and the long winning streak actually helped Argos win many games in spite of all

Fort Wayne Semistate Champions of 1979. Front: Tim Montgomery, Chuck Evans, Dave Calhoun, Mark Malone, Kevin Heuer, Don O'Dell; back row: Coach Phil Weybright, Mike Scheetz, Doug Jennings, Rich Tuttle, Bill O'Dell, Bob Daughtery and Assistant Coach Lee Zumbaugh.

the pressure involved. "I'm sure we would have lost one or two along the line if it hadn't been for the crowds and the momentum associated with the winning streak," the Argos coach admitted. "Our fans have been so supportive and our kids so proud of the streak that it was really pretty hard for us to play a flat game," he said.

A small town boy from New Paris, Indiana, Weybright confessed that he had passed up some offers to move up to a larger school in his eight years at Argos. "I've had feelers from larger schools, but I really didn't want to leave these kids. It's very flattering to get those offers, but after 13 years in this school system I'm not sure I'd be happy anywhere else.

"We don't have football here at Argos, and we don't have a wrestling program—basketball is the big thing. I make the rules, the kids accept them, and so it's a lot easier to coach here.

"Just for example we had four or five players who could dunk the ball on our 1981 team which was more power-oriented than our state tournament club, and yet we haven't had a dunk shot in three years. They're afraid they might miss one and that would hurt the team."

Weybright notes that all but two or three schools on the Argos schedule had larger enrollments, which makes the winning streak more incredible.

He said, "We've been contacted about games by bigger schools, they want us to come to their place and bring our 1,000 fans, and give us $500. I'd like to play teams like South Bend LaSalle and Warsaw but down the road it would destroy our program.

Weybright understood that his winning streak was nearing the end at the start of the 1981–82 season. "We will be competitive, but it won't be anything like it has been for the last three seasons," he conceded. "Plymouth has the talent to own the sectional for two or three years—I'm afraid this is it for us."

After the loss to Glenn, Weybright said, "We were happy to start out with a 6–0 record. We struggled early, almost lost our opener to Tippecanoe Valley, almost lost to North Miami and Knox, then seemed to turn things around."

Glenn turned the trick with extremely patient 50 percent shooting from the field, a 22-of-28 performance at the free throw stripe and good help from the bench. Jeff Tinkey's three-point play and nine Glenn free throws locked it up down the stretch.

For Jim Waller's Glenn ball club it was sweet retribution for nine losses to Argos during that 76-game streak (including a 113–57 rout in 1979) and one other defeat in sectional play. And the Falcons still were celebrating the next night when they lost the holiday tourney windup to a 3–5 Triton opponent.

"Our community handled the loss pretty well and I was glad to see that," Weybright said. "Our fans could see with one minute to go that

Mrs. Rose Ann O'Dell and Argos Police Chief Bill Walters stand by a large trash can outside the restaurant (Grandma's Kitchen) where Mrs. O'Dell works (it is owned by her father, John Snyder).

it was going to end and the Glenn crowd began to yell 76–and–1."

Weybright looked at it in a philosophical way, saying that it was probably for the best. "It removed some of the pressure and all good teams learn from their losses. I could see that pressure was starting to bother some of our players, and in this respect it probably helped to have the streak come to an end."

"I didn't mind losing to Glenn. Jim Waller [Glenn coach] showed a lot of class. This will help his program and maybe take some pressure off him. Some of our games against them had been one-sided and not everyone understood why." Ironically, a short time later Waller gave up the Glenn job after receiving several threatening letters.

Weybright wasn't sure how much of an impact the Argos streak would make on Indiana high school basketball now and in the future.

"It's hard to believe that such a thing could happen. I'll never forget this experience and I'm sure that our players feel the same way. I suppose in a couple of years when I lean back in my easy chair, it will look even better."

Argos Record

February 4, 1978—Argos 58, LaVille 57
February 10, 1978—Argos 77, Culver 47
February 11, 1978—Argos 78, North Miami 59
February 15, 1978—Argos 64, Tippecanoe Valley 55
February 17, 1978—Argos 65, Glenn 40
February 21, 1978—Argos 67, Washington Twp. 55
February 24, 1978—Argos 105, Mishawaka Marian 73
November 22, 1978—Argos 75, North Miami 58
December 1, 1978—Argos 67, Knox 40
December 9, 1978—Argos 73, Oregon-Davis 53
December 12, 1978—Argos 67, Tippecanoe Valley 53
December 15, 1978—Argos 82, Kewanna 48
December 16, 1978—Argos 70, Jimtown 60
December 20, 1978—Argos 69, Glenn 51
December 21, 1978—Argos 86, Culver 58
January 5, 1979—Argos 100, LaCrosse 57
January 6, 1979—Argos 84, North Liberty 62
January 12, 1979—Argos 88, Caston 61
January 18, 1979—Argos 87, Bremen 51
January 19, 1979—Argos 64, Culver Military 55
January 20, 1979—Argos 54, LaVille 53
January 26, 1979—Argos 76, LaVille 53
January 27, 1979—Argos 101, Washington Twp. 59
February 2, 1979—Argos 82, Triton 57
February 9, 1979—Argos 68, Culver 57
February 16, 1979—Argos 113, Glenn 57
February 20, 1979—Argos 102, Bremen 54
February 23, 1979—Argos 68, Mishawaka Marian 39

November 21, 1979—Argos 108, North Miami 52
November 30, 1979—Argos 68, Knox 42
December 8, 1979—Argos 67, Oregon-Davis 55
December 14, 1979—Argos 79, Kewanna 40
December 15, 1979—Argos 85, Jimtown 54
December 20, 1979—Argos 78, Glenn 53
December 21, 1979—Argos 96, Triton 64
January 14, 1980—Argos 91, LaCrosse 47
January 5, 1980—Argos 76, North Liberty 54
January 11, 1980—Argos 60, Caston 40
January 16, 1980—Argos 74, North Liberty 64
January 18, 1980—Argos 74, Glenn 45
January 19, 1980—Argos 71, LaVille 55
January 25, 1980—Argos 54, LaVille 50
January 26, 1980—Argos 105, Washington Twp. 36
February 1, 1980—Argos 76, Triton 53
February 8, 1980—Argos 104, Culver 48
February 15, 1980—Argos 72, Glenn 49
February 19, 1980—Argos 89, Bremen 56
February 23, 1980—Argos 78, Tippecanoe Valley 68
February 26, 1980—Argos 103, Mishawaka Marian 55
November 19, 1980—Argos 63, North Miami 54
November 22, 1980—Argos 69, Tippecanoe Valley 57
November 28, 1980—Argos 72, Knox 48
December 6, 1980—Argos 57, Oregon-Davis 50
December 12, 1980—Argos 107, Kewanna 37
December 17, 1980—Argos 78, Jimtown 24
December 18, 1980—Argos 67, Triton 53
December 19, 1980—Argos 67, Glenn 47
January 3, 1981—Argos 106, LaCrosse 44
January 9, 1981—Argos 89, Caston 66
January 10, 1981—Argos 89, North Liberty 44
January 15, 1981—Argos 76, Glenn 60
January 16, 1981—Argos 77, Culver Military 39
January 17, 1981—Argos 74, LaVille 64
January 23, 1981—Argos 45, LaVille 42
January 24, 1981—Argos 95, Washington Twp. 28
January 30, 1981—Argos 79, Triton 61
February 6, 1981—Argos 67, Culver 57
February 13, 1981—Argos 86, Glenn 62
February 17, 1981—Argos 67, Bremen 53
February 20, 1981—Argos 81, Mishawaka Marian 44
November 21, 1981—Argos 56, Tippecanoe Valley 49
November 25, 1981—Argos 53, North Miami 48
November 28, 1981—Argos 67, Westville 49
December 4, 1981—Argos 54, Knox 50
December 11, 1981—Argos 78, Jimtown 36
December 12, 1981—Argos 64, Oregon-Davis 44

24

It Wasn't Just Another Sightseeing Trip for Plymouth

It was billed by most of the experts as just another sight-seeing trip, but Coach Jack Edison and his Plymouth Pilgrims enjoyed Indianapolis' Market Square Arena so much they'd "kinda like to go back" someday.

Ranked no better than fourth in the Final Four for Indiana's 72nd state high school basketball showcase, Plymouth knocked off a strong Indianapolis Cathedral ball club in the afternoon (62–59) and then scrambled from behind against Gary Roosevelt in two overtimes, 75–74, in the title bout.

Plymouth, with its enrollment of 894, became the smallest school to rule Hoosier Hysteria since Milan's legendary state title march in 1954.

Veteran observers called the March 27, 1982, showcase one of the most entertaining in the hardwood classic's long history. Roosevelt nipped No. 1 ranked and previously unbeaten Evansville Bosse on Renaldo Thomas' last second shot in the second afternoon game, 58–57.

Plymouth's two-overtime scorcher with Roosevelt in the final game was the longest state title match since little Wingate downed South Bend in five overtimes for the 1913 championship. It was the tournament's second overtime final in five years—Muncie Central had to go one extra period in 1977 to shake off Terre Haute South, 65–64. (One year later Muncie came back to lock up No. 7—tops in the Hoosier state.)

Scott Skiles and Phil Wendel—Plymouth's goal dust twins in the backcourt—were the big guns for the Pilgrims who presented a much different look from most state championship clubs in recent years. No

Plymouth starter was taller than 6–2, and the champs carved out their nifty 28–1 record without a single black player on the roster.

The only other all-white teams to wear the crown in almost 40 years were Carmel in 1977, Lafayette Jeff in 1964, and Milan in 1954.

Skiles, a deceivingly pudgy 6–1 guard who was Indiana's top scorer in regular season stats with a 30.2 average, erupted for a near-record 39 points in the championship game and a record-tying 69 for the two state final battles. His 39-point blast was just one short of the final game tourney record set by Carmel's Dave Shepherd in 1970.

Skiles established a school record with 1,788 career points, a one-season record with 850, and as a junior he tallied 53 points in one game against Concord and 56 two weeks later against Mishawaka Penn. Skiles, who also averaged 7.2 rebounds and 5 assists, led all juniors with his 27.9 average the preceding year and Wendel's stats at the other guard position were just as remarkable. Phil averaged 16.8-ppg his junior year and 17.6 on the state championship club. He also was good for six assists per game.

Three of Plymouth's proudest going for the goal: Phil Wendel, Ron Sissel, and Scott Skiles.

Skiles sank the last-second shot from 22 feet that sent the final game into its first overtime period deadlocked at 60–60. Roosevelt was sitting comfortably on a 57–54 cushion with only 68 seconds of regulation play on the clock.

Roosevelt's Thomas also missed a chance to nail it down at the foul line in the last three seconds of the first overtime. Renaldo sank a free toss to put Gary in a 65–65 tie and then his bonus attempt bounced off the rim.

Skiles was 13-for-25 from the field and 13-for-17 at the foul stripe. He exploded for 25 of his 39 in the fourth quarter and in the two overtime periods.

Wendel also came through with 16 big points in the championship clash, hitting seven of his 11 shots from the field, and he was rewarded later in post-game ceremonies when IHSAA directors named him winner of the Trester Award. The award is presented each year to the State Final's outstanding player based on mental attitude, scholarship, and citizenship.

Roosevelt (22-6) had put much pressure on the well-disciplined Plymouth outfit after the Pilgrims held leads of 22-14 at the quarter and 30-25 at the half. Roosevelt stormed into a 45-38 lead at the end of three quarters and appeared to be on the way to the Gary school's second state title.

Skiles, Wendel, and the rest of the Plymouth crew refused to be counted out, however. The Pilgrims regained the lead at 46-45, and the rest of the struggle was a see-saw affair that kept the capacity MSA crowd on the edge of their seats. The lead changed hands eight times before Roosevelt grabbed its 57-54 edge with just a few seconds remaining.

Plymouth still trailed 60-58 with only four seconds to go, and things looked pretty bleak for Pilgrim supporters. Coach Edison called a time out to stop the clock, but the Big Red had to go the full length of the floor to have a shot.

Roosevelt denied Skiles the ball on the inbounds pass, but he got it down the sideline on a lob pass from Todd Samuelson. Roosevelt's defender had a hand in his face, but Skiles' shot was on the mark. That put it in overtime, 60-60.

Skiles and front-line replacement Mark Stukenborg hit two quick buckets to put Plymouth ahead in the second extra period, 69-65. Roosevelt never caught up, although Thomas' final basket in a 19-point performance closed the gap to 75-74 with only seven seconds on the board.

Roosevelt stopped the clock with a time-out, but Plymouth was an excellent ball-handling team, and the Pilgrims had no trouble moving the ball downcourt to use up those last seven seconds. Gary opponents couldn't even get close enough to the ball for an intentional foul.

It ended one of the most exciting tournaments in memory, with all three games decided by a total of just five points. And all four teams in the State Finals cast shot better than 50 percent in all three games—another first for this tradition-rich high school basketball extravaganza.

Against Cathedral, Plymouth had to be concerned about containing 6-10 Notre Dame recruit Ken Barlow underneath and 6-3 junior standout Scott Hicks. Barlow got 22 points and Hicks 18, but Barlow was in foul trouble almost all the way and his playing time was limited to 23 minutes.

The picture says it all.

Skiles came through with another strong 30-point performance on 11 of 21 shooting from the floor, Ron Sissel had 10, and Wendel eight. Plymouth led by 14–12, 28–23, and 42–38 quarter scores.

Cathedral held an early 12–6 lead before Plymouth reeled off 16 straight points, and then the Irish led briefly at 33–32, 53–52, and 55–54, but the Pilgrims got eight of the next 10 points to take charge.

Plymouth sank some key free throws near the end, and time after time Cathedral missed its big chances at the foul line. The Irish hit only seven of 19 at the foul line. It was without a doubt the most crippling statistic for the 27–3 Indianapolis city champs on their first trip to the State Finals.

Cathedral Coach Tom O'Brien praised Skiles and his Plymouth teammates. "You can't take anything away from Plymouth. They are very well coached, they jump at you, they trap you, and when you have men on Skiles, he dishes the ball off so well. You get this far in the tournament with this much pressure and you have to hit your free throws and you have to execute. We've been a 70 percent free throw shooting team all year, but we're a young ball club, and today we didn't do either."

"We had a lot of apprehensions about Barlow, and especially Hicks, coming into this game. They tried to isolate Barlow in the second half and started lobbing the ball in to him which was very effective," Coach Edison explained.

"We looked upon both teams as momentum teams. Either one of us could have broken the game open at any time. Nothing Skiles does surprises me, and I guess I take some things for granted. I'm used to his play, but some people who see him for the first time are shocked. They come up to me and say, 'Hey, he's more than just a shooter.' "

Big comebacks were nothing unusual for Coach Edison and his talented Plymouth ball club. The Pilgrims were all but written off in the state tournament's regional round when Elkhart Memorial built a whopping 49–35 lead with 4:38 to go in the third quarter. And Skiles was riding the bench following an untimely behind-the-back pass to get a better perspective for the game-winning push that would come later.

"I was thinking about getting the bus started and getting out of here," Coach Edison deadpanned for a South Bend writer after the Pilgrims roared back in the fourth quarter to yank it out of the fire, 77–74.

"Great strategy on my part," added the Plymouth coach. "Get so far down that we can be happy at the end of the quarter when we're only six behind."

Plymouth had cut the overwhelming margin to six by the end of the third quarter and actually regained the lead at 6:46 of the final period—its first lead since early in the opening quarter. From that point, the game see-sawed with 11 more lead changes to the wire.

Skiles put the Pilgrims in front for good on a free throw with 51 seconds on the clock, and then Wendel clinched it 20 seconds later when fouled by Memorial's Tom Granitz. On the same play Elkhart's Ernie Jones was whistled for grabbing the rim.

Wendel converted two of the three free shots, and Plymouth kept

Scott Skiles being double-teamed by LaSalle in the Semistate. Mayor William Hudnut (right) doesn't seem to appreciate seeing his Cathedral team go down under the Big Red Machine.

possession, thanks to the technical. Front-line reserve Jamie Johnson produced more insurance with a rebound shot.

Meantime, Memorial Coach Steve Johnson must have been wondering what he had to do to beat Plymouth. Early in the year Memorial's Chargers held a four-point lead with eight seconds to go only to lose to Plymouth in overtime, 93–91.

Once again Skiles led all scorers with 33 points even though he was on the bench for 4½ minutes in the third quarter. Scott got 19 of his 33 in the first half and then came back strong with 11 in the fourth quarter. Edison decided that his tremendously talented star needed a rest in that third quarter, when Plymouth turned it over nine times, but when Skiles returned he was under control.

Much of the credit for the big win giving Plymouth its fourth Elkhart regional title in the last 11 years also should go to Johnson and another reserve player, Mark Stukenborg. Johnson netted 13 points in an important relief role and Stukenborg eight. They contributed six each when the Pilgrims bounced from behind in the fourth-quarter stretch drive. The Chargers were led by Jones with 27 and Terry Coleman with 15.

One week later Plymouth had to go overtime to down Marion, 56–55, and then wipe out an eight-point lead in the fourth quarter to slip past South Bend LaSalle, 77–71, in the Fort Wayne Semistate. LaSalle led the Pilgrims 60–52 at the end of three quarters.

Plymouth's come-from-behind win over LaSalle in the Semistate

Todd Samuelson is being congratulated after the State Final.

final avenged the only regular season loss for the Pilgrims. Plymouth was an impressive 73–57 winner over highly regarded LaSalle in the South Bend Invitational final at mid-season, and then LaSalle handed the Pilgrims their only setback in the 64–62 regular season windup.

Skiles turned in another outstanding performance with 30 points for Plymouth, Wendel had 16, and Sissel 13. Johnson came off the bench with another key 8-point effort, and the Pilgrims outscored LaSalle 25–11 in the tide-turning fourth quarter. Reggie Bird answered with a strong 25-point performance for LaSalle's losers.

Plymouth took charge in the afternoon by outscoring Marion's 22–3 Giants by a 25–14 margin in the second quarter, but the Giants battled back behind Joseph Price and James Blackmon to trail only 41–37 at the three-quarter mark and lead briefly at 49–47 with 2:49 remaining in regulation time.

Wendel scored two big buckets for Plymouth at the end of the fourth quarter, and Marion never led in the extra period. Skiles put Plymouth ahead 54–53 with 40 seconds to go in the overtime and then

Top: Scott Skiles and friends being given the IHSAA championship plaque. Bottom: Phil Wendel seems more self-conscious being hugged by his mother after receiving the Trester Award than he ever did on court.

Ron Sissel and net at the Plymouth celebration. Jack Edison's thoughts during the gym rally are manifest.

passed to Sissel inside for a 56–53 cushion. Skiles wound up with 19 points and seven rebounds, Sissel added 15, and Wendel a dozen.

Blackmon (only a junior) scored a game high 20 for Marion, but Price was limited to 14 by the Plymouth defense. Edison credited Barry Peterson and Johnson for shutting off the 6-5 Notre Dame recruit who was just 37 points short of Dave Colescott's 1,529 career record at Marion.

"Price and Blackmon you don't stop one-on-one," Edison said after the overtime scorcher. "They are superior kids, and you double up on them when you can. We didn't lose our composure [when Marion came back], and I'm sure Coach (Bill) Green must be proud. They were down most of the game."

Someone estimated that the Plymouth High School gym was jammed with 8,000 fans from all over Marshall County, when Coach Edison brought his state champions home to a noisy celebration on a Sunday afternoon.

School officials pointed out quickly that the Plymouth gym seats only 5,500, but fans of all ages occupied every inch of space, even the playing floor.

"Maybe if it was a Muncie or a Marion, you could take all this a little more in stride," Coach Edison rationalized for visiting writers. "For a town and a school of our small size, it's a once-in-a-lifetime thing."

Once might be just about all that a community could stand,

because the emotional celebration started about 2 P.M. and lasted well past the supper hour. Ten firetrucks from Plymouth and surrounding small towns met the Pilgrims along the return route.

Bill Nixon, who coached Plymouth's state championship football team in 1977, and who coached many of these state basketball champs on the school's baseball team, spoke of amazing similarities relating to the two state title winners.

Nixon's Plymouth football team had to go two overtimes to beat Jasper in the 1977 Class AA state championship football game, just like Edison's basketball team needed two extra periods to beat Gary Roosevelt for the state basketball championship.

"It's noteworthy that probably the two most publicized athletes in our school's history figured prominently in both championship games," Nixon recalled. "Pete Buchanan was a superstar for our football team on both offense and defense [Buchanan owns virtually all the football records], and Skiles has done the same thing in basketball."

Nixon also mentioned a special togetherness that has been a strong foundation with the coaches, the players, and the entire student body.

"I'm still not real sure what happened down there Saturday," the 37-year-old Edison told the big crowd of Plymouth celebrants. "But I'm glad that we were able to represent our area with so much class. Now a lot of people with very little knowledge of Plymouth will think of us in a better light. They will know that we're not just good farmers." Many Bremen, Argos, Rochester, and Culver people turned out to salute the Pilgrims.

For years the colleges and the pros have tried to copy the enthusiasm and excitement that characterize the high school basketball scene in Indiana. One must admit after the 1982 State Finals and the Plymouth homecoming that followed, they're not even close to the real thing.

Not recruited by any of the major colleges with much enthusiasm before the state tournament, Skiles became the center of attention in the weeks that followed. He was the No. 1 hitter on a baseball team with state title aspirations, and he was named to the Indiana All-Star basketball team that would play Kentucky's finest preps in June.

Skiles finally put his name on a Michigan State basketball scholarship, but almost anything that happens in college seems certain to fall far short of the storybook finish he authored at Plymouth.

Michigan State's Jud Heathcote beamed at the very thought of young Scott doing many of the same things for his Spartans in the Big 10 conference for the next four years. Heathcote came to Plymouth to sign Skiles a short time after the state tourney, and his comments were lined with great expectations.

"Scott Skiles is a great player and a winner," the Michigan State coach said. "He comes from a winning program, and he is a winning individual. He has great guard skills and court awareness that you cannot coach. A player either has it or he doesn't."

Heathcote's flattering remarks on Skiles' talents echoed endless tributes that were showered on Coach Edison and his entire Plymouth team. It was a rare team-oriented bunch, known for its precision passing and total unselfishness and put together by a low-key coach.

Edison was right on target when he said, "They're good shooters and good ball-handlers. But the thing I appreciate most is their unselfish attitude and the way they show no concern at all for personal glory. They always see the open man, and this really helps our total team concept."

He could have been talking about the whole team—not just Skiles and Wendel.

Plymouth's state championship Pilgrims (1982). Front row: manager Gary Johnson, Pete Rockaway, Todd Samuelson, Larry Johns, Phil Wendel, Scott Skiles, manager Bill Mays; back row: Coach Jack Edison, Mark Stukenborg, Jamie Johnson, Tim Meckstroth, Barry Peterson, Ron Sissel, Assistant Coach Mike Pettibone.

IF YOU ARE ALIVE, lucid and reasonably cognizant of the world around you and didn't enjoy what you saw at Market Square Arena Saturday, the message is clear.

You should go in for log rolling, wrist wrestling or cribbage—basketball isn't your game.

They have been playing the Indiana high school basketball tournament since 1911 and they may need another 11 years into the next century before they come up with a better afternoon and night of basketball.

We Hoosiers have a cute little colloquialism for excitement in basketball. It's called a "barnburner." Well, the kids who participated Saturday got the barn, the farm and most of the neighborhood. There weren't enough fire departments in Indiana to handle the heat.

The state finals lasted for two overtimes past three games and the participants were separated by a grand total of five points. There were miracle shots and mystical shots. At some point during the championship game, they should have blown the whistle and called it a draw—nobody deserved to lose. Nobody should have lost.

THE TITLE CONTEST—two overtimes—should have been bronzed and etched on everyone's memory.

Gary Roosevelt's Renaldo Thomas got it half the distance and in the basket in less than five seconds to get past Bosse and into the final game. Plymouth's Scott Skiles, who has the recuperative powers of a wounded jungle cat, did him a half click of the clock better to send the Plymouth-Roosevelt title game into the first of two overtimes.

They shouldn't even waste time discussing the 75-74 Plymouth title victory. They should wrap it, stamp it "special" and ship it up Pennsylvania Street to the Indiana Basketball Hall of Fame.

Don't touch it. You can't improve on it—even Michelangelo couldn't get it.

For years I've believed that 1954 —Milan 32, Muncie Central 30— never would be duplicated. Well, folks, it was tied Saturday night. I won't live to see a better championship game—I hope, because if I do I won't live through it.

★

IT'S SIMPLE ENOUGH to explain the game: This is a ball, that is a basket; the object is to put the ball in the basket.

It also is a puzzle, a contest, a war, and, at different times, a test of intelligence, skill and strength. People who teach the game or study its mysteries often end up wondering if it's really so complicated or they're just simple.

The idea is to get it in the basket, but you can deliver it by a multitude of methods.

There were two games in the state high school basketball tournament finals in Market Square Arena Saturday afternoon—two games played with a basketball, but remarkably different.

Plymouth, a 62-59 winner, and Cathedral passed, picked, maneuvered and tried to mold many of the games' components into unified plans of action.

GARY ROOSEVELT and Evansville Bosse put on a demonstration that had a closer kinship to an air battle over the Philippine Sea. People in the second deck at MSA must have thought they were looking down on a bombing raid.

In the first game they were looking for the good shot; in the second they were letting it go from the launching pad. Yet, the shooting percentages were about the same.

It's an indisputable fact that shots don't fly off the chalkboard into the basket. The game can be coached down to its finest component, but once the ball goes in the air the human element takes over.

Cathedral lost because it couldn't hit a lick at the free throw line. The Irish were a miserable four of 14 shooting when the clock was stopped in the second half. And down the stretch when they had an opportunity to pad a lead they were somewhere below zero.

ROOSEVELT WHIPPED Bosse, 58-57, because for one moment there was a perfect wedding of boy and basketball.

Bosse's Derrick Dowell had put the state's No. 1 ranked team in front with five seconds to play. So Roosevelt had to travel the length of the floor in five seconds—something few teams ever do.

The Panthers had some luck with the in-bounds pass, getting it to midcourt. And the right man caught it.

Traveling in a tight arc, Renaldo Thomas covered the remaining distance in less than four seconds. But he went in deep and from a bad angle. There are several dozen pros who can't hit the shot.

Thomas put it up with just the right amount of everything and that was all she wrote. A bombsaway battle was decided by the most delicate shot of the afternoon.

ROOSEVELT IS NOT a good free throw shooting team and Coach Ron Heflin joked that his main conscious thought when Thomas got the ball was, "Please don't foul him."

Cathedral never really got into the flow of the game against the Pilgrims—a fact that may be attributed to Plymouth's savvy play.

And there also was the fact that the Irish, like many others along the way, couldn't handle Plymouth's Scott Skiles. Perhaps, as one man says, "He doesn't play like a guard, look like a guard or shoot like a guard," but he's all basketball player.

Skiles scored 30 points and had to be responsible for a dozen more. He is skillful at dumping off the ball and kept the defense unsettled the entire 32 minutes.

Tony Hinkle says the best player is the one who takes his team the farthest. So, while there were many vying for that honor, the afternoon session belonged to Skiles and Thomas—they took their teams one more step.

Bob Collins,
Indiana Star

Plymouth

Season Record (28–1)
1981–82

Plymouth	68	LaVille	51
Plymouth	93	Elkhart Memorial (Overtime)	91
Plymouth	78	Mishawaka	61
Plymouth	64	Triton	49
Plymouth	104	LaPorte	82
Plymouth	65	Bremen	50
Plymouth	75	Valparaiso	59
Plymouth	78	South Bend St. Joseph's	54
Plymouth	57	South Bend Riley	55
Plymouth	73	South Bend LaSalle	57
Plymouth	66	Wawasee	55

Plymouth	98	Concord	84
Plymouth	87	Rochester	74
Plymouth	71	Logansport	52
Plymouth	77	Northwood	62
Plymouth	86	Penn	76
Plymouth	82	Warsaw	46
Plymouth	71	Goshen	64
Plymouth	95	Culver Community	49
Plymouth	90	Tippecanoe Valley	41
Plymouth	62	South Bend LaSalle	64

Sectional

| Plymouth | 72 | Bremen | 37 |
| Plymouth | 55 | Argos | 47 |

Regional (Elkhart)

| Plymouth | 72 | Manchester | 55 |
| Plymouth | 77 | Elkhart Memorial | 74 |

Semistate (Fort Wayne)

| Plymouth | 56 | Marion (Overtime) | 55 |
| Plymouth | 77 | South Bend LaSalle | 71 |

State Finals (Indianapolis MSA)

| Plymouth | 62 | Indianapolis Cathedral | 59 |
| Plymouth | 75 | Gary Roosevelt (2 Overtimes) | 74 |

Appendices

State Champion Coaches, Records

1911	Crawfordsville, Dave Glascock	16–2
1912	Lebanon, Claude Whitney	16–3
1913	Wingate, Jesse Wood	22–3
1914	Wingate, Len Lehman	19–5
1915	Thorntown, Chet Hill	22–5
1916	Lafayette, C. F. Apking	20–4
1917	lebanon, Alva Staggs	26–2
1918	Lebanon, Glenn Curtis	28–2
1919	Bloomington, Cliff Wells	23–3
1920	Franklin, Ernest Wagner	29–1
1921	Franklin, Ernest Wagner	29–4
1922	Franklin, Ernest Wagner	31–4
1923	Vincennes, John Adams	34–1
1924	Martinsville, Glenn Curtis	22–7
1925	Frankfort, Everett Case	27–2
1926	Marion, Gene Thomas	27–2
1927	Martinsville, Glenn Curtis	26–3
1928	Muncie Central, Pete Jolly	28–2
1929	Frankfort, Everett Case	25–2
1930	Washington, Burl Friddle	30–1
1931	Muncie Central, Pete Jolly	24–5
1932	New Castle, Orville Hooker	28–3
1933	Martinsville, Glenn Curtis	21–8
1934	Logansport, Cliff Wells	28–4
1935	Anderson, Archie Chadd	22–9
1936	Frankfort, Everett Case	29–1–1
1937	Anderson, Archie Chadd	26–7
1938	Fort Wayne South, Burl Friddle	29–3
1939	Frankfort, Everett Case	26–6

Year	Team, Coach	Record
1940	Hammond Tech, Lou Birkett	25–6
1941	Washington, Marion Crawley	27–5
1942	Washington, Marion Crawley	30–1
1943	Fort Wayne Central, Murray Mendenhall	27–1
1944	Evansville Bosse, Herman Keller	19–7
1945	Evansville Bosse, Herman Keller	25–2
1946	Anderson, Charles Cummings	22–7
1947	Shelbyville, Frank Barnes	25–5
1948	Lafayette Jeff, Marion Crawley	27–3
1949	Jasper, Leo O'Neill	21–9
1950	Madison, Ray Eddy	27–1
1951	Muncie Central, Art Beckner	26–4
1952	Muncie Central, Jay McCreary	25–5
1953	South Bend Central, Elmer McCall	25–5
1954	Milan, Marvin Wood	28–2
1955	Indianapolis Crispus Attucks, Ray Crowe	31–1
1956	Indianapolis Crispus Attucks, Ray Crowe	31–0
1957	South Bend Central, Elmer McCall	30–0
1958	Fort Wayne South, Don Reichert	28–2
1959	Crispus Attucks, Bill Garrett	26–5
1960	East Chicago Washington, John Baratto	28–2
1961	Kokomo, Joe Platt	29–1
1962	Evansville Bosse, Jim Myers	26–2
1963	Muncie Central, Dwight Tallman	28–1
1964	Lafayette Jeff, Marion Crawley	28–1
1965	Indianapolis Washington, Jerry Oliver	29–2
1966	Michigan City Elston, Doug Adams	26–3
1967	Evansville North, Jim Rausch	27–2
1968	Gary Roosevelt, Louis Mallard	22–5
1969	Indianapolis Washington, Bill Green	31–0
1970	East Chicago Roosevelt, Bill Holzbach	28–0
1971	East Chicago Washington, John Molodet	29–0
1972	Connersville, Myron Dickerson	27–2
1973	New Albany, Kirby Overman	21–7
1974	Fort Wayne Northrop, Bob Dille	28–1
1975	Marion, Bill Green	28–1
1976	Marion, Bill Green	23–5
1977	Carmel, Eric Clark	22–7
1978	Muncie Central, Bill Harrell	27–3
1979	Muncie Central, Bill Harrell	24–5
1980	Indianapolis Broad Ripple, Bill Smith	29–2
1981	Vincennes, Gunner Wyman	26–2
1982	Plymouth, Jack Edison	28–1

YEAR-BY-YEAR IN THE CHAMPIONSHIP

1911	Crawfordsville 24, Lebanon 17
1912	Lebanon 51, Franklin 11
1913	Wingate 15, South Bend 14 (5 OTs')

1914	Wingate 36, Anderson 8
1915	Thorntown 33, Montmorenci 10
1916	Lafayette Jefferson 27, Crawfordsville 26
1917	Lebanon 34, Gary 26
1918	Lebanon 24, Anderson 20
1919	Bloomington 18, Lafayette Jeff 15
1920	Franklin 31, Lafayette Jeff 13
1921	Franklin 35, Anderson 22
1922	Franklin 26, Terre Haute Garfield 15
1923	Vincennes 27, Muncie 18
1924	Martinsville 36, Frankfort 30
1925	Frankfort 34, Kokomo 20
1926	Marion 30, Martinsville 23
1927	Martinsville 26, Muncie 23
1928	Muncie 13, Martinsville 12
1929	Frankfort 29, Indianapolis Tech 23
1930	Washington 32, Muncie 21
1931	Muncie 31, Greencastle 23
1932	New Castle 24, Winamac 17
1933	Martinsville 27, Greencastle 24
1934	Logansport 26, Indianapolis Tech 19
1935	Anderson 23, Jeffersonville 17
1936	Frankfort 50, F. W. Central 24
1937	Anderson 33, Huntingburg 23
1938	F. W. South Side 34, Hammond 32
1939	Frankfort 36, Franklin 22
1940	Hammond Tech 33, Mitchell 21
1941	Washington 39, Madison 33
1942	Washington 24, Muncie Burris 18
1943	Fort Wayne Central 45, Lebanon 40
1944	Evansville Bosse 39, Kokomo 35
1945	Evansville Bosse 46, South Bend Riley 36
1946	Anderson 67, Fort Wayne Central 53
1947	Shelbyville 68, Terre Haute Garfield 58
1948	Lafayette Jeff 54, Evansville Central 41
1949	Jasper 62, Madison 61
1950	Madison 67, Lafayette Jeff 44
1951	Muncie Central 60, Evansville Reitz 58
1952	Muncie Central 68, Indianapolis Tech 49
1953	South Bend Central 42, Terre Haute Gerstmeyer 41
1954	Milan 32, Muncie Central 30
1955	Indianapolis Attucks 97, Gary Roosevelt 74
1956	Indianapolis Attucks 79, Lafayette Jeff 57
1957	South Bend Central 67, Indianapolis Attucks 55
1958	Fort Wayne South Side 63, Crawfordsville 34
1959	Indianapolis Attucks 92, Kokomo 54
1960	East Chicago Washington 75, Muncie Central 59
1961	Kokomo 68, Indianapolis Manual 66 (OT)
1962	Evansville Bosse 84, East Chicago Washington 81
1963	Muncie Central 65, South Bend Central 61
1964	Lafayette Jeff 58, Huntington 55
1965	Indianapolis Washington 64, Fort Wayne North Side 57

1966	Michigan City Elston 63, Indianapolis Tech 52
1967	Evansville North 60, Lafayette Jeff 58
1968	Gary Roosevelt 68, Indianapolis Shortridge 60
1969	Indianapolis Washington 79, Gary Tolleston 76
1970	East Chicago Roosevelt 76, Carmel 62
1971	East Chicago Washington 70, Elkhart 60
1972	Connersville 80, Gary West Side 63
1973	New Albany 84, South Bend Adams 79
1974	Fort Wayne Northrop 59, Jeffersonville 56
1975	Marion 58, Loogootee 46
1976	Marion 82, Rushville 76
1977	Carmel 53, East Chicago Washington 52
1978	Muncie Central 65, Terre Haute South 64 (OT)
1979	Muncie Central 64, Anderson 60
1980	Indianapolis Broad Ripple 73, New Albany 66
1981	Vincennes Lincoln 54, Anderson 52
1982	Plymouth 75, Gary Roosevelt 74 (2 OT's)

AWARDS FOR MENTAL ATTITUDE
Gimbel Award

1917	Claude Curtis, Martinsville
1918	Ralph Esarey, Bloomington
1919	Walter Cross, Thorntown
1920	Harold Laughlin, Bedford
1921	Ralph Marlow, Sandusky
1922	Reece Jones, Vincennes
1923	Maurice Robinson, Anderson
1924	Phillip Kessler, Richmond
1925	Russell Walter, Kokomo
1926	Richard Williams, Evansville Central
1927	Franklin Prentice, Kendallville
1928	Robert McCarnes, Logansport
1929	Emmett Lowerey, Indianapolis Tech
1930	Kenneth Young, LaPorte
1931	Norman Cotton, Terre Haute Wiley
1932	Jess McAnally, Greencastle
1933	James Seward, Indianapolis Shortridge
1934	Arthur Gosman, Jasper
1935	James Lyboult, Richmond
1936	Steve Sitko, Fort Wayne Central
1937	Robert Menke, Huntingburg
1938	Robert Mygrants, Hammond
1939	Jim Myers, Evansville Bosse
1940	Duane Conkey, Mitchell
1941	Donald Server, Madison
1942	Kenneth Brown, Jr., Muncie Burris
1943	Dave Laflin, Lebanon

IHSAA Medal

1944   Walter McFatridge, Jr., Kokomo

Trester Award

The inscription on the Arthur L. Trester Mental Attitude Award reads as follows: *The Recipient of This Award, While a Student in Grade Twelve, was Nominated by the Principal and Coach; Excelled in Mental Attitude, Athletic Ability, Scholarship and Leadership During the Four Years of High School; Participated as a State Finalist in This Sport and Was Selected by Members of the IHSAA Executive Committee.*

1945	Max Allen, Indianapolis Broad Ripple
1946	Robert Cripe, Flora
1947	Ronald Bland, Terre Haute Garfield
1948	Lee Hamilton, Evansville Central
1949	James Schooley, Auburn
1950	Pat Klein, Marion
1951	Robert Jewell, Indianapolis Attucks
1952	Joseph Sexson, Indianapolis Tech
1953	Harley Andrews, Terre Haute Gerstmeyer
1954	Bob Plump, Milan
1955	James Henry, New Albany
1956	Dennis Tepe, Elkhart
1957	Robert Perigo, Lafayette Jeff
1958	Richard Haslam, Crawfordsville
1959	James Rayl, Kokomo
1960	Robert Cantrell, East Chicago Washington
1961	Dick and Tom VanArsdale, Indianapolis Manual
1962	John Wilson, Evansville Bosse
1963	Greg Samuels, Terre Haute Garfield
1964	Mike Weaver, Huntington
1965	Edward Bopp, Indianapolis Washington
1966	James Cadwell, Michigan City Elston
1967	Charles Nelson, Fort Wayne South Side
1968	James Nelson, Gary Roosevelt
1969	Joe Sutter, Marion
1970	James Trout, Loogootee
1971	Jerry Lamberson, New Castle
1972	Mark Inman, Jeffersonville
1973	Garry Abplanalp, Franklin
1974	Don and Jon McGlocklin, Franklin
1975	Steve Walker, Lebanon
1976	David Colescott, Marion
1977	Mark Herrmann, Carmel
1978	Jack Moore, Muncie Central
1979	Malcom Cameron, Terre Haute South
1980	Jeff Todd, Marion
1981	Karl Donovan, Vincennes Lincoln
1982	Phil Wendel, Plymouth

Index

The following index of names of people, teams, and fieldhouses covers the text only (not introductions and appendices). A number in italic indicates that the person named appears only in the photo on that page (if he appears in both the text and photo on a given page, the number will not be italicized).